The Illustrated Encyclopedia of Major

# Aircraft of World War II

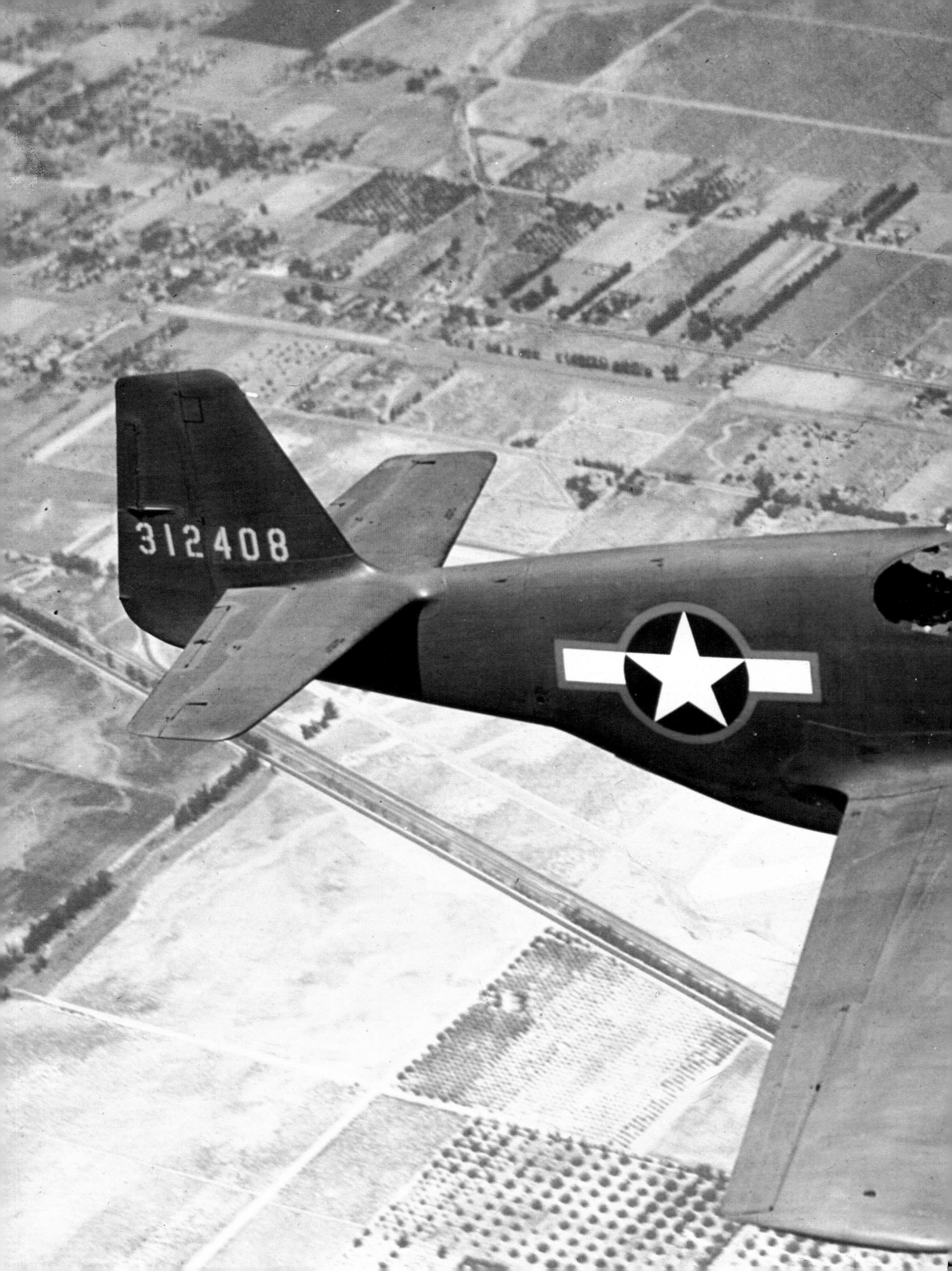
312408

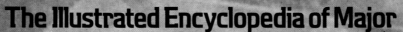

The Illustrated Encyclopedia of Major

# Aircraft of World War II

## Francis K. Mason

## CRESCENT BOOKS
### New York

**Crescent Books**

First English edition published by Temple Press
an imprint of Newnes Books 1983

All rights reserved.
This edition published by Crescent Books,
a division of Crown Publishers, Inc.
h g f e d c b a

Printed and bound in Italy

Created and produced by Stan Morse
Aerospace Publishing Ltd
10 Barley Mow Passage
London W4 4PH

All correspondence concerning the content of this volume
should be addressed to Aerospace Publishing Ltd. Trade
enquiries should be addressed to Crescent Books,
New York.

ISBN: 0-517-405059

Library of Congress Catalog Card Number: 82-46 093

**PICTURE ACKNOWLEDGEMENTS**

The Publishers wish to thank the following people and organizations for their help in supplying photographs for this book.

**Jacket front:** John MacClancy Collection. **Jacket back:** US Navy. **Pages 2/3:** John MacClancy Collection. **6:** US Navy. **11:** Imperial War Museum. **14:** US Air Force. **15:** RAF Museum, Hendon. **17:** US Air Force. **20:** US Air Force. **21:** RAF Museum, Hendon. **22:** US Navy. **23:** Imperial War Museum. **24:** Imperial War Museum. **27:** US Air Force. **28:** John MacClancy Collection. **29:** US Air Force. **30:** US Navy. **31:** Popperfoto. **35:** John MacClancy. **37:** Bundesarchiv. **38:** Imperial War Museum. **39:** Imperial War Museum. **40:** US Navy. **41:** McDonnell Douglas. **44:** Fleet Air Arm Museum. **45:** Charles E. Brown-RAF Museum, Hendon. **46:** RAF Museum, Hendon. **47:** Imperial War Museum. **51:** Imperial War Museum. **57:** Imperial War Museum. **59:** US Navy. **60:** Grumman Aerospace Corporation. **61:** US Navy. **62:** Grumman Aerospace Corporation. **63:** Charles E. Brown-RAF Museum, Hendon. **64:** Charles E. Brown-RAF Museum, Hendon. **65:** Charles E. Brown-RAF Museum, Hendon. **66:** Charles E. Brown-RAF Museum, Hendon. **67:** Charles E. Brown-RAF Museum, Hendon. **68:** Charles E. Brown-RAF Museum, Hendon. **69:** Imperial War Museum. **71:** Military Archive and Research Service. **72:** John MacClancy Collection. **77:** Bundesarchiv. **83:** John MacClancy Collection. **86:** US Navy. **93:** US Navy. **94:** John MacClancy Collection. **96:** Lockheed Corporation. **101:** Imperial War Museum. **103:** Charles E. Brown-RAF Museum, Hendon. **104:** John MacClancy Collection. **105:** Military Archive and Research Service. **109:** US Air Force. **110:** US Air Force. **118:** US Navy. **127:** US Air Force. **128:** US Air Force. **129:** US Air Force. **130:** US Air Force. **131:** US Air Force. **133:** Imperial War Museum. **144:** Imperial War Museum. **145:** Popperfoto. **149:** Fox Photos. **150:** Charles E. Brown-RAF Museum, Hendon. **154:** Imperial War Museum. **155:** US Navy. **156:** Imperial War Museum.

# Contents

# Aichi D3A 'Val'

Famous for its part in the treacherous raid on Pearl Harbor, and later for its sinking of the British carrier HMS *Hermes* and cruisers HMS *Cornwall* and *Devonshire*, the Aichi D3A mirrored the Japanese approach to the 'Stuka' concept. This D3A1 Model 11 served with the Yokosuka Kokutai in 1940.

## History and Notes

Although thought to be obsolescent when Japan entered the war, the Aichi D3A with fixed spatted landing gear was the first Japanese aircraft to drop bombs on American targets when aircraft of this type took part in the great raid on Pearl Harbor on 7 December 1941. Designed to a 1936 carrier-based dive-bomber requirement, the prototype was flown in January 1938 with a 710-hp (430-kW) Nakajima Hikari 1 radial. Production D3A1s had slightly smaller wings and were powered by the 1,000-hp (746-kW) Mitsubishi Kinsei 43 radial. A dorsal fin extension considerably improved the aircraft's manoeuvrability, although the armament of only two forward-firing 7.7-mm (0.303-in) machine-guns, with another of the same calibre in the rear cockpit, was undeniably puny. After limited land-based operations in China and Indo-China, D3A1s were flown in all major carrier actions during the first 10 months of the war and sank more Allied naval vessels than any other Axis aircraft. Among British casualties in D3A1 attacks were HMS *Hermes* (the world's first carrier to be sunk by carrier aircraft), and the cruisers HMS *Cornwall* and HMS *Dorsetshire*. Heavy losses among D3A1s during and after the Battle of the Coral Sea, however, forced withdrawal by most of the survivors to land bases. In 1942 the D3A2 was introduced with increased fuel capacity and more powerful engine, but by 1944 the aircraft were hopelessly outclassed by American fighters; a small number was subsequently employed in kamikaze attacks. Production amounted to 476 D3A1s and 1,016 D3A2. The Allied reporting name was 'Val'.

## Specification: Aichi D3A2

**Origin:** Japan
**Type:** two-seat shipborne dive-bomber
**Powerplant:** one 1,300-hp (970-kW) Mitsubishi Kinsei 54 radial piston engine
**Performance:** maximum speed 267 mph (430 km/h) at 20,340 ft (6200 m); climb to 9,845 ft (3000 m) in 5.76 minutes; service ceiling 34,450 ft (10500 m); range 840 miles (1352 km)
**Weights:** empty 5,666 lb (2570 kg); maximum take-off 8,378 lb (3800 kg)
**Dimensions:** span 47 ft 2 in (14.38 m); length 33 ft 5⅜ in (10.20 m); height 12 ft 7½ in (3.85 m); wing area 375.7 sq ft (34.90 ²)

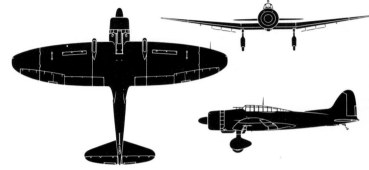

**Aichi D3A 'Val'**

**Armament:** two forward-firing 7.7-mm (0.303-in) type 97 machine-guns in the nose and one flexible 77-mm (0.303-in) Type 92 gun in the rear cockpit, plus one 551-lb (250-kg) bomb under the fuselage and two 132-lb (60-kg) bombs under the wings

Despite their many outstanding successes in the early months of the Pacific war, many of the Japanese aircraft, such as the Aichi D3A dive bomber, were obsolescent by European standards but were marginally superior to anything the British and Americans had available in the Far East, and were present in far greater numbers.

# Arado Ar 234

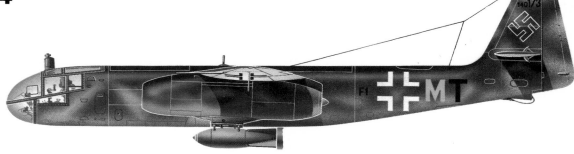

An Arado Ar 234B-2 of 9.KG 76, commanded by Major Hans-Georg Bätcher and based at Rheine and Achmer. II/KG 76 became fully operational in February 1945, losing its first aircraft in action on 24 February with P-47s near Segelsdorf.

## History and Notes

The world's first turbojet-powered bomber, the Arado Ar 234 Blitz (Lightning) was originally conceived as a twin-jet high-speed reconnaissance aircraft late in 1940. Delayed by slow delivery of the Junkers 004B turbojets, the Ar 234 V1 prototype was not first flown until 15 June 1943; this aircraft featured an auxiliary trolley, which was jettisoned on take-off, in place of conventional landing gear. Further prototypes followed, including the Ar 234 V6 and V8 which were powered by four 1,764-lb (800-kg) thrust BMW 003A-1 turbojets.

When production finally started, it was of the twin-jet Ar 234B which featured conventional nosewheel landing gear, the mainwheels retracting into a slightly widened centre fuselage. The Ar 234B-1 was an unarmed reconnaissance aircraft which first served with 1./Versuchsverband Oberbefehlshaber der Luftwaffe late in 1944, and soon after with Sonderkommando Hecht and Sperling. These units were replaced in 1945 by 1.(F)/33, 1.(F)/100 and 1.(F)/123, and many reconnaissance sorties were flown over the UK. The bomber version was the Ar 234B-2, which could carry a bombload of 4,409 lb (200 kg), and other variants included the Ar 234B-2/b reconnaissance aircraft, the Ar 234B-2/1 pathfinder and Ar 234B-2/r long-range bomber. Ar 234B-2 bombers joined KG 76 in January 1945 and carried out a number of daring and hazardous raids before the end of the war. A small number of Ar 234s was also employed as night-fighters with Kommando Bonow, but the four-jet Ar 234C, although just beginning to appear at the end of the war, failed to reach squadron service. Many other advanced projects were in hand when hostilities ceased.

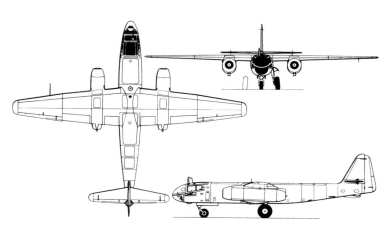

## Specification: Arado Ar 234B-2
**Origin:** Germany
**Type:** single-seat tactical light bomber
**Powerplant:** two 1,764-lb (800-kg) thrust BMW 003A-1 turbojet
**Performance:** maximum speed 461 mph (742 km/h) at 19,685 ft (6000 m); climb to 19,685 ft (6000 m) in 12.8 minutes; service ceiling 32,810 ft (10000 m); range 1,013 miles (1630 km)
**Weights:** empty 11,464 lb (5200 kg); maximum take-off 21,605 lb (9800 kg)
**Dimensions:** span 46 ft 3½ in (14.44 m); length 41 ft 5½ in (12.64 m); height 14 ft 1½ in (4.29 m); wing area 284.17 sq ft (27.3 m²)
**Armament:** bombload of up to 4,409 lb (2000 kg); some aircraft carried two rear-firing 20-mm guns

**Arado Ar 234B-2**

Photo-reconnaissance versions of the Arado Ar 234 served with 1. Versuchsverband Oberbefehlshaber der Luftwaffe, and flew numerous high-altitude photo sorties over Britain, their high speed rendering them immune to interception.

# Armstrong Whitworth Albemarle

An Armstrong Whitworth Albemarle Mk V special transport of No. 297 Sqn, RAF, normally based at Stoney Cross, but flown out to the Mediterranean to participate in the airborne assault on Sicily that month.

## History and Notes

Performing the lesser known but vital tasks of glider tug and paratrooping pathfinder and troop transport, the unattractive Albemarle was originally designed to a 1938 medium bomber requirement, using a composite construction of wood and steel, intended to facilitate sub-contract manufacture outside the aircraft industry. The first prototype crashed, and the second flew on 20 March 1940, being followed by 32 aircraft produced as bombers but not accepted as such by the RAF. Repeated changes in A. W. Hawkesley's production line caused by numerous modifications delayed delivery to the RAF until January 1943, by which time the Hercules XI-powered Albemarle Mk I was being produced as a special transport for use by the airborne forces. Albemarle Mk I glider tugs, plus Albemarle II, V and VI special transports followed, together with Albemarle Mk VI glider tugs. Only one Wright Double Cyclone-powered Albemarle Mk IV was built. Production of the Albemarle totalled 602, of which a small number was supplied to Russia. The glider tug first went into action towing Horsa gliders during the invasion of Sicily, and during the Normandy landings of 6 June 1944 flew as pathfinders for the 6th Airborne Division, dropping men of the 22nd Independent Parachute Company; later they towed gliders during the Arnhem operation. In all, Albemarles equipped seven RAF squadrons.

**Specification:** Armstrong Whitworth Albemarle Mk I (Special Transport)
**Origin:** UK
**Type:** four-crew transport/glider tug
**Powerplant:** two 1,590-hp (1186-kW) Bristol Hercules XI radial piston engines
**Performance:** maximum speed 265 mph (426 km/h) at 10,500 ft (3200 m); initial climb rate 980 ft (299 m) per minute; service ceiling 18,000 ft (5485 m); range 1,300 miles (2092 km)
**Weights:** empty 21,800 lb (9888 kg); maximum take-off 36,500 lb (16556 kg)
**Dimensions:** span 77 ft 0 in (23.47 m); length 59 ft 11 in (18.26 m); height 15 ft 7 in (4.75 m); wing area 803.5 sq ft (74.65 m²)
**Armament/Accommodation:** two 0.303-in (7.7-mm) machine-guns in dorsal turret; accommodation for up to 12 fully armed paratroops

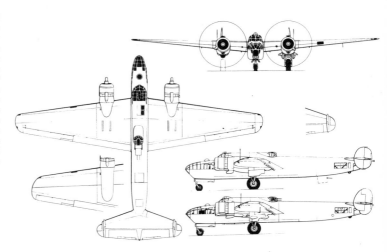

**Armstrong Whitworth Albemarle (top view and scrap view: first prototype)**

Despite production delays, the Albemarle came to be employed in the transport and glider tug roles in almost all the major airborne assault operations by the RAF in the last two years of the war.

# Armstrong Whitworth Whitley

Although withdrawn from Bomber Command when the emphasis shifted to the four-engine bombers, the Whitley continued to give good service with Coastal Command. The Whitley Mk VII shown here carried the markings of No. 502 (Ulster) Sqn based at Holmsley South in 1943.

## History and Notes

Rugged workhorse of RAF Bomber Command at the start of the war, the twin-engine Whitley had been designed to a 1934 requirement and first flew on 4 June 1935. The Whitley Mk I (Tiger IX radial engines) and Whitley Mk II (Tiger VIII) had been largely relegated to training duties by September 1939, and Merlin X-powered Whitley Mk Vs were being delivered to the RAF, remaining in production from 1939 until 1943. A total of 1,476 was built. Whitleys carried out the majority of the controversial leaflet raids during the first year of the war and joined in Bomber Command's night offensive over Europe from 1940 onwards, making their last raid (on Ostend) on 29-30 April 1942. Whitley Mk Vs of Nos 51 and 78 Squadrons took part in the first RAF raid on Berlin of 25/26 August 1940. The Whitley Mk V was used in early paratroop attacks on the Italian viaduct at Tragino on 10 February 1941 and in the Bruneval raid of 27/28 February 1942; it was also used as a glider tug for the Airspeed Horsa glider. The Whitley Mk VII served with RAF Coastal Command, entering service in March 1941 for anti-submarine duties over the Atlantic; aircraft of No. 502 Squadron were the first to be equipped with the long-range ASV Mk II radar, and achieved the first U-boat kill with ASV when *U-206* was sunk in the bay of Biscay on 30 November 1941.

**Specification:** Armstrong Whitworth Whitley Mk V
**Origin:** UK
**Type:** five-crew long-range heavy bomber
**Powerplant:** two 1,145-hp (854-kW) Rolls-Royce Merlin X inline piston engines
**Performance:** maximum speed 222 mph (357 km/h) at 17,000 ft (5180 m); initial climb rate 800 ft (244 m) per minute; service ceiling 17,600 ft (5365 m); range 1,650 miles (2655 km) with 3,000-lb (1361-kg) bombload or 470 miles (756 km) with 8,000-lb (3175-kg) bombload
**Weights:** empty 19,330 lb (8768 kg); maximum take-off 33,500 lb (15196 kg)
**Dimensions:** span 84 ft 0 in (25.60 m); length 69 ft 3 in (21.11 m); height 15 ft 0 in (4.57 m); wing area 1,137.0 sq ft (105.63 m²)
**Armament:** one 0.303-in (7.7-mm) machine-gun in nose turret and four 0.303-in (7.7-mm) machine-guns in power-operated tail turret, plus a maximum bombload of 7,000 lb (3175 kg), usually comprising 14 bombs of 500 lb (227 kg) each

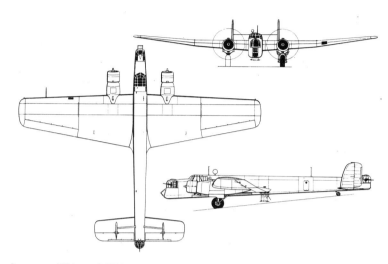

**Armstrong Whitworth Whitley Mk III**

The Whitley bomber was immensely rugged and, despite a somewhat sluggish performance, was widely used by RAF Bomber Command during the first two years of the war, particularly in the oft-criticized leaflet 'raids' over Germany in the first months.

# Avro Anson

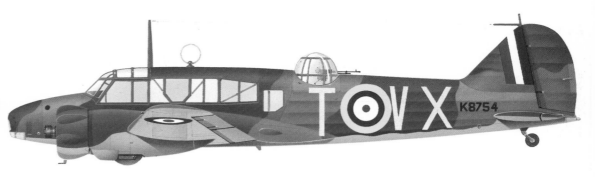

Representative of the Ansons which undertook anti-submarine patrols over the North Sea from the first days of the war is this Mk I of No. 206 Sqn based at Manston. Ansons served on no fewer than 57 RAF squadrons.

## History and Notes

Anachronistic relic of pre-war RAF expansion, the Anson was originally the result of a coastal reconnaissance aircraft requirement, and was developed from a six-seat commercial aircraft. It first flew on 24 March 1935 and, powered by Cheetah engines, the Anson Mk I entered service with No. 48 Squadron in March 1936, and was the first RAF aircraft with a retractable landing gear, albeit manually operated. The Anson subsequently served with 12 squadrons of Coastal Command up to the beginning of the war, when the first Lockheed Hudsons were just beginning to arrive from America. Nevertheless Ansons were retained on short-range coastal reconnaissance duties in diminishing numbers until 1942, occasionally having brushes with the enemy. By the beginning of the war, however, the Anson was already in use as an aircrew trainer for navigators, wireless operators and air gunners, and it was for this long and priceless service that the 'faithful Annie' is best remembered. Jacobs- and Wright-powered Anson Mks III and IV aircraft were shipped to Canada to equip the growing numbers of flying schools under the Commonwealth Air Training Scheme, Canadian manufacturers also producing the Anson Mks II, V and VI. Light transport conversions from the Anson Mk I resulted in the Anson Mks X, XI and XII, some of which were employed as air ambulances; the Anson Mk XI was powered by Cheetah XIX engines driving Fairey-Reed metal propellers, and the Anson Mk XII had Cheetah XVs driving constant-speed Rotol propellers. Production, which continued after the war with the Anson Mks 19, 20, 21 and 22, reached a total of 11,020 aircraft, including 2,882 built in Canada.

## Specification: Avro Anson Mk 1
**Origin:** UK
**Type:** three-crew general-reconnaissance aircraft
**Powerplant:** two 350-hp (261-kW) Armstrong Siddeley Cheetah IX radial piston engines
**Performance:** maximum speed 188 mph (302 km/h) at 7,000 ft (2135 m); initial climb rate 720 ft (219 m) per minute; service ceiling 19,000 ft (5790 m); range 790 miles (1271 km)
**Weights:** empty 5,375 lb (2438 kg); maximum take-off 8,000 lb (3629 kg)
**Dimensions:** span 56 ft 6 in (17.22 m); length 42 ft 3 in (12.87 m); height 13 ft 1 in (3.99 m); wing area 463.0 sq ft (43.01 m²)
**Armament:** one fixed forward-firing 0.303-in (7.7-mm) machine-gun in nose and one 0.303-in (7.7-mm) machine-gun in dorsal turret, plus provision to carry up to 360 lb (163 kg) of bombs

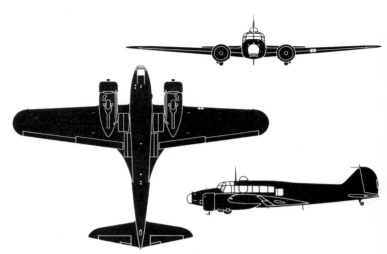

**Avro Anson Mk X**

Serving as a coastal patrol aircraft at the beginning of the war, the Anson was quickly replaced by the Lockheed Hudson, and was then used almost exclusively as a trainer. A late production Anson Mk I is pictured here.

# Avro Lancaster

In order to carry the 22,000-lb (9976-kg) 'Grand Slam' bomb, the Lancaster B.Mk I (Special) had two turrets removed and a cutaway fuselage. The bombs were dropped on the Bielefeld viaduct by No. 617 Sqn.

## History and Notes

Undisputedly the finest night heavy bomber of the war, the four-engine Lancaster was developed when the two-Vulture Manchester proved a failure on account of its engines. Designer Roy Chadwick substituted four Rolls-Royce Merlins in the new bomber, which first flew on 9 January 1941, the first RAF squadron (No. 44) being completely equipped with Lancaster Mk Is (of which 3,544 were built) in January 1942. The type's first bombing raid was carried out on Essen on 10-11 March that year; one month later Lancasters dropped the first 8,000-lb (3629-kg) bomb (also on Essen) and followed with the first 12,000-lb (5443-kg) bomb on 15-16 September 1943, and the first 22,000-lb (9979-kg) bomb on 14 March 1945. The Lancaster Mk II (of which 300 were built) was powered by 1,650-hp (1231-kW) Bristol Hercules VI radials and the Lancaster Mk III (2,990 built) by Packard-built Merlin 28, 38 or 224 engines. These versions came to constitute Bomber Command's main force equipment, being fitted with Gee, H2S and all manner of other navigation and bombing radar aids. Lancaster Mk I (Special) aircraft were adapted to carry the special mines used in the famous dams raid by No. 617 Squadron. Later wartime versions included the Lancaster Mk VI with Merlin 87s driving four-blade propellers, the Lancaster Mk I (FE), prepared for Far Eastern service, and the Lancaster Mk VII (built by Austin) with revised dorsal turret. Total Lancaster production was 7,366 including 422 Lancaster Mk Xs built in Canada. Lancasters dropped a total of 608,612 tons of bombs and flew 156,000 operational sorties during the war.

## Specification: Avro Lancaster Mk I
**Origin:** UK
**Type:** seven-crew night heavy bomber
**Powerplant:** four 1,460-hp (1089-kW) Rolls-Royce Merlin XX inline piston engines
**Performance:** maximum speed 287 mph (462 km/h) at 11,500 ft (3505 m); climb to 20,000 ft (6095 m) in 41.6 minutes; service ceiling 24,500 ft (7470 m); range with 14,000-lb (6350-kg) bombload 1,660 miles (2671 km) or with 22,000-lb (9979-kg) bombload 1,040 miles (1674 m)
**Weights:** empty 36,900 lb (16738 kg); maximum take-off with 14,000 lb (6350 kg) of bombs 68,000 lb (30845 kg)
**Dimensions:** span 102 ft 0 in (31.09 m); length 69 ft 6 in (21.18 m); height 20 ft 0 in (6.10 m); wing area 1,297.0 sq ft (120.49 m²)
**Armament:** two 0.303-in (7.7-mm) guns in nose, dorsal and ventral turrets (the last later deleted), and four 0.303-in (7.7-mm) guns in tail turret, plus a normal bombload of up to 14 1,000-lb (454-kg) bombs

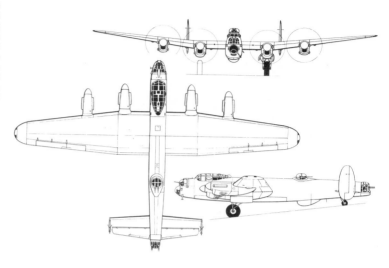

**Avro Lancaster B.Mk III**

Most famous night bomber of all time, the Lancaster served on a total of 65 squadrons of the RAF, and eventually carried the heaviest bomb dropped by aircraft in the war, the 22,000-lb (9976-kg) 'Grand Slam'. A Merlin-powered Lancaster Mk I is shown.

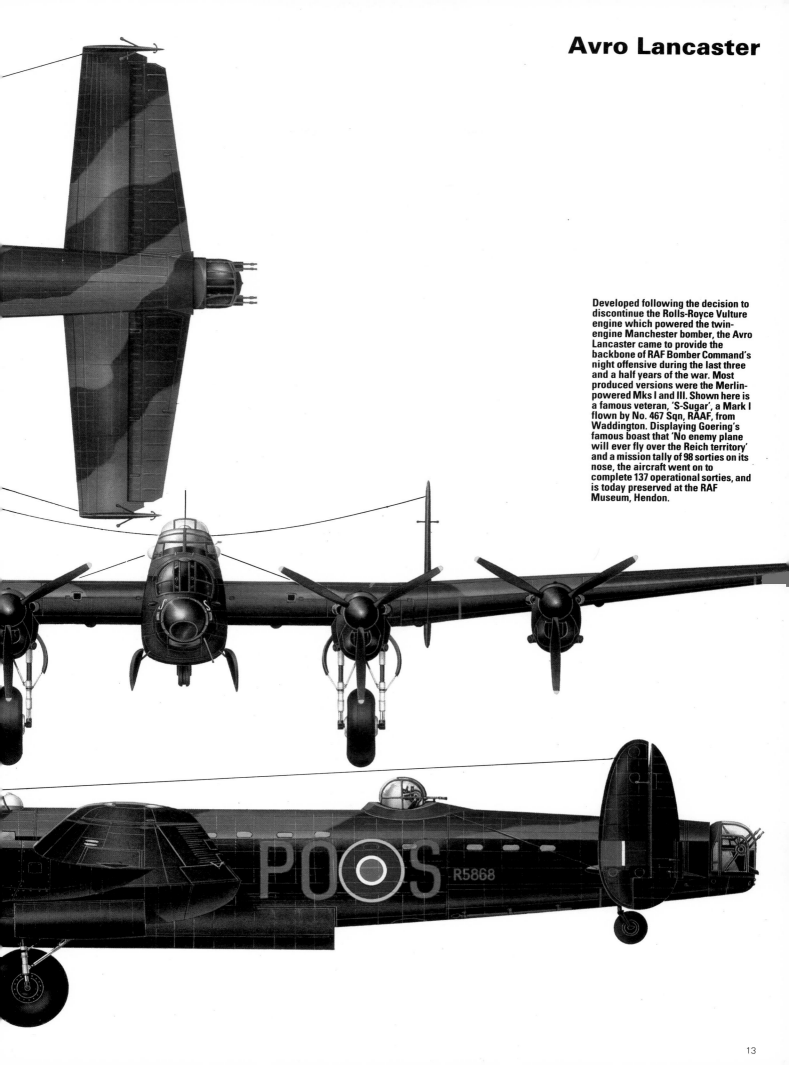

# Avro Lancaster

Developed following the decision to discontinue the Rolls-Royce Vulture engine which powered the twin-engine Manchester bomber, the Avro Lancaster came to provide the backbone of RAF Bomber Command's night offensive during the last three and a half years of the war. Most produced versions were the Merlin-powered Mks I and III. Shown here is a famous veteran, 'S-Sugar', a Mark I flown by No. 467 Sqn, RAAF, from Waddington. Displaying Goering's famous boast that 'No enemy plane will ever fly over the Reich territory' and a mission tally of 98 sorties on its nose, the aircraft went on to complete 137 operational sorties, and is today preserved at the RAF Museum, Hendon.

# Bell P-39 Airacobra

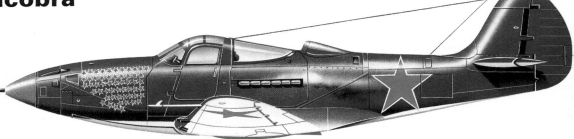

No fewer than 4,924 P-39Ns and P-39Qs were shipped to the Soviet Union, many of them over the Alaska-Siberian route from America. A number of Soviet P-39 pilots achieved very high victory scores, including Captain Grigori A. Rechkalov of the 9th Guards Fighter Division (44 victories with P-39s out of a total of 58).

## History and Notes

The radical P-39 single-seat fighter was designed around the 37-mm T-9 cannon which had given impressive demonstrations in 1935, the hub-firing arrangement of this gun dictating the midship location of the Allison inline engine behind the cockpit, driving the propeller by an extension shaft; this in turn led to adoption of a nosewheel landing gear. The prototype XP-39 was first flown in April 1939; production P-39Ds entered service with the USAAC in 1941 and first saw combat in the Pacific theatre in April 1942. P-39Ds also served with US forces in Europe but suffered heavily in action; they also flew with one RAF squadron (No. 601) but persistent problems caused them to be withdrawn after scarcely a single action. The Airacobra flew with much better results with three USAAF groups based in North Africa from the end of 1942. The P-39D was followed by the P-39F, which introduced an Aeroproducts propeller in place of the former Curtiss type, the P-39J with V-1710-59 engine, the P-39K with -63 engine and Aeroproducts propeller, and the P-39L with -63 engine and Curtiss propeller. The P-39M introduced the -83 engine with larger-diameter propeller. Final and most-built versions were the P-39N and P-39Q with -85 engine; production amounted to 2,095, bringing the total of all P-39s to 9,558. Of these, no fewer than 4,773 were shipped to the Soviet Union in response to Stalin's desperate appeals for military assistance.

**Specification:** Bell P-39N Airacobra
**Origin:** USA
**Type:** single-seat interceptor fighter
**Powerplant:** one 1,200-hp (895-kW) Allison V-1710-85 inline piston engine
**Performance:** maximum speed 399 mph (642 km/h) at 9,700 ft (2955 m); climb to 15,000 ft (4570 m) in 3.8 minutes; service ceiling 38,500 ft (11735 m); range 750 miles (1207 km)
**Weights:** empty 5,657 lb (2566 kg); maximum take-off 8,200 lb (3720 kg)
**Dimensions:** span 34 ft 0 in (10.36 m); length 30 ft 2 in (9.19 m); height 12 ft 5 in (3.78 m); wing area 213.0 sq ft (19.79 m²)
**Armament:** one hub-firing 37-mm gun, two 0.5-in (12.7-mm) machine-guns in nose decking, and four 0.3-in (7.62-mm) guns in the wings, plus provision for one 500-lb (227-kg) bomb under the fuselage

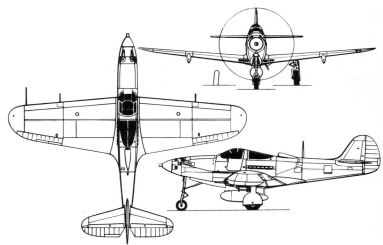

**Bell P-39Q Airacobra**

Though fast and heavily armed, the Airacobra never achieved the popularity of its contemporary trio, the P-38, P-47 and P-51, among the Western Allies; it was somewhat tricky to fly and unforgiving of handling mistakes, particularly during landing.

# Blackburn Skua

Although the Skua was originally conceived as a dive bomber, suitable targets were rare and the aircraft served in an ad hoc capacity, sometimes being used as a fleet fighter, its wing armament of four machine-guns in theory being no lighter than that of the Sea Gladiator.

## History and Notes

Occupying a niche unique in British naval aviation, the Blackburn Skua was a two-seat fighter/dive-bomber which gave valuable service in the first two years of the war. Designed to a 1934 specification, the prototype Skua first flew on 9 February 1937, being powered by an 840-hp (627-kW) Bristol Mercury IX radial; this and a second aircraft were termed Skua Mk Is, but the production aircraft were Skua Mk IIs with 890-hp (664-kW) Perseus XIIs. By the outbreak of war 154 of the 190 aircraft on order had been delivered and were serving with Nos 800, 801, 803 and 806 Squadrons. It was a Skua, flown by Lieutenant B. S. McEwen RN of No. 803 Squadron from HMS *Ark Royal*, which shot down the first German aircraft to fall to British aircraft guns (a Dornier Do 18 over the North Sea on 25 September 1939). During the Norwegian campaign Skuas of Nos 800 and 803 Squadrons flew from Hatston in the Orkneys to Bergen where they dive-bombed and sank the German cruiser *Königsberg* on 10 April 1940. Skuas of No. 801 Squadron took part in the defence of Dunkirk during the famous evacuation, while others from *Ark Royal* attacked the French fleet in Oran harbour in September 1940. Skuas remained in front-line service until August 1941, when they were replaced by Fulmars and Sea Hurricanes, and were relegated to training and target towing duties. Similar to the Skua was the Blackburn Roc turret fighter, of which 136 were produced.

## Specification: Blackburn Skua Mk II
**Origin:** UK
**Type:** two-seat shipborne fighter/dive-bomber
**Powerplant:** one 890-hp (664-kW) Bristol Perseus XII radial piston engine
**Performance:** maximum speed 225 mph (362 km/h) at 6,500 ft (1980 m); initial climb rate 1,580 ft (482 m) per minute; service ceiling 20,200 ft (6155 m); range 435 miles (700 km)
**Weights:** empty 5,496 lb (2493 kg); maximum take-off 8,228 lb (3732 kg)
**Dimensions:** span 46 ft 2 in (14.07 m); length 35 ft 7 in (10.84 m); height 12 ft 6 in (3.81 m); wing area 319.0 sq ft (29.64 m²)
**Armament:** four 0.303-in (7.7-mm) machine-guns in the wings and one in the rear cockpit, plus one 500-lb (227-kg) bomb

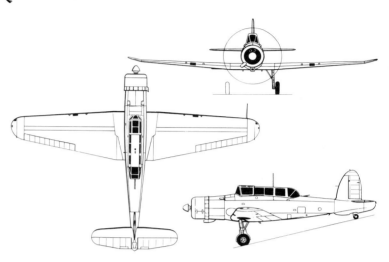

**Blackburn Skua Mk II**

The Fleet Air Arm's Blackburn Skua served aboard a number of British aircraft carriers at the beginning of the war and gave good service, particularly over the North Sea; during the Norwegian campaign of 1940 it operated from airfields ashore to protect the British Expeditionary Force.

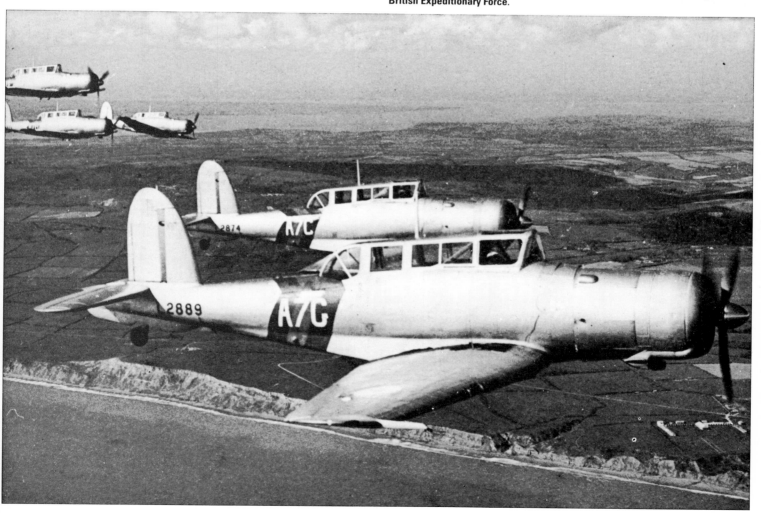

# Bloch 151/152/155

Despite its ability to survive much greater battle damage than other French fighters of 1940, the Bloch 152 nevertheless suffered the heaviest casualties; of the 632 aircraft taken on charge, about 270 were lost to enemy action in the Battle of France.

## History and Notes

Outmoded and handicapped by a radial engine of inadequate power, the Bloch 151 series fighters constituted the bulk of French fighter resistance during the Battle of France in 1940. Nevertheless they packed a powerful punch and, flown with skill and bravery, inflicted surprisingly heavy casualties on the Luftwaffe. Like so many wartime French aircraft, the Bloch 150 had stemmed from a 1934 requirement, but the prototype M.B. 150-01 failed to leave the ground for its first flight on 17 July 1936. Development continued, however, and after a successful flight by the M.B.150-01M on 29 September 1937 the type eventually entered production as the M.B.151 with Gnome-Rhône 14 N 35 radial, and the M.B.152 with 14 N 25 and 49 engines. By mid-January 1940 the Armée de l'Air had received 138 M.B.151s and 274 M.B.152s, but many were still without essential components. The situation had improved by the time of the German attack in the West when the number of M.B.152s had risen to 363 in service with five *groupes de chasse*. A new variant, the M.B.155 with two additional 7.5-mm (0.295-in) guns, started delivery just before the armistice, but only a few were flown during the Battle of France. Typifying the nature of operations flown by the French fighters was that during 3 June, when 300 bombers attacked the Paris area; the M.B.152s were caught in the climb by Bf 109Es and in the fight that followed four German aircraft were shot down for the loss of nine M.B.152s with three more damaged. However, against the combat loss of some 270 M.B.151s and M.B.152s during May and June, their pilots had destroyed a total of 146 German aircraft. Production of the M.B.151 and M.B.152 totalled 593.

## Specification: Bloch 152

**Origin:** France
**Type:** single-seat fighter
**Powerplant:** one 870-hp (649-kW) Gnome-Rhône 14 N 25 radial piston engine
**Performance:** maximum speed 299 mph (482 km/h) at 16,405 ft (5000 m); climb to 16,405 ft (5000 m) in 6.0 minutes; service ceiling 32,810 ft (10000 m); range 581 miles (935 km)
**Weights:** empty 4,453 lb (2020 kg); normal loaded 5,842 lb (2650 kg)
**Dimensions:** span 34 ft 5⅜ in (10.50 m); length 29 ft 10¼ in (9.10 m); height 9 ft 11⅓ in (3.03 m); wing area 186.4 sq ft (17.32 m²)

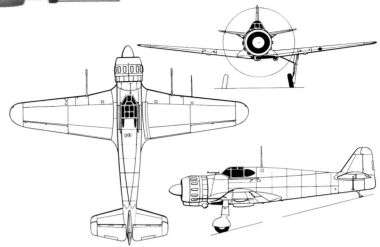

**Bloch 152**

**Armament:** two 20-mm HS404 cannon and two 7.5-mm (0.295-in) MAC 1934 machine-guns

Red and yellow striping identified aircraft of the Armée de l'Air de l'Armistice (the air force permitted by the Germans in unoccupied France after 1940). These Bloch 152s equipped 2ᵉ Escadrille, GC I/1, at Lyon-Bron in 1942.

# Boeing B-17 Fortress

RAF Bomber and Coastal Commands also flew the B-17, the Fortress Mks I, II and III corresponding to the B-17C, B-17E and B-17G respectively. The Fortress Mk II of No. 220 Sqn at Ballykelly depicted here carried the colour scheme of Coastal Command's maritime reconnaissance squadrons.

## History and Notes

Pursuing an operational theory that high flying, heavily armed bombers were the surest means of striking strategic targets in daylight, the US Army Air Corps issued a requirement in 1934 for which the Boeing Model 299 was designed and first flown on 28 July 1935. Twelve YB-17s entered service in 1937 and were followed by small numbers of B-17Bs and B-17Cs in 1940-1, and by the B-17D in 1941. The B-17E introduced the enlarged vertical tail surfaces and tail gun position characteristic of all subsequent B-17s, as well as power-operated twin-gun turrets aft of the cockpit and below the centre fuselage. 512 B-17Es were produced, this version being the first US Army Air Forces heavy bomber to see combat in Europe with the 8th Air Force. A total of 3,400 B-17Fs, with enlarged one-piece nose transparency, was produced during 1942-3, and these were followed by the principal variant, the B-17G, which, in reply to calls for improved nose armament to counter the Luftwaffe's head-on attacks, introduced the two-gun 'chin' turret; production totalled 8,685 aircraft by Boeing, Douglas and Lockheed-Vega. The Fortress was deployed principally in Europe during the war, with much smaller numbers in the Far East. They carried out many epic raids, large formations of bombers, each bristling with heavy machine-guns and providing mutual protection against enemy fighters, pounding across the daylight skies over Hitler's Reich. In due course heavy losses forced the Americans to introduce escort fighters – the P-38, P-47 and P-51. One temporary expedient involved the use of a small number of B-17s modified as YB-40 'escort' aircraft, some aircraft carrying up to 30 machine-guns. Fortresses (B-17Ds and B-17Fs) served in small numbers with RAF Bomber and Coastal Commands.

## Specification: Boeing B-17G Flying Fortress

**Origin:** USA
**Type:** 10-crew daylight medium/heavy bomber
**Powerplant:** four 1,200-hp (895-kW) Wright Cyclone R-1820-97 radial piston engines
**Performance:** maximum speed 287 mph (462 km/h) at 25,000 ft (7620 m); climb to 20,000 ft (6095 m) in 37.0 minutes; service ceiling 35,600 ft (10850 m); range with 6,000-lb (2722-kg) bombload 2,000 miles (3219 km)
**Weights:** empty 36,135 lb (16391 kg); maximum take-off 72,000 lb (32660 kg)
**Dimensions:** span 103 ft 9 in (31.62 m); length 74 ft 9 in (22.78 m); height 19 ft 1 in (5.82 m); wing area 1,420.0 sq ft (131.92 m²)

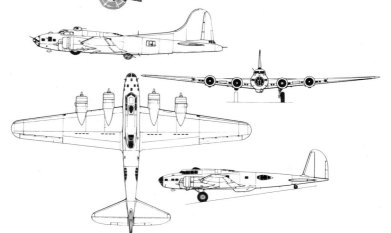

**Boeing B-17C (top view: B-17F)**

**Armament:** twin 0.5-in (12.7-mm) gun turrets under nose, aft of cockpit, under centre fuselage and in tail, and single-gun mountings in sides of nose, in radio operator's hatch and in waist (beam) positions, plus a maximum bombload of 17,600 lb (7983 kg)

A formation of B-17G Fortress bombers of the USAAF's 381st Bomb Group (Heavy), based at Ridgewell, England, in 1944; aircraft carrying the letters VE were from the 532rd Squadron, those with VP from the 533rd. Tight formation allowed mutual defence from the B-17's many guns.

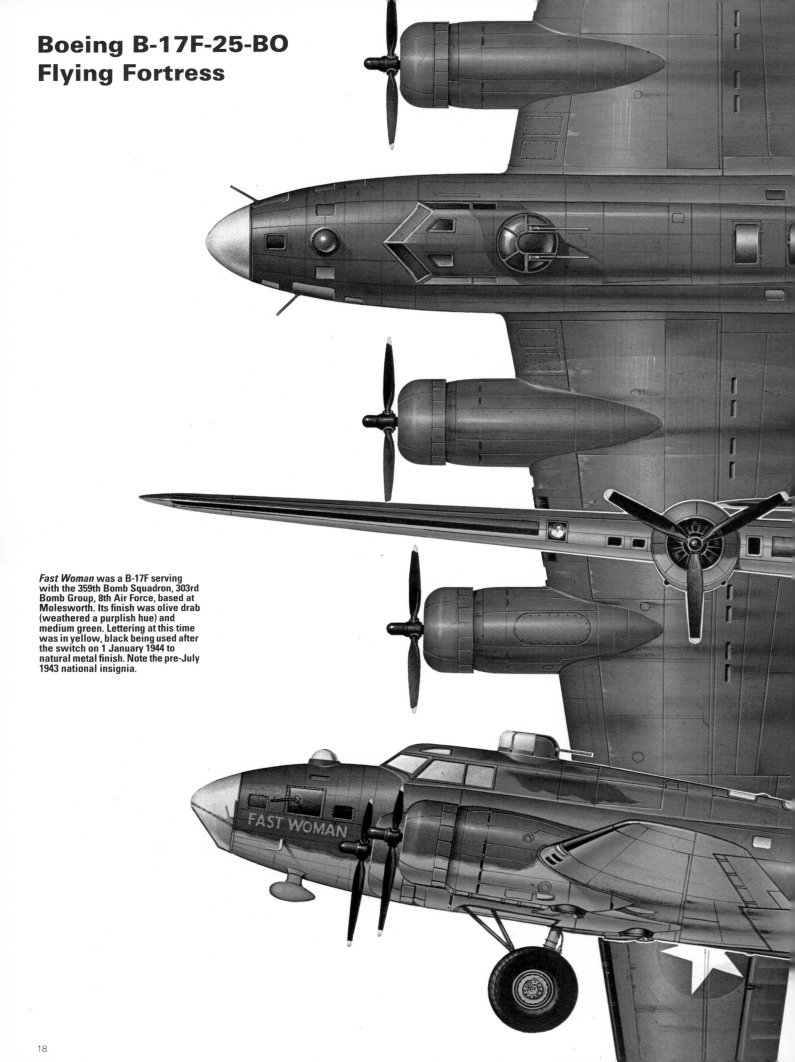

# Boeing B-17F-25-BO Flying Fortress

*Fast Woman* was a B-17F serving with the 359th Bomb Squadron, 303rd Bomb Group, 8th Air Force, based at Molesworth. Its finish was olive drab (weathered a purplish hue) and medium green. Lettering at this time was in yellow, black being used after the switch on 1 January 1944 to natural metal finish. Note the pre-July 1943 national insignia.

FAST WOMAN

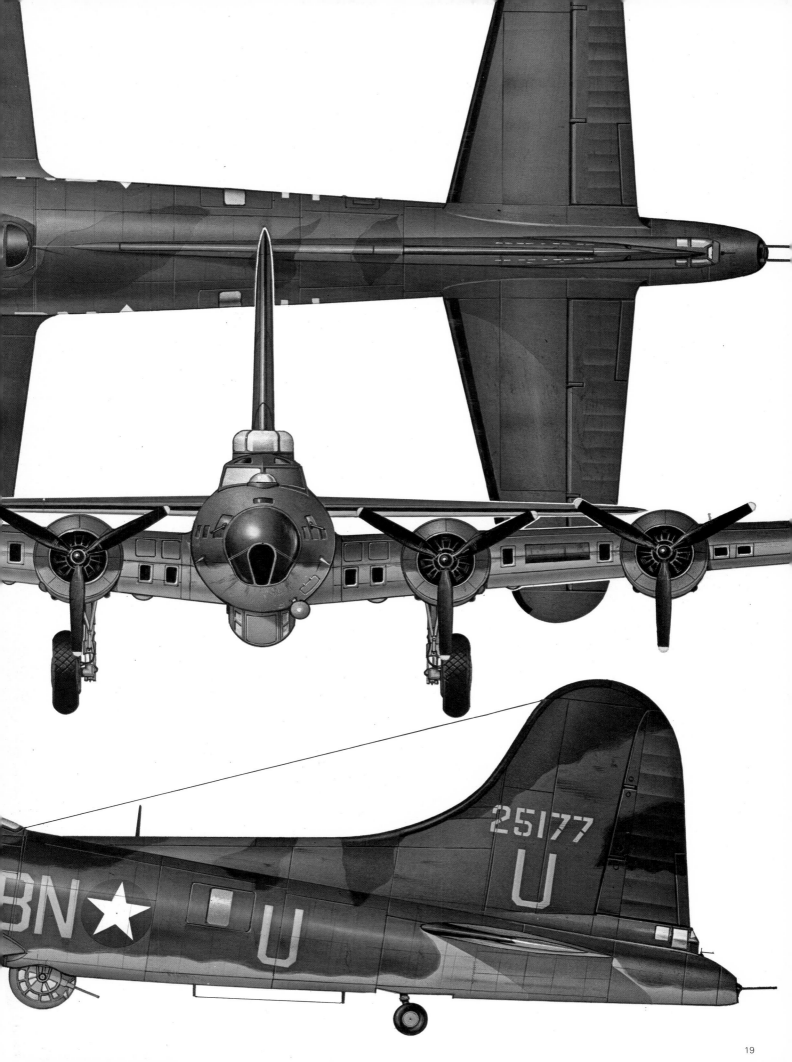

25177
U

BN ★ U

# Boeing B-29 Superfortress

A feature of the B-29's gun armament was the use of remotely-controlled turrets, periscopically sighted by gunners located within the fuselage. The aircraft illustrated, carrying BTO (bombing through overcast) radar, was based on Tinian for the final heavy raids on Japan.

## History and Notes

Design of the B-29 heavy bomber started in 1940 to meet a US Army Air Corps requirement for a 'Hemisphere Defense Weapon', an aircraft capable of carrying 2,000 lb (907 kg) of bombs for 5,333 miles (8582 km) at 400 mph (644 km/h); only after the Japanese attack on Pearl Harbor put an end to America's isolationism was the project given top priority, and the first XB-29 was flown on 21 September 1942. The very big four-engine mid-wing bomber had by then been ordered in large numbers and in 1943 the decision was taken to deploy the B-29 only against Japan, concentrating the new bombers in the XX Bomber Command on bases in India and China. The first YB-29s were delivered to the 58th Bomb Wing in July 1943 and were followed by B-29-BWs three months later. Production was concentrated at Boeing Wichita (BW), Bell, Atlanta (BA), Martin, Omaha (MO), and a new Boeing-run factory at Renton (BN). Four groups of B-29s moved to India early in 1944, making their first raid on Bangkok on 5 June, and on the Japanese mainland 10 days later. For the first nine months the B-29s were principally employed in high-level daylight raids, but on 9 March 1945 they switched to low-level night attacks with devastating incendiary raids on Japanese cities (the first of which on Tokyo caused 80,000 deaths). Two other main versions of the B-29 appeared during the war, the B-29A-BN with four-gun forward upper turret and increased wing span, and the B-29B-BA with reduced gun armament and increased bombload. The B-29-45-MOs Enola Gay and Bock's Car of the 393rd Bomb Squadron dropped the atomic bombs 'Little Boy' and 'Fat Boy' on Hiroshima and Nagasaki on 6 and 9 August 1945 respectively, bringing the war to an end. Total B-29 production was 3,970.

**Specification:** Boeing B-29A Superfortress
**Origin:** USA
**Type:** 10-crew heavy strategic bomber
**Powerplant:** four 2,200-hp (1641-kW) Wright R-3350-57 radial piston engines
**Performance:** maximum speed 358 mph (576 km/h) at 25,000 ft (7620 m); climb to 20,000 ft (6095 m) in 38 minutes; service ceiling 31,800 ft (9695 m); range 4,100 miles (6598 km)
**Weights:** empty 71,360 lb (32369 kg); maximum take-off 141,100 lb (64003 kg)
**Dimensions:** span 142 ft 3 in (43.36 m); length 99 ft 0 in (30.18 m); height 29 ft 7 in (9.01 m); wing area 1,736.0 sq ft (161.27 m²)
**Armament:** four-gun turret over nose, two-gun turrets under nose, under and over rear fuselage, all of 0.5-in (12.7-mm) calibre, and one 20-mm and two 0.5-in (12.7-mm) guns in tail, plus a bombload of up to 20,000 lb (9072 kg)

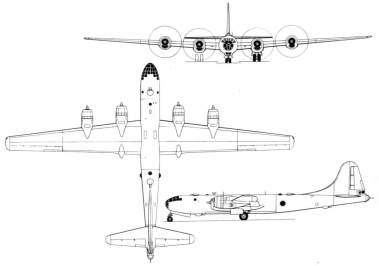

**Boeing B-29A Superfortress**

The mighty Superfortress. One of the most remarkable achievements of the war was the design, development and production of this bomber in the space of four years. All B-29s were assigned to the assault on Japan, the two aircraft seen here – YB-29s – being flown by the 58th Bomb Wing (Very Heavy).

# Boulton Paul Defiant

A Defiant in the markings of No. 264 Sqn, the pennant below the cockpit denoting the aircraft of the commanding officer, Squadron Leader P.A. Hunter, who was shot down and killed on 24 August 1940 in the Battle of Britain. The Defiant was subsequently transferred to the night fighting role.

## History and Notes

Perpetuating the elderly and fallacious single-engine two-seat fighter formula born in 1917 with the Bristol F.2B fighter, the Boulton Paul Defiant was schemed in 1937 as the smallest aircraft capable of accepting a two-man crew, a single Rolls-Royce Merlin inline engine and a four-gun power-operated turret located close to the centre of gravity capable of heavy fire towards the flanks of the aircraft. The prototype Defiant was first flown on 11 August 1937, and the type joined No. 264 Squadron in December 1939. Powered by a 1,030-hp (768-kW) Merlin III inline engine, the Defiant Mk I was armed with four 0.303-in (7.7-mm) Browning machine-guns in the dorsal turret, but was totally devoid of fixed forward-firing armament, and the turret could not be trained to fire directly forwards. The fighter was flown with some success during the Dunkirk evacuation, German pilots being misled by the type's superficial resemblance to 'conventional' single-seat fighters, but during the Battle of Britain Nos 141 and 264 Squadrons suffered disastrous losses to German pilots who were now fully aware of the type's armament and performance limitations.

The Defiant was thus retasked with night-fighting, a role for which it was much better suited. Defiant Mk I aircraft at first operated 'blind', but Defiant Mk IA aircraft had AI Mk IV or Mk VI radar. The Defiant Mk II was already in service, being a day fighter with the more powerful 1,260-hp (940-kW) Merlin XX, and this version was also rapidly converted into a night-fighter. Other roles undertaken by the Defiant were air-sea rescue, radar calibration and countermeasures and, in the Defiant Mk III version produced by conversion of Defiant Mk Is, target towing. Production ceased in February 1943 after the building of 1,060 Defiants.

## Specification: Boulton Paul Defiant Mk II
**Origin:** UK
**Type:** two-seat night-fighter
**Powerplant:** one 1,260-hp (940-kW) Rolls-Royce Merlin XX inline piston engine
**Performance:** maximum speed 315 mph (507 km/h) at 16,500 ft (5030 m); initial climb rate 2,050 ft (625 m) per minute; service ceiling 31,800 ft (9690 m); range 480 miles (772 km)
**Weights:** empty 6,150 lb (2892 kg); maximum take-off 8,600 lb (3901 kg)
**Dimensions:** span 39 ft 4 in (11.99 m); length 35 ft 4 in (10.77 m); height 12 ft 2 in (3.71 m); wing area 250.0 sq ft (23.23 m²)
**Armament:** four 0.303-in (7.7-mm) Browning machine-guns in dorsal turret

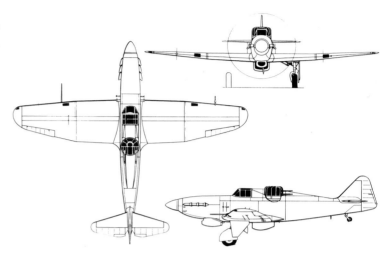

**Boulton Paul Defiant NF.Mk II**

Designed as a two-seat interceptor fighter armed only with a four-gun power-operated turret, the Defiant had a brief moment of glory over Dunkirk, but the two squadrons which were committed in the Battle of Britain were decimated by German single-seat fighters.

# Brewster F2A Buffalo

One of the most successful users of the Buffalo was the Finnish air force, ranged as it was against large numbers of obsolescent Russian aircraft in 1942. The aircraft shown here belonged to HLeLv 24, and was flown by Heimo Lampi who gained 14 victories.

## History and Notes

The first monoplane fighter to enter operational service with the US Navy, the Buffalo first flew as the XF2A-1 prototype in December 1937, and the F2A-1 initial production version became operational with VF-3 aboard the USS *Saratoga* in June 1940. These 11 aircraft were powered by the 940-hp (701-kW) R-1820-34 radial, and were followed by the improved F2A-2. This model had redesigned vertical tail surfaces and, more importantly, an uprated engine in the form of the 1,200-hp (895-kW) R-1820-40. Reports of British and French combat experience in Europe had by this time revealed that most US combat aircraft were deficient in a number of important respects, and the F2A-3 was produced to remedy at least some of these defects in the Buffalo series. Thus the 43 F2A-2s were followed by 108 F3A-3 aircraft with a measure of armour protection and lengthened nose, but otherwise similar to the F2A-2. These 162 aircraft comprised the entire production of the F2A for the US services, and the type saw only very limited combat use, largely with VMF-221 in the Battle of Midway in 1942, when this US Marine Corps squadron suffered devastating losses.

Other aircraft were built to meet export orders. The B-239 was the export version of the F2A-1, and 44 were built against a Finnish order. Next came the B-339, which was produced in the B-339B and B-339D versions (40 and 72 respectively) against Belgian and Dutch orders. The two versions were essentially land-based versions of the F2A-1, and 38 of the Belgian order were diverted to the UK, which also accepted 170 B-339E aircraft under the designation Buffalo Mk I. The final production version was the B-439, an export version of the F2A-3, 20 of which were ordered by the Netherlands for service in the Dutch East Indies. All 20 aircraft were delivered to the USAAF, which later passed 17 to the Royal Australian Air Force. The Buffaloes were recognized as unsuited to European operations (though the Finns enjoyed great success against the Russians), and most export aircraft served in the Far East, suffering dismal defeat at the hands of Japanese pilots over Malaya, Burma and the Dutch East Indies.

## Specification: Brewster F2A-3
**Origin:** USA
**Type:** single-seat shipboard fighter
**Powerplant:** one 1,200-hp (895-kW) Wright R-1820-40 radial piston engine
**Performance:** maximum speed 321 mph (516 km/h) at 16,500 ft (5030 m); initial climb rate

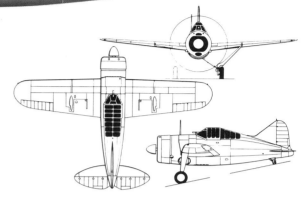

**Brewster F2A-3 Buffalo**

2,290 m (698 m) per minute; service ceiling 32,300 ft (10120 m); maximum range 965 miles (1650 km)
**Weights:** empty 4,732 lb (2146 kg); maximum take-off 7,159 lb (3247 kg)
**Dimensions:** span 35 ft 0 in (10.67 m); length 26 ft 4 in (8.02 m); height 12 ft 1 in (3.68 m); wing area 208.9 sq ft (19.41 m²)
**Armament:** four 0.5-in (12.7-mm) Browning machine-guns, two in nose and two in wings.

First monoplane fighter to serve on a US Navy squadron, the F2A Buffalo was already obsolete when America entered the war, and suffered heavy casualties in its only major Pacific combat with the US Marine Corps, the Great Battle of Midway.

# Bristol Beaufighter

An early Beaufighter TF.Mk X of No. 455 Sqn equipped for anti-shipping strike duties with eight underwing rockets; later aircraft featured a dorsal fin extension found necessary to improve directional stability when carrying a torpedo. Rocket and torpedo Beaufighters served together in special anti-shipping strike wings.

## History and Notes

Cornerstone of the UK's early night-fighter defences and the RAF's first purpose-built night-fighter, the twin-engine Beaufighter first arrived in service in small numbers at the beginning of the German night *Blitz* in September 1940, having first flown on 17 July 1939. The Beaufighter Mk I with Bristol Hercules radials was produced in two forms, the Mk IF for Fighter Command and the Mk IC for Coastal Command, the former equipped with AI Mk IV radar gaining its first confirmed night victory on 19 November 1940. The Beaufighter Mk IIF followed, powered with two Rolls-Royce Merlin XX inline engines, joining home-based night-fighter squadrons in 1941, by which time the heavily-armed fighter was achieving a respectable toll of enemy night raiders. The Beaufighter Mk VI, also produced in Mk VIF and Mk VIC versions, reverted to Hercules radials, but of increased power, the Mk VIC introducing a Vickers gun to fire aft from the navigator's hatch. By 1942 Beaufighters were flying with a sharply dihedralled tailplane, and the Beaufighter Mk VI also introduced an extended dorsal fin to counter take-off swing. Underwing rockets and an 18-in (457-mm) torpedo were carried by some Beaufighter Mk VIC aircraft. As the Mosquito had almost exclusively assumed the night-fighting role, the definitive ASV-equipped Beaufighter TF.Mk X was delivered to Coastal Command as a long-range strike fighter, employing torpedo, rockets, bombs and guns. Beaufighters served in the Mediterranean and the Far East, giving outstanding service against the Japanese in Burma. Production of the Beaufighter (which was also undertaken in Australia) continued until September 1945, 5,562 aircraft being produced.

**Specification:** Bristol Beaufighter Mk VIF
**Origin:** UK
**Type:** two-seat night-fighter
**Powerplant:** two 1,670-hp (1246-kW) Bristol Hercules VI or XVI radial piston engines
**Performance:** maximum speed 333 mph (536 km/h) at 15,600 ft (4755 m); climb to 15,000 ft (4570 m) in 7.8 minutes; service ceiling 26,500 ft (8075 m); range 1,480 miles (2382 km)
**Weights:** empty 14,600 lb (6623 kg); maximum take-off 21,600 lb (9798 kg)
**Dimensions:** span 57 ft 10 in (17.63 m); length 41 ft 8 in (12.70 m); height 15 ft 10 in (4.82 m); wing area 503.0 sq ft (46.73 m²)
**Armament:** four 20-mm cannon in nose, two 0.303-in (7.7-mm) machine-guns in port wing, and four 0.303-in (7.7-mm) machine-guns in starboard wing.

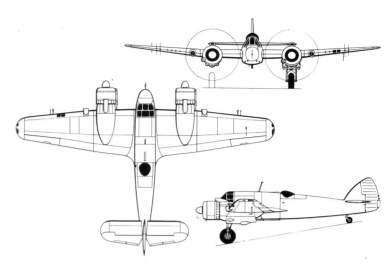

**Bristol Beaufighter Mk IF**

The Beaufighter was the RAF's first purpose-designed night fighter and pioneered the science of radar-directed interception. Powerful and heavily-armed, the aircraft served on almost every front during the war in a variety of roles and gained a fine reputation in the Mediterranean and Far East.

# Bristol Beaufort

A Beaufort Mk I in the markings of No. 22 Sqn. It was Flying Officer Kenneth Campbell of this squadron who, in a Beaufort, carried out a magnificent torpedo attack on the German warships in Brest harbour, scoring a direct hit on the *Gneisenau*; Campbell was shot down and killed, but won a posthumous Victoria Cross.

## History and Notes

Until superseded by the torpedo-carrying Beaufighter, the Beaufort was the RAF's standard torpedo-bomber from 1940 to 1943, replacing the aged Vickers Vildebeest biplane. First flown on 15 October 1938, the Beaufort Mk I, of which early versions were powered by 1,010-hp (753-kW) Bristol Taurus II radials (later replaced by Taurus VIs), joined No. 22 Squadron in December 1939 and carried out their first minelaying sortie on 15-16 August 1940. Beauforts also dropped the RAF's first 2,000-lb (907-kg) bomb on 7 May. Total production of the Beaufort Mk I was 965, and this version was followed by the Beaufort Mk II with American Pratt & Whitney Twin Wasp radials, production continuing until 1943, by which time 415 had been produced. The final Beaufort Mk IIs were completed as trainers with the two-gun dorsal turret deleted. Beauforts equipped six Coastal Command squadrons in the United Kingdom and four in the Middle East, their most famous operations being carried out against the German warships *Scharnhorst* and *Gneisenau* on 6 April 1941 in Brest harbour (which earned a posthumous VC for Flying Officer K. Campbell of No. 22 Squadron), and during the warships' escape up the English Channel early in 1942. Beauforts were also very active while based on Malta, attacking Axis shipping being sailed to North Africa. The Beaufort Mks V-IX were built in Australia for the RAAF in the Far East, production totalling 700.

**Specification:** Bristol Beaufort Mk I
**Origin:** UK
**Type:** four-crew torpedo-bomber
**Powerplant:** two 1,130-hp (843-kW) Bristol Taurus VI radial engines
**Performance:** maximum speed 265 mph (426 km/h) at 6,000 ft (1830 m); service ceiling 16,500 ft (5030 m); range 1,600 miles (2574 km)
**Weights:** empty 13,100 lb (5942 kg); maximum take-off 21,228 lb (9629 kg)
**Dimensions:** span 57 ft 10 in (17.62 m); length 44 ft 3 in (13.49 m); height 14 ft 3 in (4.34 m); wing area 503.0 sq ft (46.73 m²)
**Armament:** two 0.303-in (7.7-mm) machine-guns in nose and dorsal turret (some aircraft had a rear-firing machine-gun under the nose and two in beam-firing positions), plus a bombload up to 2,000 lb (907 kg) or one 1,605-lb (728-kg) 18-in (457-mm) torpedo

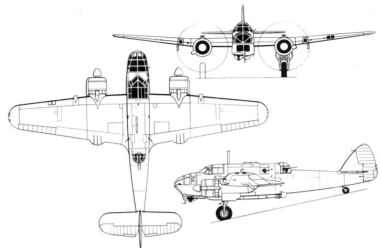

**Bristol Beaufort Mk I**

**Early Beaufort Mk Is of RAF Coastal Command's No. 217 Sqn; based at St Eval in Cornwall during the first two years of the war, the Squadron's Beauforts flew minelaying and anti-shipping missions over the English Channel before moving to the Far East.**

# Bristol Blenheim

The Blenheim Mk IV continued to give steadfast service well into the war, spearheading the British day bomber force throughout the first two years. The aircraft shown served with LeLv 42 of the Finnish air force late in 1942 at the beginning of the Continuation War.

## History and Notes

At the beginning of the war the RAF's principal twin-engine light bomber was the Blenheim, the aircraft having first entered service in its Mk I form with No. 114 Squadron in March 1937. Capable of outpacing the then-current RAF biplane fighters, the Blenheim Mk I was being replaced by the Blenheim Mk IV as a home-based bomber in 1939, the latter featuring a longer nose with conventional 'stepped' cockpit windscreen. The short-nose Blenheim Mk IF continued in service throughout 1940 as a night fighter with Fighter Command, however, having been fitted with a tray of four 0.303-in (7.7-mm) machine-guns under the fuselage; some of these aircraft pioneered the RAF's first airborne interception radar, gaining the world's first night AI victory on 22 July 1940. Bomber Command's Blenheim Mk IVs continued in service for three years, making many memorable raids during that time, their last operation being flown on 18 August 1942. This version also served with Coastal Command both as a fighter (the Blenheim Mk IVF) and as an anti-shipping bomber, and in a period of six months in 1941 sank 70 enemy ships. Blenheim MK IVs flew with the RAF in the Mediterranean and Middle East until 1943, and in the Far East participated in the defence of Singapore and in the Burma campaign. The Blenheim Mk V with Mercury XXX, whose principal version was the tropicalized Blenheim Mk VD, entered service in North Africa at the end of 1942, but was found to be too slow and vulnerable and was soon withdrawn from service. A total of about 4,440 Blenheims was produced.

## Specification: Bristol Blenheim Mk IV
**Origin:** UK
**Type:** three-crew light bomber
**Powerplant:** two 920-hp (686-kW) Bristol Mercury XV radial piston engines
**Performance:** maximum speed 266 mph (428 km/h) at 11,800 ft (3595 m); initial climb rate 1,500 ft (457 m) per minute; service ceiling 22,000 ft (6705 m); range 1,460 miles (2350 km)
**Weights:** empty 9,790 lb (4441 kg); maximum take-off 13,500 lb (6124 kg)
**Dimensions:** span 56 ft 4 in (17.17 m); length 42 ft 7 in (12.98 m); height 9 ft 10 in (2.99 m); wing area 469.0 sq ft (43.57 m²)
**Armament:** one fixed forward-firing 0.303-in (7.7-mm) machine-gun in nose and two 0.303-in (7.7-mm) machine-guns in dorsal turret, plus a bombload of 1,000 lb (454 kg) internally and 320 lb (145 kg) externally

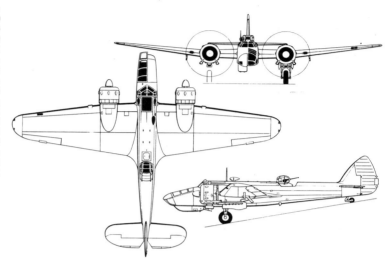

**Bristol Blenheim Mk V**

Obsolescent at the outbreak of war, the Blenheim Mk I nevertheless continued to serve as a night fighter; this radar-equipped Mk IF with four-gun pack under the fuselage flew with No. 54 Operational Training Unit.

# Cant Z.1007 Alcione

Built largely of wood, the attractive Cant Z.1007 had a creditable performance. However, like so many Italian aircraft, the defensive armament was puny and many Airone (Heron) bombers fell to equally mediocre British fighters.

## History and Notes

Product of Cantieri Riuniti dell'Adriatico (always abbreviated to 'Cant'), which since the mid-1920s had been synonymous with Italian flying-boats and floatplanes, the three-engine Z.1007 Alcione (Kingfisher) was designed by Filippo Zappata during 1937 as a logical development of his Z.506B Airone (Heron) floatplane, itself a military counterpart of the commercial Z.506A. With three 840-hp (627-kW) Isotta Fraschini Asso engines, the prototype was first flown in May 1937, and gained a favourable response from the Regia Aeronautica test establishments, particularly on account of its easily maintained all-wood construction. Early production aircraft were armed with four 7.7-mm (0.303-in) machine-guns in dorsal turret, beam hatches and ventral position, but later Alciones had 12.7-mm (0.5-in) guns in the turret and ventral position. Production got under way in 1939 and the first aircraft joined the Regia Aeronautica later that year. The main production version, the Z.1007bis, was powered by three 1,000-hp (746-kW) Piaggio radials, and featured larger fuselage, increased wing area and strengthened landing gear; most aircraft also changed to a twin-finned tail unit. Z.1007s were used in the torpedo-bombing role, particularly in operations against the Malta convoys, but were mainly employed in night bombing operations over the Aegean, Malta and, to a lesser extent, in North Africa. On account of its weak gun defence, however, the Z.1007 proved a sitting duck for mid-war Allied fighters, yet remained in service until September 1943, while some also served on the Russian Front. The metal-construction, twin-engine Z.1018 Leone (Lion) was developed from the Alcione, but scarcely entered service before the Italian surrender.

## Specification: Cant Z.1007bis Alcione

**Origin:** Italy
**Type:** five-crew medium bomber/torpedo-bomber
**Powerplant:** three 1,000-hp (746-kW) Piaggio P.XI bis RC 40 radial piston engines
**Performance:** maximum speed 280 mph (450 km/h) at 13,780 ft (4200 m); initial climb rate 1,542 ft (470 m) per minute; service ceiling 26,575 ft (8100 m); range 800 miles (1280 km) with full bomb load
**Weights:** empty 19,005 lb (8620 kg); maximum take-off 30,029 lb (13621 kg)
**Dimensions:** span 81 ft 4½ in (24.80 m); length 60 ft 2½ in (18.35 m); height 17 ft 1½ in (5.22 m); wing area 753.5 sq ft (70.00 m²)
**Armament:** one 7.7-mm (0.303-in) Breda-SAFAT machine-gun in each of two beam hatches, and single 12.7-mm (0.5-in) Breda-SAFAT machine-guns in dorsal turret and ventral position, plus a bombload of up to 4,409 lb (2000 kg) internally and up to 2,205 lb (1000 kg) under wings, or two 1,000-lb (454-kg) torpedoes as an alternative to the internal bombload

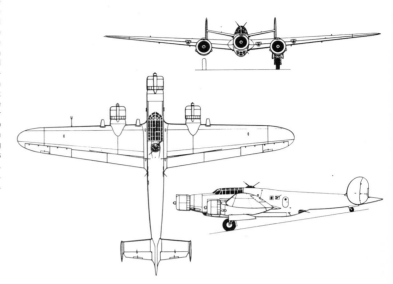

**CANT Z.1007bis**

The big Cant Z.1007 tri-motor bomber was produced in both single- and twin-fin versions and served side-by-side on the same squadrons; these aircraft belonged to the 230ª Squadriglia BT, 95° Gruppo BT, 35° Stormo BT, which operated over Greece in the campaign of 1941.

# Consolidated B-24 Liberator

On account of its very long range, the Liberator was ideal as a maritime patrol aircraft, serving with both the US Navy and RAF Coastal Command based in Britain. This PB4Y-1 of US Navy squadron VPB-110 was based in the UK during the winter of 1944-5.

## History and Notes

Produced in larger numbers than any other American aircraft during the war (and any other four-engine aircraft in history) the B-24 did not enter the design stage until 1939, and the prototype XB-24 was flown on 29 December that year. Minor development batches followed in 1940 before the first major production version, the B-24D, appeared late in 1941. A policy decision to concentrate B-24s primarily in the Pacific theatre (where its long range was used to good effect) resulted in most of the 2,738 B-24Ds being deployed against Japan, but the 8th and 9th Air Forces in Europe and North Africa also received the aircraft, one of their outstanding raids being the attack on the Ploesti oil refineries on 1 August 1943. 791 B-24Es with changed propellers were produced before production switched to the B-24G, of which 430 were built. This version introduced a two-gun nose turret to counter German head-on fighter attacks and was followed by 3,100 B-24Hs. Major production version was the B-24J, of which 6,678 were built, incorporating a Motor Products nose turret, new-type autopilot and bombsight. The B-24L (1,667 built) featured two manually operated tail guns in a Consolidated turret, and the B-24M (2,593 built) introduced a Motor Products two-gun tail turret. This huge manufacturing effort (which produced a total of 18,313 aircraft in five and a half years) involved Consolidated, Douglas, Ford and North American plants, the total including many aircraft for the RAF (in which Liberators served with 42 squadrons) and US Navy (with whom Liberators served under the designation PB4Y) and also the 25-passenger C-87 version, of which 282 were produced.

## Specification: Consolidated B-24J Liberator
**Origin:** USA
**Type:** eight/10-crew daylight medium/heavy bomber
**Powerplant:** four 1,200-hp (895-kW) Pratt & Whitney R-1830-65 radial piston engines
**Performance:** maximum speed 290 mph (467 km/h) at 25,000 ft (620 m); climb to 20,000 ft (6095 m) in 25 minutes; service ceiling 28,000 ft (8535 m); range 2,000 miles (3219 km) with an 8,800-lb (3992-kg) bombload
**Weights:** empty 36,500 lb (16556 kg); maximum take-off 65,000 lb (29484 kg)
**Dimensions:** span 110 ft 0 in (33.53 m); length 67 ft 2 in (20.47 m); height 18 ft 0 in (5.49 m); wing area 1,048.0 sq ft (97.36 m²)
**Armament:** two-gun turrets in nose, tail, upper fuselage aft of cockpit and under centre fuselage, and single flexible guns in waist (beam) positions for a total of 10 0.5-in (12.7-mm) machine-guns, plus a normal bombload of 8,800 lb (3992 kg)

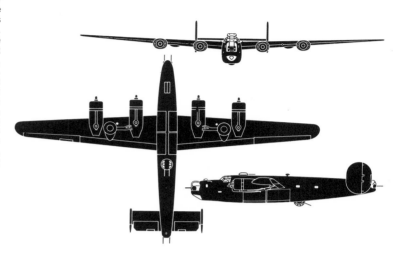

**Consolidated B-24J Liberator**

The USAAF employed a unique expedient to assist in assembling its large formations of bombers, using a brightly painted aircraft (in this case covered with polka dots and an illuminated 'I' on the rear fuselage) on which component leaders would formate. Once the whole formation had caught up, the 'assembly ship' returned to base.

# Consolidated PBY Catalina

Catalinas flew with a total of 18 squadrons of the RAF, almost all with Coastal Command. This Catalina Mk IV of No. 210 Sqn, with ASV Mark II radar, was based at Sullom Voe in the Shetlands for patrol duties over the Denmark Straits in 1944-5.

## History and Notes

The prototype of the graceful Catalina flying-boat was the XP3Y-1 which first flew on 28 March 1935. Giving it a substantial bomb-carrying capability brought it into the patrol bomber category so that production aircraft were termed PBY-1s, and these first equipped US Navy Patrol Squadron VP-11F in October 1936. Similar PBY-2s and PBY-3s followed into service in 1937-8. The PBY-4, introduced in 1938, featured 1,050-hp (783-kW) Pratt & Whitney R-1830-72 radials and large transparent blister fairings over the beam gunners' positions, previously covered by sliding hatches. By the end of 1941 some 16 US Navy squadrons were flying the PBY-5 with -92 engines and modified fin shape; in addition five squadrons were still equipped with earlier versions. At the time of Pearl Harbor the first examples of the PBY-5A amphibian were being delivered. Meanwhile substantial orders for PBY-4s and PBY-5s had been ordered by the UK, and within three years these totalled 685, many of them being delivered to the air forces of Canada, Australia and New Zealand, as well as RAF Coastal Command. A version with heightened fin and rudder, and search radar carried in a fairing above the cockpit, was the PBY-6A, 112 being delivered to the US Navy, 48 to Russia and 75 to the USAAF (as the OA-10B). Production was also undertaken in Canada by Canadian Vickers and Boeing, the version which joined the RCAF being called the Canso, while the Naval Aircraft Factory at Philadelphia produced the PBN-1 Nomad with improvements to hull and tip floats. Total production of all versions of the PBY was 3,290 in the US and Canada, plus an unknown quantity built in Russia as the GST.

**Specification:** Consolidated B-24J Liberator
**Origin:** USA
**Type:** eight/10-crew daylight medium/heavy bomber
**Powerplant:** four 1,200-hp (895-kW) Pratt & Whitney R-1830-65 radial piston engines
**Performance:** maximum speed 290 mph (467 km/h) at 25,000 ft (620 m); climb to 20,000 ft (6095 m) in 25 minutes; service ceiling 28,000 ft (8535 m); range 2,000 miles (3219 km) with an 8,800-lb (3992-kg) bombload
**Weights:** empty 36,500 lb (16556 kg); maximum take-off 65,000 lb (29484 kg)
**Dimensions:** span 110 ft 0 in (33.53 m); length 67 ft 2 in (20.47 m); height 18 ft 0 in (5.49 m); wing area 1,048.0 sq ft (97.36 m²)
**Armament:** two-gun turrets in nose, tail, upper fuselage aft of cockpit and undercentre fuselage, and single flexible guns in waist (beam) positions for a total of 10 0.5-in (12.7-mm) machine-guns, plus a normal bombload of 8,800 lb (3992 kg)

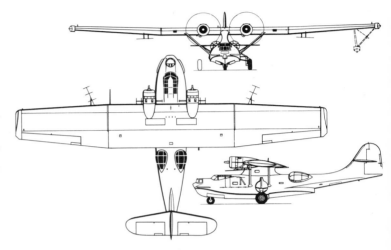

**Consolidated PBY-5A Catalina**

Capable of remaining on patrol for 24 hours at a time, the PBY-5 Catalina equipped 16 US Navy patrol squadrons when America entered the war in 1941. The aircraft is here seen on patrol over the Aleutians in the North Pacific and is carrying early ASV radar.

# Curtiss P-40 Warhawk

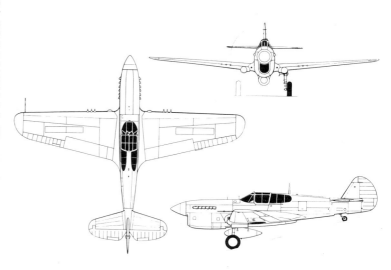

A P-40L of the 325th Fighter Group based in Tunisia, flying escort duties for medium bombers of the USAAF's 47th bomb Wing in 1943. Adequate in combat against Italian aircraft, the P-40 was generally inferior to other contemporary British and American fighters.

## History and Notes

America's most important fighter at the time of the Japanese attack on Pearl Harbor, the P-40 continued to give valuable service for the remainder of the war, though it never matched the excellence of the famous P-38/P-47/P-51 trio. It had, after all, first flown as the X17Y (later the P-36 with Pratt & Whitney R-1830 radial) and been re-engined as the XP-40 with supercharged Allison V-1710 inline engine in October 1938. Large orders followed, but most P-40As went to the RAF (as the Tomahawk Mk I). The P-40B followed with cockpit armour and an armament of two 0.5-in (12.7-mm) and four 0.3-in (7.62-mm) guns (the Tomahawk Mk IIA in the RAF). The P-40C (Tomahawk Mk IIB) featured self-sealing fuel tanks. The P-40D introduced a slightly shortened nose with radiator moved forward and deepened, this marked change in appearance being identified by a change of name to Kittyhawk in the RAF (all P-40s in American service being termed Warhawks); the P-40D corresponded with the Kittyhawk Mk I in RAF service. The first major USAAF version was the P-40E (Kittyhawk Mk IA), with six 0.5-in (12.7-mm) wing guns, 2,320 being built. A Packard-built Rolls-Royce Merlin powered the P-40F (Kittyhawk Mk II). Most-produced version was the P-40N (of which 5,219 were built), this version reverting to the Allison V-1710 engine and featuring shackles for up to 1,500 lb (680 kg) of bombs; in RAF service it became the Kittyhawk Mk IV. The majority of USAAF P-40s served in the Pacific, although many served in the Mediterranean theatre alongside the RAF's Tomahawks and Kittyhawks. Total USAAF production was 12,014, 1,182 Tomahawks and 3,342 Kittyhawks being built on British contracts.

**Specification:** Curtiss P-40N-20 Warhawk (Kittyhawk Mk IV)
**Origin:** USA
**Type:** single-seat fighter/fighter-bomber
**Powerplant:** one 1,360-hp (1015-kW) Allison V-1710-81 inline piston engine
**Performance:** maximum speed 378 mph (609 km/h) at 10,500 ft (3200 m); climb to 15,000 ft (4570 m) in 6.7 minutes; service ceiling 38,000 ft (11580 m); range 240 miles (386 km)
**Weights:** empty 6,000 lb (2722 kg); maximum take-off 11,400 lb (5171 kg)
**Dimensions:** span 37 ft 4 in (11.38 m); length 33 ft 4 in (10.16 m); height 12 ft 4 in (3.76 m); wing area 236.0 sq ft (21.92 m²)
**Armament:** six 0.5-in (12.7-mm) machine-guns in the wings, plus a bombload of up to three 500-lb (227-kg) bombs

**Curtiss P-40C**

Although P-40Bs and P-40Cs were in combat with the Japanese from the start of the Pacific war, the P-40E, shown here, was the first version to serve with the USAAF in Europe and the Middle East in 1942.

# Curtiss SB2C Helldiver

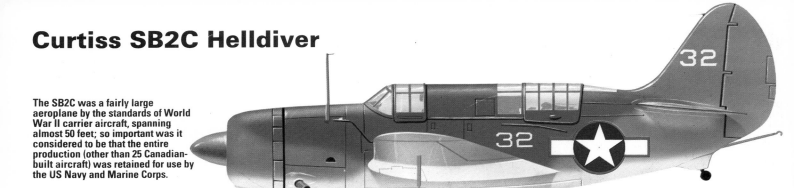

The SB2C was a fairly large aeroplane by the standards of World War II carrier aircraft, spanning almost 50 feet; so important was it considered to be that the entire production (other than 25 Canadian-built aircraft) was retained for use by the US Navy and Marine Corps.

## History and Notes

Last of a long line of Curtiss aircraft to carry the name Helldiver (the earlier aircraft being inter-war biplanes), the SB2C was first flown as the XSB2C-1 on 18 December 1940. Production SB2C-1s featured an enlarged fin and rudder assembly, increased fuel capacity and four 0.5-in (12.7-mm) guns in the wings. The SB2C-1C carried an armament of two 20-mm guns in the wings. The SB2C-3 appeared in 1944 with more powerful engine, and the SB2C-4 had provision to carry eight 5-in (127-mm) rockets or 1,000 lb (454 kg) of bombs under the wings (in addition to the 1,000-lb/454-kg internal bombload); the SB2C-4E carried radar in a small pod under the wing. The SB2C-5 carried increased fuel. Production amounted to 7,199 of all aircraft, including 300 by Fairchild in Canada, 984 by the Canadian Car and Foundry, and 900 produced for the USAAF as the A-25A (most of which were taken over by the US Marine Corps and re-designated SB2C-1A). Helldivers first went into action on 11 November 1943 with a raid by VB-17 on Rabaul. During 1944 they gradually replaced the Douglas SBD Dauntless, and were in constant action against the Japanese. Some 26 Canadian-built aircraft were supplied to the UK.

## Specification: Curtiss SB2C-4 Helldiver
**Origin:** USA
**Type:** two-seat scout-bomber
**Powerplant:** one 1,900-hp (1417-kW) Wright R-2600-20 radial piston engine
**Performance:** maximum speed 295 mph (476 km/h) at 16,700 ft (5090 m); initial climb rate 1,800 ft (549 m) per minute; service ceiling 29,100 ft (8870 m); range 1,165 miles (1875 km)
**Weights:** empty 10,547 lb (4784 kg); maximum take-off 16,616 lb (7537 kg)
**Dimensions:** span 49 ft 9 in (15.16 m); length 36 ft 8 in (11.17 m); height 13 ft 2 in (4.01 m); wing area 422.0 sq ft (39.20 m²)
**Armament:** two fixed forward-firing 20-mm guns in the wings and two 0.3-in (7.62-mm) flexible guns in the rear cockpit, plus a bombload of 1,000 lb (454 kg) under the wings and 1,000 lb (454 kg) internally.

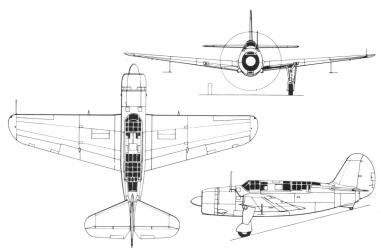

Curtiss SB2C Helldiver

The Curtiss Helldiver was flown in large numbers by the US Navy and Marine Corps in the last two years of the Pacific war. Pictured here are SB2Cs from the carrier USS *Ticonderoga*, returning from a raid on Japan in the last weeks of the war.

# de Havilland Mosquito

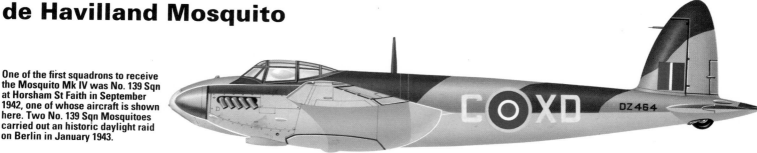

One of the first squadrons to receive the Mosquito Mk IV was No. 139 Sqn at Horsham St Faith in September 1942, one of whose aircraft is shown here. Two No. 139 Sqn Mosquitoes carried out an historic daylight raid on Berlin in January 1943.

## History and Notes

The Mosquito was one of the greatest military aircraft of all time, possessing a speed that, until the advent of jet aircraft, put it virtually beyond the reach of any defending fighter. Conceived in 1938 as a private venture to employ a primarily wooden structure to offset dependence on strategic materials, the twin-Merlin aircraft first flew on 25 November 1940. It entered RAF service first as a photo-reconnaissance aircraft (Mosquito Mk I) in mid-1941, then as a high-speed unarmed bomber (Mosquito B.Mk IV) in May 1942 and as a night-fighter with four 20-mm and four 0.303-in (7.7-mm) guns (Mosquito NF.Mk II) in the same month. The Mosquito T.Mk III was a trainer and the Mosquito FB.Mk VI a fighter-bomber capable of carrying two 500-lb (227-kg) bombs in the rear of the bomb bay. In 1944 the Mosquito B.Mk IX joined Bomber Command's night offensive, carrying a single 4,000-lb (1814-kg) bomb in an enlarged bomb bay, a weapon it later carried to Berlin. Mosquito B.Mk IXs were also fitted with 'Oboe', the pathfinding radar device. Developed from the Mk IX was the Mosquito B.Mk XVI, also a 4,000-lb (1814-kg) bomb-carrier but with pressure cabin and wing drop-tank provision. Photo-reconnaissance versions included the Mosquito PR.Mk VIII and PR.Mk XVI high altitude aircraft, the very long-range PR.Mk XVI high altitude aircraft, and the very long-range PR.Mk 34, intended for the Far East. As a night-fighter the Mk II was followed by the Mosquito NF.Mks XII and XIII with airborne radar (Mk VIII), the Mosquito NF.Mk XVII with American Mk X radar, and the Mosquito NF.Mk 30 high-altitude night-fighter. The anti-shipping Mosquito FB.Mk XVIII carried a 57-mm Molins gun in the nose. Total Mosquito production was 7,781, including aircraft built in Canada and Australia.

## Specification: de Havilland Mosquito PR.Mk 34
**Origin:** UK
**Type:** two-seat photo-reconnaissance aircraft
**Powerplant:** two 1,710-hp (1276-kW) Rolls-Royce Merlin 76 or 113 inline piston engines
**Performance:** maximum speed 425 mph (684 km/h) at 30,500 ft (9295 m); climb to 15,000 ft (4570 m) in 7.2 minutes; service ceiling 36,000 ft (10970 m); range 3,500 miles (5633 km)
**Weights:** empty 16,631 lb (7544 kg); maximum take-off 25,500 lb (11567 kg)
**Dimensions:** span 54 ft 2 in (16.51 m); length 41 ft 6 in (12.65 m); height 15 ft 3 in (4.65 m); wing area 454.0 sq ft (42.18 m²)
**Armament:** none

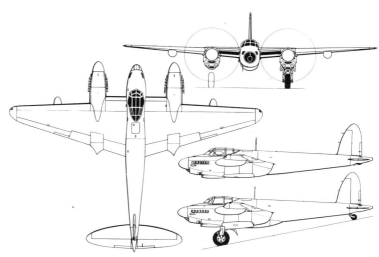

de Havilland Mosquito B.Mk XVI (upper view: B.Mk IX)

The superb Mosquito epitomized the fast light bomber whose sole protection lay in its ability to outrun any fighter opposition by reason of its very high speed. Built almost entirely of wood, it was powered by two Rolls-Royce Merlins.

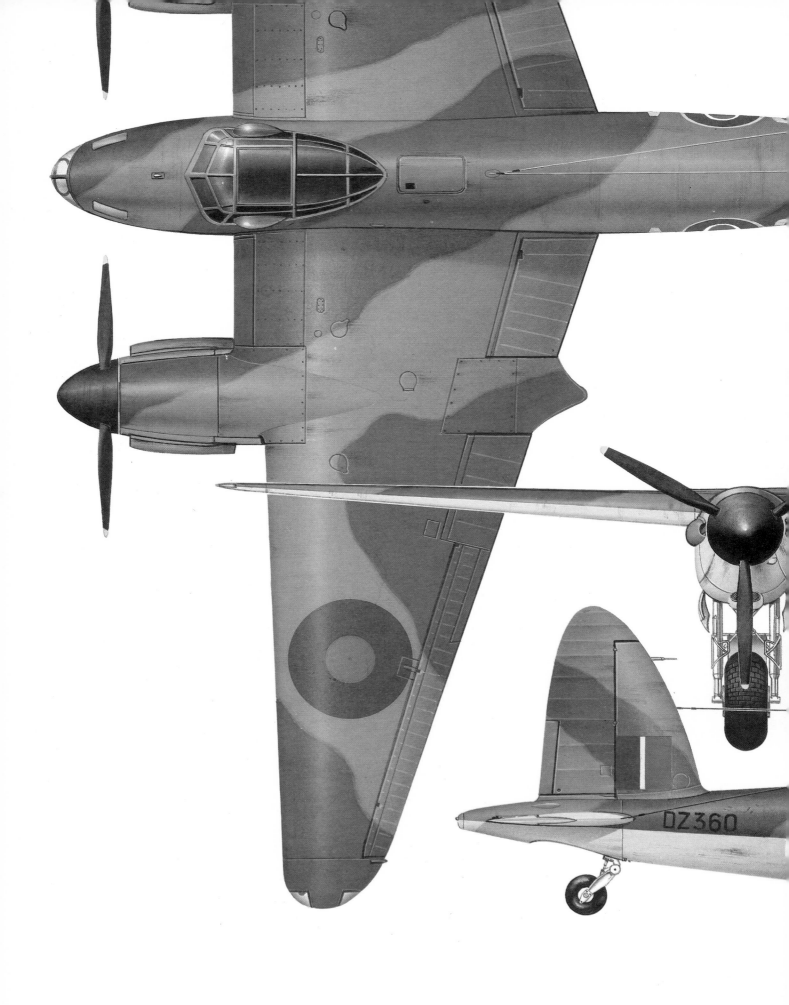

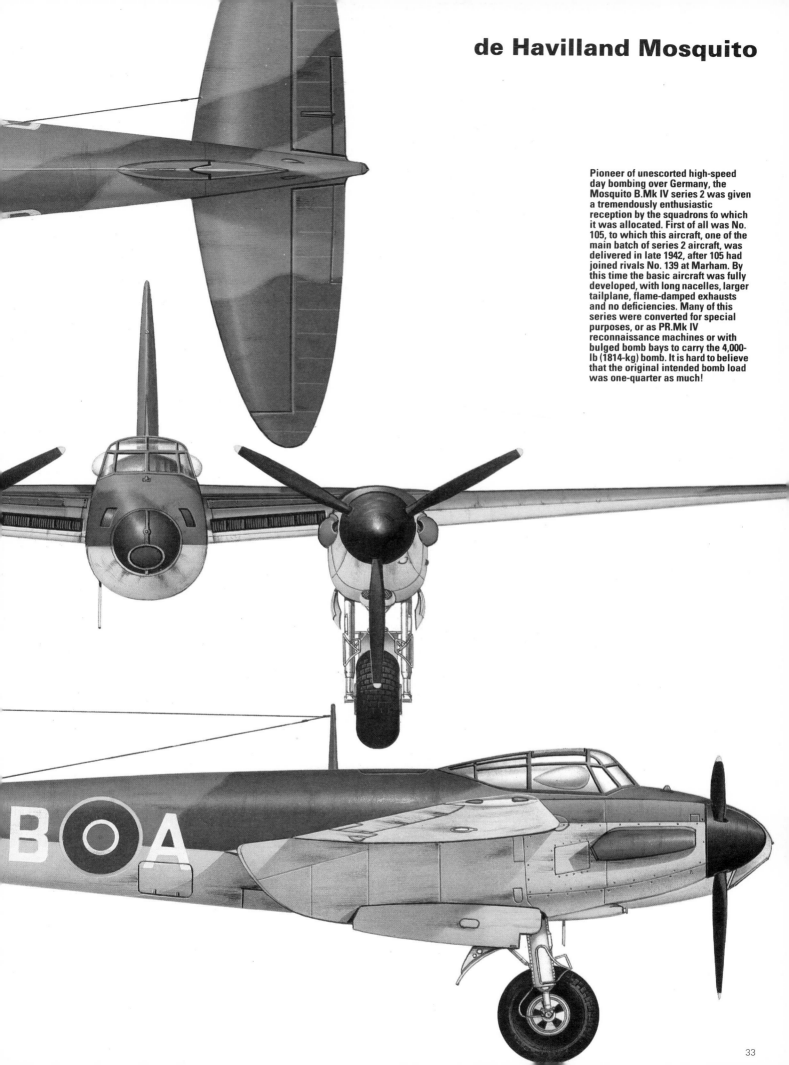

# de Havilland Mosquito

Pioneer of unescorted high-speed day bombing over Germany, the Mosquito B.Mk IV series 2 was given a tremendously enthusiastic reception by the squadrons to which it was allocated. First of all was No. 105, to which this aircraft, one of the main batch of series 2 aircraft, was delivered in late 1942, after 105 had joined rivals No. 139 at Marham. By this time the basic aircraft was fully developed, with long nacelles, larger tailplane, flame-damped exhausts and no deficiencies. Many of this series were converted for special purposes, or as PR.Mk IV reconnaissance machines or with bulged bomb bays to carry the 4,000-lb (1814-kg) bomb. It is hard to believe that the original intended bomb load was one-quarter as much!

# Dewoitine D.520

One of the relatively small number of D.520s which had been completed prior to the German attack in the West on 10 May 1940. There is little doubt that had the French aircraft industry succeeded in meeting all its delivery schedules in 1939 and 1940, fortunes would have been very different for the French air force.

## History and Notes

Best of all French fighters at the time of the great German attack in the West of May 1940 was the Dewoitine D.520, although it was probably no better than the RAF's Hurricane Mk I; moreover, no more than 36 had been delivered to a single *groupe de chasse* when the blow fell. Although the need for a fighter to replace the D.510 had been acknowledged as long ago as 1934, the D.520's design was not started until November 1936; the prototype was flown by Marcel Doret on 2 October 1938. Such delays were symptoms of the lethargy and procrastination that pervaded the French aircraft industry immediately before the war. Indeed it was not until 2 November 1939 that the first production D.520 was flown. First to receive the new fighter was GC 1/3, and this *groupe* first met the Luftwaffe on 13 May, shooting down three Hs 126s and an He 111 without loss. Some 43 other aircraft were quickly delivered to GC II/3, GC II/7, GC III/3 and GC III/6, and as new aircraft were completed Aéronavale Escadrilles AC 1, 2, 3, and 4 were equipped with a further 52 before the armistice was signed. As production of the D.520 continued in the Vichy (unoccupied) zone, a number of French pilots escaped to the UK, and in due course a total of 235 D.520s served with Vichy forces in France and 202 in Africa. Highest-scoring French fighter pilot was Adjutant Pierre Le Gloan, a pilot of GC III/6 who destroyed 18 enemy aircraft (out of his eventual total of 22) while flying D.520s. Total production of the aircraft was 775.

**Specification:** Dewoitine D.520S (first 558 aircraft)
**Origin:** France
**Type:** single-seat fighter
**Powerplant:** one 930-hp (694-kW) Hispano-Suiza 12Y45 inline piston engine
**Performance:** maximum speed 332 mph (535 km/h) at 18,045 ft (5500 m); climb to 13,125 ft (4000 m) in 5.82 minutes; service ceiling 33,630 ft (10250 m); normal range 553 miles (890 km)
**Weights:** empty 4,685 lb (2125 kg); normal loaded 5,897 lb (2675 kg)
**Dimensions:** span 33 ft 5½ in (10.20 m); length 28 ft 8¾ in (8.76 m); height 8 ft 5⅛ in (2.57 m); wing area 171.7 sq ft (15.95 m²)
**Armament:** one 20-mm HS404 hub-firing cannon and four 7.5-mm (0.295-in) MAC 1934 M39 machine-guns in the wings

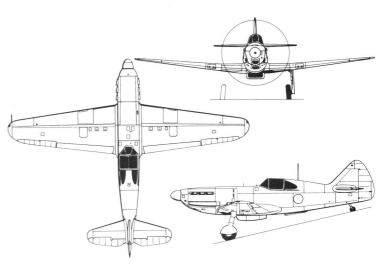

Dewoitine D.520

A factory-fresh D.520 (no. 494) at Toulouse prior to delivery to the Vichy air force in March 1942. Following the 'Torch' landings in North Africa eight months later, the Germans seized the air force's 1,876 aircraft, which included 246 D.520s.

# Dornier Do 17

A Dornier Do 17Z-2 of 1. Staffel, Kampfgeschwader 2 'Holzhammer', based at Tatoi, Greece in May 1941. The emblem of 1./KG 2, an eagle carrying a bomb, is painted underneath the cockpit.

## History and Notes

Designed to meet a commercial requirement for a high-speed mailplane issued in 1933, the attractive twin-engine Dornier Do 17 first appeared in prototype form with single fin and rudder, but the exceptionally slim fuselage resulted in the aircraft being abandoned on account of cramped accommodation. Rescued from oblivion, the prototypes were re-evaluated as high-speed bombers and, with twin fins and rudders, the Do 17 was ordered into production as the Do 17E and Do 17F, bomber and reconnaissance versions respectively, in 1936; both versions saw considerable service in the Spanish Civil War from 1937 onwards. Other pre-war versions were the Do 17M bomber and the Do 17P reconnaissance aircraft, these being standard service aircraft with the Luftwaffe during 1939-40, the former with 900-hp (671-kW) Bramo radials and the latter with 865-hp (645-kW) BMW 132N radials.

The most important version was the Do 17Z which featured a deepened and extensively glazed nose, and some idea of the importance attached to this version by the Luftwaffe may be gained by the 352 aircraft on operational charge at the end of 1939. These four-seat bombers were produced in a number of versions, the Do 17 Z-1 having an armament of four 7.92-mm (0.31-in) guns and a bombload of 1,102 lb (500 kg), the Do 17 Z-2 having 1,000-hp (746-kW) Bramo engines and an armament of up to eight 7.92-mm (0.31-in guns and a bombload of 2,205 lb (1000 kg), the Do 17Z-3 being photo-reconnaissance aircraft, the Do 17Z-4 being a dual-control trainer and the Do 17Z-6 and Do 17Z-10 Kauz (Screech Owl) being night-fighters; the last, produced in 1940, featured a nose armament of two 20-mm and four 7.92-mm (0.31-in) guns.

## Specification: Dornier Do 17Z-2

**Origin:** Germany
**Type:** four-crew medium bomber
**Powerplant:** two 1,000-hp (746-kW) Bramo 323P radial piston engines
**Performance:** maximum speed 255 mph (410 km/h) at 13,125 ft (4000 m); service ceiling 26,900 ft (8200 m); maximum range 845 miles (1360 km)
**Weights:** empty 11,486 lb (5210 kg); maximum take-off 18,937 lb (8590 kg)
**Dimensions:** span 59 ft 0⅝ (18.00 m); length 52 ft 9¾ in (16.10 m); height 14 ft 11¼ in (4.55 m); wing area 592.01 sq ft (55.00 m²)
**Armament:** bombload of up to 2,205 lb (1000 kg) and a variable defensive armament of up to eight 7.92-mm (0.31-in) MG 15 flexible guns disposed around crew cabin

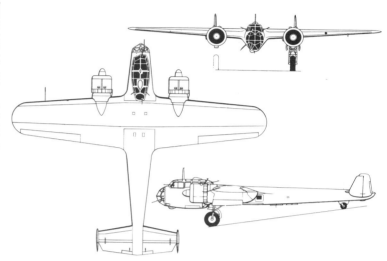

Dornier Do 17Z-2

Two Do 17Zs, also of KG 2, seen during the Blitz of the Low Countries. The Do 17 was the least effective of the Do 17/Ju 88/He 111 trio used during the early years, being slower and carrying less bombload than the other two.

# Dornier Do 18

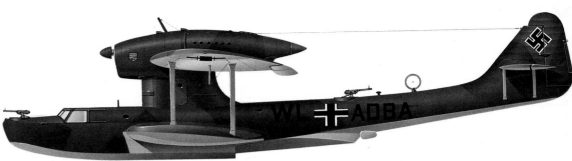

A small number of Do 18s was used for training in coastal reconnaissance and air-sea rescue work. This Do 18D was flown by the FFS(See), Flugzeugführerschule, or maritime pilot school, in the summer of 1939.

## History and Notes

The attractive Dornier Do 18 flying-boat originated as a commercial aircraft ordered by the airline Deutsche Lufthansa in 1934 to replace the highly successful but ageing Wal (Whale). Extensively cleaned up and modernized, the first Do 18 VI was flown on 15 March 1935 and the first military variant, the Do 18D, was operational with the Luftwaffe in September 1938; powered by two tandem-aligned Jumo 205C engines and with four-man crew, the Do 18D-1 and Do 18D-2 carried single flexible 7.92-mm (0.31-in) machine-guns in bow and midships positions.

By the outbreak of war the Do 18G, with 880-hp (656-kW) Jumo 205D engines, a 13-mm (0.51-in) bow gun and a turret-mounted 20-mm cannon amidships, had entered production and joined earlier versions with the *Küstenfliegergruppen* (coastal reconnaissance groups) for duties over the North Sea and Baltic. After about 100 aircraft (including some 70 Do 18Gs) had been completed, production was halted, but the flying-boats continued in service until 1942. The Do 18H trainer was produced by converting some Do 18Gs to include dual controls, and the Do 18N air-sea rescue aircraft were also modified from Do 18Gs to carry ambulance equipment, working with the *Seenotstaffeln* (air-sea rescue squadrons) in France, Denmark, the Netherlands and Norway. It was incidentally a coastal reconnaissance Do 18 of 2./Kü Fl Gr 106 that was the first German aircraft to fall victim to British air action in the war when it was shot down by Blackburn Skuas from HMS *Ark Royal* over the North Sea on 26 September 1939.

## Specification: Dornier Do 18G-1

**Origin:** Germany
**Type:** four-crew coastal reconnaissance flying-boat
**Powerplant:** two 880-hp (6461kW) Junkers Jumo 205D inline piston engines in tandem
**Performance:** maximum speed 162 mph (260 km/h) at sea level; climb to 3,280 ft (1000 m) in 7.9 minutes; service ceiling 13,780 ft (4200 m); range 2,174 miles (3500 km)
**Weights:** empty 12,900 lb (5850 kg); maximum take-off 22,046 lb (10000 kg)
**Dimensions:** span 77 ft 9 in (23.70 m); length 63 ft 2 in (19.25 m); height 17 ft 5½ in (5.32 m); wing area 1,049 sq ft (97.5 m²)
**Armament:** one 13-mm (0.51-in) MG 131 gun in bow flexible mounting and one 20-mm MG 151 gun in midships turret, plus 220 lb (100 kg) of bombs

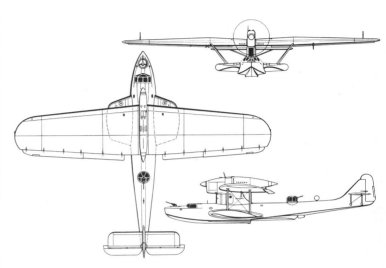

**Dornier Do 18**

The Do 18D was the first version of this flying boat to enter service with the Luftwaffe's Küstenfliegergruppen (coastal groups); an early Do 18D-1 of 2./KüFlGr 506 is seen here taking off at Kiel in September 1938.

# Dornier Do 217

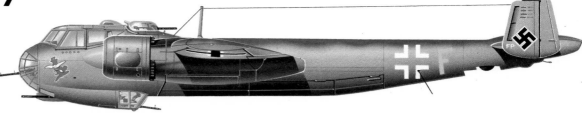

The Dornier Do 217E was widely used in the anti-shipping role over the Atlantic and North Sea from 1941 to 1943. This Do 217E-2 (with ship tally on the fin) served with 6.Staffel, Kampfgeschwader 40, at Bordeaux-Mérignac late in 1942.

## History and Notes

Just as the Dornier Do 17 bomber was entering Luftwaffe service, the manufacturers put forward proposals for a larger and faster version; this was the Do 217, whose Do 217 V1 prototype with two 1,075-hp (802-kW) Daimler-Benz DB 601A inline engines was first flown in August 1938. Directional stability problems led to larger tail surfaces on pre-production Do 217A-0 reconnaissance aircraft, which joined the Luftwaffe in 1940 and carried out clandestine flights over Soviet territory in that year. First production version was the Do 217E-1 bomber with two 1,550-hp (1156-kW) BMW 801MA radials, a crew of four or five, and a bombload of 4,409 lb (2000 kg); it first joined II./KG 40 in France in March 1941; the Do 217E-2 followed with dorsal turret added and 13-mm (0.51-in) gun in addition to the normal armament of one 13-mm (0.51-in), one 15-mm (0.59-in) and up to five 7.92 (0.31-in) guns; the Do 217E-3 with additional armour and the Do 217E-5, adapted to carry two Henschel Hs 293 anti-shipping missiles, were other versions.

The Dornier Do 217J night-fighter, with FuG 202 radar, two 20-mm and four 7.92 (0.31-in) guns in the nose, joined the Luftwaffe in 1942; the Do 217K bomber was powered by 1,700-hp (1268-kW) BMW 801D engines and was produced in versions adapted to carry Hs 293 or Fritz X missiles. Produced simultaneously was the Do 217M with 1,750-hp (1306-kW) DB 603As, whose sub-variants were similar to those of the Do 217K. Final main variant was the Do 217N night-fighter with DB 603As and revised nose in which were fitted four 20-mm and four 7.92-mm (0.31-in) guns plus two 20-mm upward-firing guns in a *schräge Musik* (jazz music) installation. A total of 1,730 Do 217s was built, and the type was regarded as an efficient and reliable bomber and night-fighter, on which the Luftwaffe came to rely heavily during the last three years of the war.

## Specification: Dornier Do 217M-1
**Origin:** Germany
**Type:** four-crew heavy bomber
**Powerplant:** two 1,750-hp (1306-kW) Daimler-Benz DB 603A inline piston engines
**Performance:** maximum speed 348 mph (560 km/h) at 18,700 ft (5700 m); initial climb rate 688 ft (210 m) per minute; service ceiling 31,170 ft (9500 m); normal range 1,335 miles (2150 km)
**Weights:** empty 19,845 lb (9000 kg); maximum take-off 36,817 lb (16700 kg)
**Dimensions:** span 62 ft 4 in (19.00 m); length 58 ft 4½ in (17.79 m); height 16 ft 6 in (5.03 m); wing area 613.54 sq ft (57.00 m²)
**Armament:** two 13-mm (0.51-in) and up to six 7.92-mm (0.31-in) guns, and up to 8,818 lb (4000 kg) of bombs, of which 5,511 lb (2500 kg) were carried internally

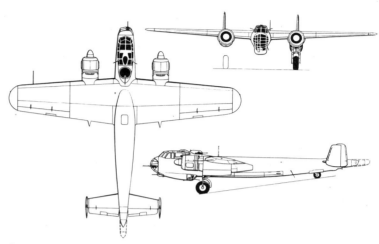

**Dornier Do 217E-2**

Bearing the insignia of Luftflotte 2, this Dornier Do 217K-1 was allocated directly to the Luftflotte headquarters, and as such was probably employed for reconnaissance duties; the Do 217K-1 was normally a night medium bomber.

# Douglas A-20/DB-7 Boston/Havoc

Known as the Havoc when serving as a night fighter in the RAF, the aircraft was also widely used in 1941 as an 'intruder bomber', the aircraft depicted here belonging to No. 23 Sqn based at Ford; their job was later taken over by Beaufighters and Mosquitoes.

## History and Notes

Conceived under Ed Heinemann's design leadership with much the same combat philosophy in mind as that of the Bristol Blenheim, the Douglas Model 7A was evolved into the DB-7 for foreign air forces in 1937, and a prototype was flown on 17 August 1939; orders were placed principally by the French government but, with the fall of France in 1940, most of the aircraft were taken over by the RAF where they were modified as night-fighters with eight 0.303-in (7.7-mm) guns in the nose as the Havoc Mk I (and later with 12 guns as the Havoc Mk II). The USAAF placed initial contracts for 206 A-20s and A-20As, based on the French DB-7, the former with turbocharged Wright R-2600-7 radials being the fastest Havoc purchased by the USAAF. Minor alterations to the nose shape identified the A-20B of which 999 were produced, while numerous DB-7Bs and DB-7Cs were repossessed from the British and Dutch respectively after Pearl Harbor. The A-20C was an attempt to standardize British and American requirements in a single version but, with gross weight advancing to 25,600 lb (11612 kg) the maximum speed fell to 342 mph (550 km/h). The A-20C was the first USAAF version to see combat, the 15th Bomb Squadron arriving in the UK in May 1942 (in fact flying its first operations in Boston Mk IIICs of the RAF's No. 226 Squadron on 4 July that year). Most-produced version was the A-20G, which followed the A-20C on the production lines, 2,850 being completed; early aircraft were armed with four 20-mm and two 0.5-in (12.7-mm) nose guns, but later versions had the cannon deleted in favour of four more 0.5-in (12.7-mm) guns; external racks doubled the bomb load to 4,000 lb (1814 kg). The A-20G was followed by 412 A-20Hs, similar but with slightly more powerful engines. Total production of all A-20s was 7,385, including no fewer than 3,125 supplied to the Soviet Union.

## Specification: Douglas A-20G Havoc
**Origin:** USA
**Type:** three-crew light attack bomber
**Powerplant:** two 1,600-hp (1194-kW) Wright R-2600-23 radial piston engines
**Performance:** maximum speed 339 mph (546 km/h) at 12,400 ft (3780 m); climb to 10,000 ft (3050 m) in 7.1 minutes; service ceiling 25,800 ft (7865 m); range 1,090 miles (1754 km)
**Weights:** empty 15,984 lb (7250 kg); maximum take-off 27,200 lb (12338 kg)

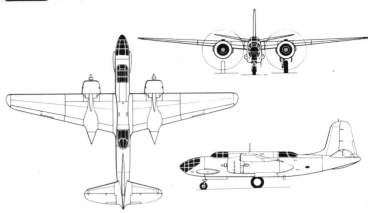

**Douglas A-20C Havoc/Boston Mk III**

**Dimensions:** span 61 ft 4 in (18.69 m); length 48 ft 0 in (14.63 m); height 17 ft 7 in (5.36 m); wing area 464.0 sq ft (43.11 m²)
**Armament:** six 0.5-in (12.7-mm) machine-guns in nose and two 0.5-in (12.7-mm) machine-guns in dorsal turret, plus a bombload of up to 2,600 lb (1179 kg)

Equivalent to the USAAF's A-20J, the Boston Mk IV served with six squadrons of the RAF, including No. 342 Sqn of the so-called Free French air force, one of whose aircraft – resplendent in invasion stripes – is seen landing in France in 1944.

# Douglas A-26 Invader

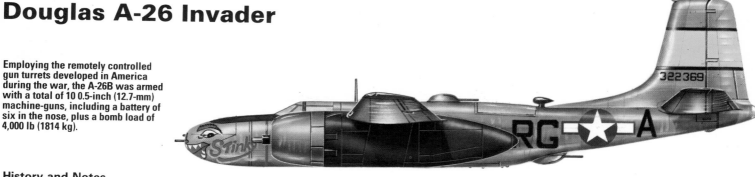

Employing the remotely controlled gun turrets developed in America during the war, the A-26B was armed with a total of 10 0.5-inch (12.7-mm) machine-guns, including a battery of six in the nose, plus a bomb load of 4,000 lb (1814 kg).

## History and Notes

Designed in 1940 to replace the A-20 Havoc and incorporating the fruits of early wartime experience, the Douglas A-26 was the last important American aircraft in the category of 'attack' bomber. The first of three prototypes, the XA-26, was flown on 10 July 1942 as a bomber with bombardier's glazed nose station; the second, the XA-26A, was a night-fighter prototype with four 20-mm guns under the fuselage and four 0.5-in (12.7-mm) guns in a remotely-controlled dorsal turret; and the third, the XA-26B, was armed with a 75-mm cannon in the nose. The heavily armoured A-26B was selected for production, capable of carrying a maximum bombload of 6,000 lb (2722 kg) plus eight 5-in (12.7-mm) rocket projectiles. A total of 1,355 A-26Bs was built, deliveries to the USAAF starting 1944 with 2,000-hp (1492-kW) Pratt & Whitney R-2800 engines; with their speed of 355 mph (572 km/h) they were among the fastest of all American wartime bombers. The only other version produced during the war was the A-26C, in which all but two of the six nose 0.5-in (12.7-mm) guns were deleted, being replaced by a transparent bombardier's station; a total of 1,091 A-26Cs was produced, most of which were delivered to the Pacific theatre; 88 A-26Cs were supplied to the US Navy. Over 5,250 A-26s were cancelled at the end of the war, although the aircraft (later redesignated the B-26 when the Martin Marauder had disappeared from service) was widely used by the post-war USAF, particularly in the Korean War.

**Specification:** Douglas A-26B-1 Invader
**Origin:** USA
**Type:** three-crew light attack bomber
**Powerplant:** two 2,000-hp (1492-kW) Pratt & Whitney R-2800-79 radial piston engines
**Performance:** maximum speed 355 mph (572 km/h) at 16,000 ft (4875 m); climb to 10,000 ft (3050 m) in 8.1 minutes; service ceiling 22,100 ft (6735 m); range 1,400 miles (2253 km)
**Weights:** empty 22,370 lb (10147 kg); maximum take-off 35,000 lb (15880 kg)
**Dimensions:** span 70 ft 0 in (21.35 m); length 50 ft 9 in (15.47 m); height 18 ft 6 in (5.64 m); wing area 540.0 sq ft (50.17 m²)
**Armament:** six 0.5-in (12.7-mm) machine-guns in nose and remotely-controlled dorsal and ventral turrets each with two 0.5-in (12.7-mm) guns, plus a bombload of up to 6,000 lb (2722 kg) and eight 5-in (127-mm) rockets

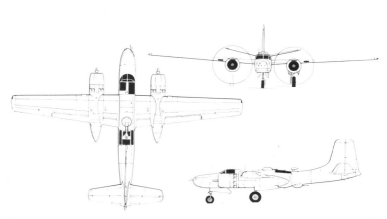

Douglas A-26B Invader

Although originally ordered before the United States entered the war, the A-26 Invader only reached operational units during the final months of hostilities, joining the 9th Air Force in Europe in November 1944. Nose armament and dorsal turret have been deleted from this picture by a wartime censor.

# Douglas SBD Dauntless

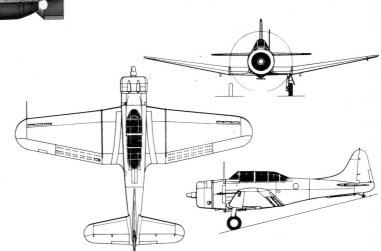

After the Allied landings in North Africa of November 1942 the French Naval Air Service was given 32 Dauntless aircraft and in 1944, after a period in training, these were flown to Cognac in Southern France to support French ground forces during the final months of the war.

## History and Notes

Developed directly from the Northrop BT-1 (the Northrop Corporation became a division of Douglas), the prototype of the SBD Dauntless two-seat carrier-borne dive bomber was in fact a much modified production BT-1. Production orders for 57 SBD-1s and 87 SBD-2s were placed in April 1939, the former being delivered to US Marine Corps bombing and scout-bombing squadrons, and the latter to US Navy scout and bombing squadrons. The SBD-3, with two additional 0.5-in (12.7-mm) guns in the nose, self-sealing tanks and R-1829-52 engine, appeared in March 1941, and by the time of Pearl Harbor in December that year 584 SBD-3s had been delivered. Some 780 SBD-4s (with 24-volt system but otherwise similar to the SBD-3 and produced at El Segundo, California) were built in 1942; photo-reconnaissance modifications, the SBD-1P, SBD-2P and SBD-3P were also produced during 1941-2. A new Douglas plant at Tulsa, Oklahoma, produced 2,409 SBD-5s with 1,200-hp (895-kW) R-1820-60 engines, following these with 451 SBD-6s with -66 engines. The USAAF took delivery of 168 SBD-3A, 170 SBD-4A and 615 SBD-5A aircraft as the A-24, A-24A and A-24B respectively, bringing the total Douglas production to 5,321 SBDs. They were unquestionably one of the USA's most important weapons in the Pacific war, and sank a greater tonnage of Japanese shipping than any other aircraft, as well as playing a key part in the great battles of Midway, the Coral Sea and the Solomons.

**Specification:** Douglas SBD-5 Dauntless
**Origin:** USA
**Type:** two-crew carrier-based scout/dive-bomber
**Powerplant:** one 1,200-hp (895-kW) Wright R-1820-60 radial piston engine
**Performance:** maximum speed 245 mph (394 km/h) at 15,800 ft (4815 m); initial climb rate 1,190 ft (363 m) per minute; service ceiling 24,300 ft (7405 m); range 1,100 miles (1770 km)
**Weights:** empty 6,675 lb (3028 kg); maximum take-off 10,855 lb (4924 kg)
**Dimensions:** span 41 ft 6¼ in (12.65 m); length 33 ft 0⅛ in (10.06 m); height 12 ft 11 in (3.94 m); wing area 325.0 sq ft (30.19 m²)
**Armament:** two fixed forward-firing 0.5-in (12.6-mm) machine-guns and two flexible 0.3-in (7.62-mm) guns in rear cockpit, plus a bombload of one 1,600-lb (726-kg) bomb under the fuselage and two 325-lb (147-kg) bombs under the wings

**Douglas SBD Dauntless**

A formation of Douglas SBD Dauntless scout bombers. This aircraft bore the brunt of carrierborne bombing duties in the Pacific between 1942 and 1944, serving aboard such famous American carriers as the USS *Lexington, Saratoga, Yorktown* and *Enterprise.*

# Douglas C-47 Skytrain

A Dakota Mk III (equivalent to the USAAF's C-47A) of the RAF's No. 24 Sqn. Though not strictly a transport squadron in an operational sense, No. 24 for many years was the RAF's principal communications squadron and flew Dakotas of all types on frequent services between the various war fronts.

## History and Notes

Probably the best known transport aeroplane of all time, whether as an airliner or military transport, the Douglas C-47 evolved from the DC-3 airliner which introduced new levels of speed and comfort to air travel during the late 1930s. First flown as a commercial aircraft on 15 December 1935, the C-47 was not ordered by the US Army Air Corps until 1940, the airline interior giving way to bucket seats along the cabin sides, and Pratt & Whitney R-1830 radials replacing the DC-3's Wright Cyclones. Some 953 C-47s were built before production switched to the C-47A with 24-volt in place of 12-volt electrical system; a total of 4,931 C-47As was built. High-altitude superchargers and R-1830-90 engine were introduced in 3,241 C-47Bs (including 133 TC-47B trainers), intended for use in South East Asia. Many other variations were produced under separate designations, of which the C-53 Skytrooper was the most important, being in effect an airline standard aircraft for military purposes. Wartime military production of the C-47 reached 10,048, plus an estimated 2,700 produced in the Soviet Union as the Lisunov Li-2. In the USAAF the C-47 became the standard transport and glider tug in service from 1942 onwards, being flown in large numbers in every airborne forces operation during the war; furthermore, some 1,895 Dakotas served with 25 RAF squadrons, the Dakota Mk I corresponding to the C-47, the Dakota Mk II to the C-53, the Dakota Mk III to the C-47A and the Dakota Mk IV to the C-47B. As late as 1961 the USAF still had over 1,000 C-47s on its inventory, and the type was also used by the US Navy as the R4D in several variants.

**Specification:** Douglas C-47 Skytrain (Dakota Mk I)
**Origin:** USA
**Type:** three-crew 27-troop military transport
**Powerplant:** two 1,200-hp (895-kW) Pratt & Whitney R-1839-92 radial piston engines
**Performance:** maximum speed 230 mph (370 km/h) at 8,500 ft (2590 m); climb to 10,000 ft (3050 m) in 9.6 minutes; service ceiling 24,000 ft (7315 m); range 1,600 miles (2575 km)
**Weights:** empty 18,200 lb (8256 kg); maximum take-off 26,000 lb (11805 kg)
**Dimensions:** span 95 ft 6 in (29.11 m); length 63 ft 9 in (19.43 m); height 17 ft 0 in (5.18 m); wing area 987.0 sq ft (91.69 m²)
**Accommodation:** 27 fully-armed troops or 25 paratroops, or 18-24 stretcher cases, or up to 10,000 lb (4536 kg) of freight

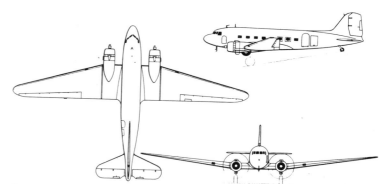

Douglas C-47 Skytrain

The C-47 (Dakota in RAF service) was the most widely used glider tug by the Allies during the war, early aircraft seen here towing Waco Hadrian assault gliders on a training flight in the USA, probably in 1943.

# Douglas C-47 Skytrain

General Eisenhower is on record as having stated that the C-47 was one of the four principal instruments of Allied victory in World War II (the others being the bazooka, Jeep and atom bomb). Typical example of the Skytrain was this C-47A-65-DL of the 81st Troop Carrier Squadron, 436th Troop Carrier Group, based at Membury in England between 3 March 1944 and February 1945 (it also took part in the airborne assault on Southern France, based at Voltone, Italy, during July and August 1944). The mission tally on 'Buzz Buggy', together with invasion stripes, suggests participation in the Normandy, South France, Nijmegen and Bastogne operations, both as a paratrooper and glider tug.

# Fairey Albacore

Introducing the 'luxury' of enclosed cabin and a Taurus engine, the Albacore was less popular with naval aircrews who generally preferred the open cockpit and rugged reliability of the older Swordfish.

## History and Notes

Wholly eclipsed by the Swordfish, which it was intended to replace, the Fairey Albacore was in essence a cleaned-up version of the celebrated 'Stringbag' with an enclosed cabin to improve the operational efficiency of the crew and a Bristol Taurus radial to provide higher performance despite considerably greater weights. First flown in December 1938, the initial prototype was fitted with a wheel landing gear while the second had twin floats. The Albacore, which was inevitably called the 'Applecore' in service, differed from the Swordfish in being used operationally only on the wheeled type of landing gear. The type entered service with the Royal Navy's Fleet Air Arm in 1940, and production amounted to 798 aircraft. The Albacore was first flown in action during attacks on Boulogne in September 1940. Most Albacores were land-based throughout their careers, but the type's brief moment of glory arrived when the Albacores from the carrier HMS *Formidable* severely damaged the Italian battleship *Vittorio Veneto* during the Battle of Cape Matapan in March 1941. After this time the Albacore was occasionally used for bombing in the Western Desert, usually at night to prevent the depredations of Axis fighters, and the type played an important part in the operations leading up to the Battle of Alamein in October 1942. In carrier operations the Albacore was operated in the North Atlantic, Arctic, Mediterranean and Indian oceans; and the type was also used with some success as a support aircraft during seaborne invasions, notably those of Sicily, Italy and northern France, the last in the hands of Royal Canadian Air Force squadrons.

## Specification: Fairey Albacore

**Origin:** UK
**Type:** three-crew naval torpedo-bomber
**Powerplant:** one 1,065-hp (794-kW) Bristol Taurus II radial piston engine
**Performance:** maximum speed 161 mph (259 km/h) at 7,000 ft (2135 m); climb to 6,000 ft (1830 m) in 8.0 minutes; service ceiling 20,700 ft (6310 m); range 820 miles (1319 km)
**Weights:** empty 7,200 lb (3266 kg); maximum take-off 12,600 lb (5715 kg)
**Dimensions:** span 50 ft 0 in (15.24 m); length 39 ft 9½ in (12.13 m); height 15 ft 3 in

**Fairey Albacore**

(4.65 m); wing area 623.0 sq ft (57.88 m²)
**Armament:** one forward-firing 0.303-in (7.7-mm) Vickers machine-gun and two 0.303-in (7.7-mm) Vickers 'K' machine-guns in the rear cockpit, plus one 18-in (457-mm) torpedo or up to 2,000 lb (907 kg) of bombs.

**The Fairey Albacore was almost wholly overshadowed by its stablemate, the Swordfish. Intended to supersede the latter, the Albacore nevertheless gave good service in the Mediterranean and North Africa. This example is seen dropping a practice 18-inch torpedo.**

# Fairey Barracuda

The Barracuda, shown here with anti-submarine radar and underwing depth bombs, was delayed for two years by design adaptation for the Merlin engine following the discontinuation of the original powerplant. It was nevertheless flown to good effect in the last year of the war.

## History and Notes

Intended to replace the Albacore, itself a replacement for the Swordfish, the Barracuda was an altogether more advanced aircraft conceptually, and was designed as a high-performance monoplane to meet a 1937 requirement. The intended powerplant was the Rolls-Royce Exe, and the programme was delayed substantially when this engine was abandoned and the structure had to be revised to accommodate a Merlin engine from the same manufacturer. Thus the Barracuda prototype did not fly until 7 December 1940, and it was immediately apparent that the performance of the heavy Barracuda would be limited by the power available: the 1,260-hp (940-kW) Merlin XXX in the Barracuda Mk I and the 1,640-hp (1223-kW) Merlin 32 for the Barracuda Mks II and III. At a time when production priorities were afforded mostly to the RAF, deliveries of the Barracuda to the Fleet Air Arm were slow to start, and it was January 1943 before Barracuda Mk I began to enter service with the Fleet Air Arm. The Barracuda Mk I was little more than a service-test type, only 23 being built. The two main wartime models were thus the Barracuda Mk II with ASV Mk IIN radar (1,635 built by Fairey, Blackburn, Boulton Paul and Westland) and the Barracuda Mk III torpedo-reconnaissance version with ASV Mk X radar (912 built by the parent company). The Barracuda saw only limited service in home waters, the highpoint of its career being a highly successful strike on the German battleship *Tirpitz* in April 1944; but in the Pacific campaigns of 1944 and 1945 the Barracuda was one of the more prominent British aircraft.

## Specification: Fairey Barracuda Mk II

**Origin:** UK
**Type:** three-crew shipborne torpedo- and dive-bomber
**Powerplant:** one 1,640-hp (1223-kW) Rolls-Royce Merlin 32 inline piston engine
**Performance:** maximum speed 228 mph (367 km/h) at 1,750 ft (535 m); climb to 5,000 ft (1525 m) in 6.0 minutes; service ceiling 16,600 ft (5060 m); range 1,150 miles (1850 km)
**Weights:** empty 9,350 lb (4241 kg); maximum take-off 14,100 lb (6396 kg)
**Dimensions:** span 49 ft 2 in (14.99 m); length 39 ft 9 in (12.11 m); height 15 ft 1 in (4.60 m); wing area 367.0 sq ft (34.09 m²)
**Armament:** two 0.303-in (7.7-mm) Vickers 'K' machine-guns in the rear cockpit, plus one 1,620-lb (735-kg) torpedo, or four 450-lb 9204-kg) depth charges, or six 250-lb (113-kg) bombs

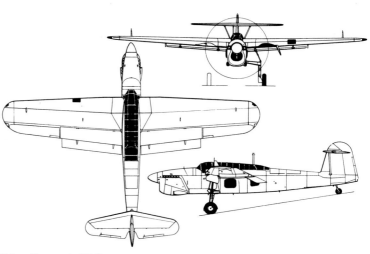

**Fairey Barracuda Mk II**

Despite its ungainly appearance the Fairey Barracuda was intended to embody experience gained with such aircraft as the Swordfish, at the same time benefitting from the monoplane configuration. Alas, entrenched demands for naval accoutrements compromised the design from the outset.

# Fairey Battle

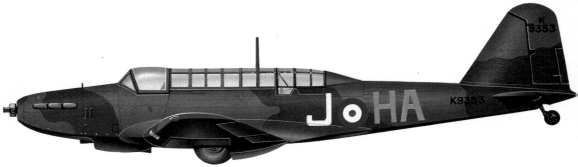

Among the Battle squadrons which were virtually annihilated during the French campaign of May 1940 was No. 218 Sqn, all its aircraft being destroyed in the efforts to halt the advancing German columns. The aircraft simply proved too slow in the face of accurate flak and swarming enemy fighters.

## History and Notes

Synonymous with the tragedy that befell France in 1940, the Fairey Battle light bomber proved hopelessly outclassed in the presence of the modern Luftwaffe at that time. Yet this aircraft had been conceived in the early 1930s as one of the key aircraft to equip the fast-expanding pre-war RAF. First flown on 10 March 1936, the Battle joined Nos 52 and 63 Squadrons in March 1937; in little over a year later Battles equipped 17 day bomber squadrons. At the outbreak of war 10 Battle squadrons accompanied the Advanced Air Striking Force to France, but within a month were suffering prohibitive losses when sent on daylight raids without fighter escort. With no suitable replacement available they remained in France and constituted the RAF's day bomber force when the German *Blitzkrieg* opened in the West on 10 May 1940. The war's first Victoria Crosses were awarded posthumously to a Battle's crew (Flying Officer D. E. Garland and Sergeant T. Gray of No. 12 Squadron) for an attack on the Maastricht bridges on 10 May, when four out of five aircraft were shot down. In an attack at Sedan on 14 May, 40 Battles from a force of 70 were destroyed. After less than a month the AASF had been decimated and the surviving Battles were withdrawn to the UK but, after a short further period of operations against the Channel ports, they were withdrawn from operations and relegated to training. Many were shipped to Canada while others undertook target towing duties. Battles supplied to Belgium fared no better in 1940 than those of the RAF.

## Specification: Fairey Battle Mk I

**Origin:** UK
**Type:** three-crew light bomber
**Powerplant:** one 1,030-hp (768-kW) Rolls-Royce Merlin III inline piston engine
**Performance:** maximum speed 241 mph (388 km/h) at 13,000 ft (3960 m); climb to 5,000 ft (1525 m) in 4.1 minutes; service ceiling 23,500 ft (7165 m); range 1,050 miles (1690 km)
**Weights:** empty 6,647 lb (3015 kg); maximum take-off 10,792 lb (4895 kg)
**Dimensions:** span 54 ft 0 in (16.46 m); length 45 ft 1¾ in (12.90 m); height 15 ft 6 in (4.72 m); wing area 422.0 sq ft (39.20 m²)
**Armament:** one fixed forward-firing 0.303-in (7.7-mm) machine-gun and one 0.303-in (7.7-mm) flexible machine-gun in the rear cockpit, plus a bombload of 1,000 lb (454 kg)

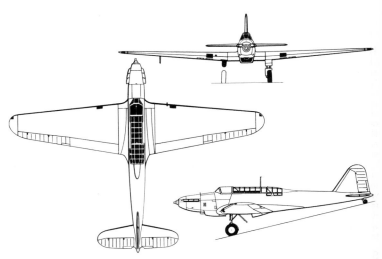

**Fairey Battle**

After the Fairey Battle's disastrous experiences in France during May 1940 as a light bomber, production switched to trainer versions, dual controls being provided in separate cockpits. Many Battles were also relegated to target towing.

# Fairey Swordfish

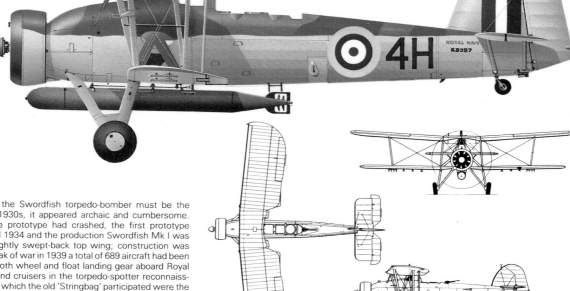

Pictured here is an early production Swordfish Mk I complete with 18-inch (45.7-cm) naval torpedo. This version had provision for interchangeable wheel or float undercarriage and served in the 'torpedo-spotter-reconnaissance' role during the early years of the war.

## History and Notes

Of all aircraft regarded as anachronisms the Swordfish torpedo-bomber must be the supreme example for, even in the early 1930s, it appeared archaic and cumbersome. Stemming from an earlier design whose prototype had crashed, the first prototype Swordfish (the TSR.II) first flew on 17 April 1934 and the production Swordfish Mk I was prepared to Specification S.38/34 with slightly swept-back top wing; construction was all-metal with fabric covering. By the outbreak of war in 1939 a total of 689 aircraft had been delivered or were on order, serving with both wheel and float landing gear aboard Royal Navy carriers, battleships, battle-cruisers and cruisers in the torpedo-spotter reconnaissance role. Among the memorable actions in which the old 'Stringbag' participated were the action at Taranto of 11 November 1940, when Swordfish aircraft from HMS *Illustrious* sank or crippled three Italian battleships; the crippling of the *Bismarck* in the Atlantic; and the suicidal attack on the German warships, *Scharnhorst*, *Gneisenau* and *Prinz Eugen* during their famous escape up the English Channel in February 1942. Production of the Swordfish was undertaken largely by Blackburn, the Swordfish Mk II being introduced with strengthened lower wing to allow eight rocket projectiles to be mounted, the Swordfish Mk III with ASV radar between the landing gear legs, and the Swordfish Mk IV conversion of the Mk II with a rudimentary enclosed cabin. Production ended on 18 August 1944, by which time a total of 2,396 Swordfish had been completed.

**Specification:** Fairey Swordfish Mk II
**Origin:** UK
**Type:** three-crew torpedo/anti-submarine aircraft
**Powerplant:** one 750-hp (560-kW) Bristol Pegasus XXX radial piston engine
**Performance:** maximum speed 138 mph (222 km/h) at sea level; initial climb rate 1,220 ft (372 m) per minute; service ceiling 19,250 ft (5865 m); range 546 miles (879 km)
**Weights:** empty 4,700 lb (2132 kg); maximum take-off 7,510 lb (3407 kg)

**Fairey Swordfish Mk II**

**Dimensions:** span 45 ft 6 in (12.87 m); length 35 ft 8 in (10.87 m); height 12 ft 4 in (3.76 m); using area 607.0 sq ft (56.39 m²)
**Armament:** one fixed forward-firing 0.303-in (7.7-mm) machine-gun and one flexible 0.303-in (7.7-mm) gun in rear cockpit, plus a weapon load of one 18-in (457-mm) torpedo or eight 60-lb (27.2-kg) rocket projectiles

**The immortal Swordfish was outwardly an anachronism without parallel in World War II; nevertheless its battle honours stand unsurpassed by any other British naval aircraft, headed by the famous attack on the *Bismarck* in the Atlantic and the raid on the Italian fleet in Taranto harbour.**

# Fairey Swordfish

Although fairly anonymous in being bare of serial number, Royal Navy ship and squadron markings, this Swordfish is shown in a colour scheme typical of around 1940-1 (the period of the Battle of Taranto) and is carrying a standard naval 18-in (457-mm) torpedo. The horizontal bar suspended from the top wing centre section, visible in the front view, is the aim-off sight, used for attacks on ships, and the emergency dinghy stowage was located in the top wing immediately outboard of the wing-fold; the rear Lewis gun is shown in the stowed position.

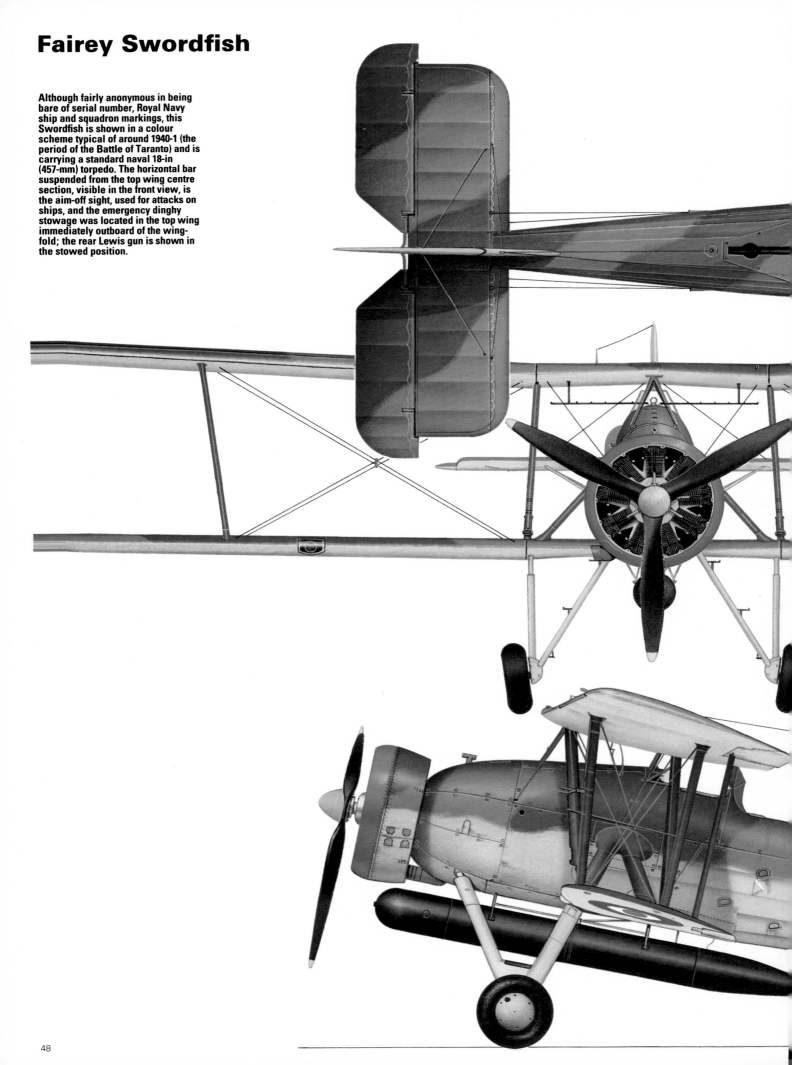

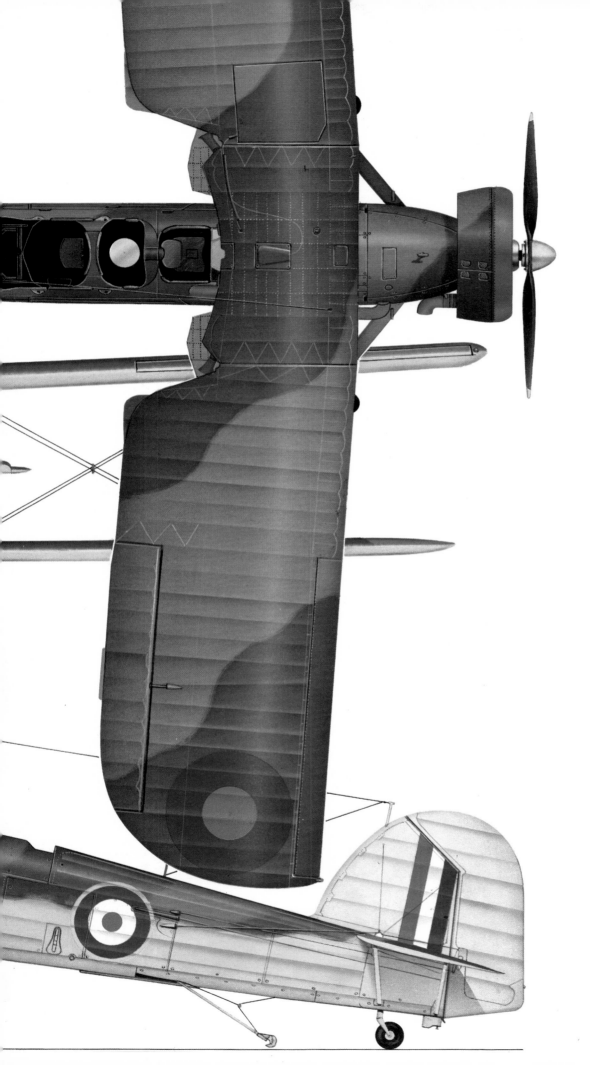

# Fairey Fulmar

Powered by the same Merlin engine as in the Hurricane, the Fulmar was considerably larger and heavier, and with a second crew member could scarcely be expected to match single-seat fighter opponents. Against enemy bombers and flying boats it proved more successful.

## History and Notes

The first true shipborne monoplane fighter for the Fleet Air Arm, the eight-gun Fairey Fulmar tends to be overlooked in the part it played in the first three years of the war, until replaced by deck-operating adaptations of the Hurricane and Spitfire, and by the Martlet. Developed from the Fairey P.4/34 light bomber prototypes which flew in 1937, the Fulmar fleet fighter prototype was flown on 4 January 1940, with production aircraft being completed soon after. Early trials showed the aircraft to have a disappointing performance, although it was recognized as being a fairly large aeroplane with the same engine as the Hurricane single-seater. In 1942, after 127 production Fulmar Mk Is had been completed, the Fulmar Mk II appeared with 1,260-hp (940-kW) Merlin XXX, an engine which raised the top speed to 272 mph (438 km/h). Fulmar Mk Is of No. 808 Squadron of the Fleet Air Arm were listed in RAF Fighter Command's order of battle during the Battle of Britain, although they were not engaged in combat. By November 1940, however, Fulmars were in action from HMS *Illustrious* at the time of the Battle of Taranto, and soon afterwards from HMS *Ark Royal* defending the vital convoys sailing to Malta. At the Battle of Cape Matapan Fulmars from HMS *Formidable* escorted the Albacores and Swordfish which torpedoed the Italian battleship *Vittorio Veneto*. Early in 1942, as Japanese naval forces sailed into the Indian Ocean to threaten Ceylon, two squadrons of Fulmars were based there as part of Colombo's air defences; when confronted for the first time by the much superior carrier-based Zero-Sen fighters the Fulmars were utterly outclassed and almost all were shot down or damaged. A total of 450 Fulmar Mk IIs was built, and some served as night-fighters.

## Specification: Fairey Fulmar Mk II
**Origin:** UK
**Type:** two-seat shipborne fighter
**Powerplant:** one 1,260-hp (940-kW) Rolls-Royce Merlin XXX inline piston engine
**Performance:** maximum speed 272 mph (438 km/h) at 16,500-ft (5030 m); initial climb rate 1,320 ft (402 m) per minutes; service ceiling 27,200 ft (8290 m); range 780 miles (1255 km)
**Weights:** empty 7,384 lb (3349 kg); maximum take-off 10,200 lb (4627 kg)
**Dimensions:** span 46 ft 4½ in (14.13 m); length 40 ft 2 in (12.24 m); height 10 ft 8 in (3.25 m); wing area 342.0 sq ft (31.77 m²)
**Armament:** eight 0.303-in (7.7-mm) machine-guns in wings, and a few aircraft also had a single flexible 0.303-in (7.7-mm) machine-gun in the rear cockpit

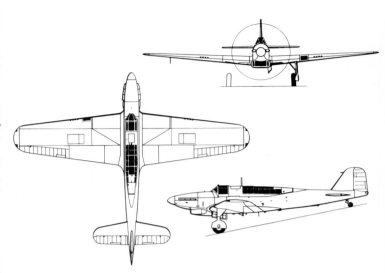

**Fairey Fulmar**

The Fleet Air Arm's first eight-gun carrierborne fighter, the Fulmar served with the Royal Navy throughout the first three years of the war and, despite poor performance, gave good service. In the Far East, however, it proved wholly inadequate against the Japanese Zero-Sen naval fighter.

# Fiat BR.20 Cicogna

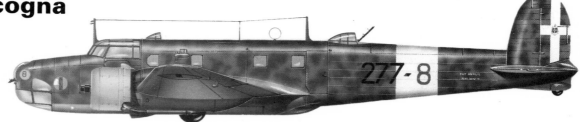

An early Fiat BR.20M belonging to the 277ª Squadriglia BT, 116° Gruppo BT, 37° Stormo BT, based at Grottaglie, South Italy, late in 1940. The unit operated over the Greco-Albanian front during the invasion of Greece, but suffered fairly heavily at the hands of RAF Hurricanes until the intervention of the Luftwaffe.

## History and Notes

A contemporary of the Bristol Blenheim Mk I and of similar performance (though able to carry three times the bombload), the Fiat BR.20 Cicogna (Stork) appeared in 1936 and, in view of a number of sporting successes and record flights by early aircraft, suggested it would become an effective addition to the Regia Aeronautica's bomber force. The first flight by the prototype on 10 February 1936 was followed by deliveries to the 13° Stormo BT in September that year, and to the 7° Stormo BT six months later. These two units took BR.20s to Spain in 1937, and in 1938-9 85 similar aircraft were exported to Japan for service in China, and one aircraft was purchased by Venezuela in 1938. At the end of 1939 the prototype of an improved version, the BR.20M, was flown with cleaned-up nose and strengthened wing; the Fiat A.80 RC 41 engines remained unchanged. When Italy entered the war in June 1940 four *stormi* (the 7°, 13° 18° and 43°) flew 148 BR.20s, roughly one-third of them the new version. Some aircraft took part in the short campaign against France, and 80 were based in Belgium for the Italian attacks on the UK in November 1940, suffering heavy casualties. BR.20 units also suffered heavily in night attacks on Malta, and in North Africa difficulties in operating the Fiat engines in desert conditions led to considerable unserviceability – a situation which the Italian aircraft industry seemed powerless to rectify. A much improved and extensively redesigned version, the BR.20-II (or BR.20bis) had been flown in 1940 and, with 1,250-hp (933-kW) Fiat A.82 RC 32 radials and a nose shape similar to that of the Heinkel He 111, entered production in 1943. By the time of the Italian armistice, however, the number of serviceable BR.20s stood at 67, out of a total of 606 produced.

## Specification: Fiat BR.20 Cicogna

**Origin:** Italy
**Type:** five/six-crew medium bomber
**Powerplant:** two 1,000-hp (746-kW) Fiat A.80 RC41 radial piston engines
**Performance:** maximum speed 267 mph (430 km/h) at 13,125 ft (4000 m); climb to 13,125 ft (4000 m) in 13.55 minutes; service ceiling 24,935 ft (7600 m); range 1,193 miles (1920 km)
**Weights:** empty 14,330 lb (6500 kg); maximum take-off 22,266 lb (10100 kg)
**Dimensions:** span 70 ft 8¾ in (21.56 m); length 52 ft 9¾ in (16.10 m); height 14 ft 1¼ in (4.30 m); wing area 796.6 sq ft (74.00 m²)
**Armament:** single 7.7-mm (0.303-in) machine-guns in nose, dorsal and ventral positions, plus a maximum bombload of 3,527 lb (1600 kg)

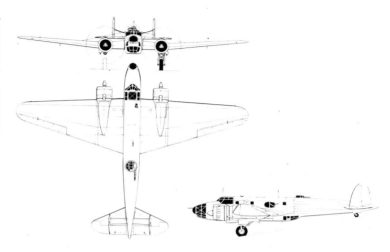

Fiat BR.20M Cicogna (middle side view: BR.20M (mod); lower side view BR.20bis)

Popularly referred to as the Cicogna (Stork), the Fiat BR.20 was an unimaginative design with no better than mediocre performance. It was however widely used during the first two years of the war, presumably on account of its useful bomb load, but was critically short of defensive armament.

# Fiat CR.42 Falco

Serving alongside the Luftwaffe at the end of the Battle of Britain, this CR.42 belonged to the 95ª Squadriglia CT, 18° Gruppo CT, 56° Stormo CT, based at Maldegen, Belgium. Unfortunately for the Regia Aeronautica the CR.42s encountered a victory-flushed RAF Fighter Command and suffered heavily.

## History and Notes

Often compared in concept and design with the Gloster Gladiator, against which it frequently fought in 1940-1, the Fiat CR.42 (Falco (Falcon)) biplane did not first fly until 1939, however, and such an anachronism is difficult to understand. Employing the same Warren truss system of interplane struts as the 1933 CR.32, from which it was developed, Celestino Rosatelli's CR.42 was powered by an 840-hp (627-kW) Fiat A74 R1C 38 radial and had a top speed of 274 mph (441 km/h). By September 1939 the Falco equipped three *stormi* and, while the RAF was hurriedly reducing its Gladiator strength, the Regia Aeronautica was increasing its CR.42 inventory, so that when Italy entered the war in June 1940 there were 330 in service with four *stormi* in the Mediterranean plus two *squadriglie* in Italian East Africa. The Falco first saw combat in the brief French campaign, and later 50 aircraft accompanied the Corpo Aero Italiano to bases in Belgium for attacks on southern England at the end of the Battle of Britain, suffering heavily to the guns of RAF Hurricanes. In the Middle East the Falco fared better, however, being more of a match for the widely-used Gladiator; during the Greek campaign one *gruppo* of three CR.42 *squadriglie* was committed and, except on a few occasions, acquitted itself well; but when Hurricanes eventually arrived the Italian biplane losses mounted steadily. In East Africa 51 crated CR.42s were received to supplement the 36 aircraft delivered to the 412ª and 413ª Squadriglie, but in due course they were destroyed in the air or on the ground, although they took a heavy toll of the antiquated aircraft of the RAF and SAAF. In the Western Desert CR.42 fighters were joined by a fighter-bomber version adapted to carry two 220-lb (100-kg) bombs, and these continued in service with the 5°, 15° and 50° Stormi Assalti until November 1942. A total of 1,781 CR.42s was built (some serving in Sweden and Hungary), but at the time of the Italian armistice in September 1943 only 64 remained serviceable.

**Specification:** Fiat CR.42 Falco
**Origin:** Italy
**Type:** single-seat fighter
**Powerplant:** one 840-hp (627-kW) Fiat A.74 R1C 38 radial piston engine

**Fiat CR.42 Falco**

**Performance:** maximum speed 274 mph (441 km/h) at 19,685 ft (6000 m); climb to 19,685 ft (6000 m) in 9.0 minutes; service ceiling 33,135 ft (10100 m); range 485 miles (780 km)
**Weights:** empty 3,933 lb (1784 kg); maximum take-off 5,060 lb (2295 kg)
**Dimensions:** span 31 ft 9⅞ in (9.70 m); length 27 ft 0⅞ in (8.26 m); height 10 ft 0⅜ in (3.05 m); wing area 241.1 sq ft (22.40 m²)
**Armament:** two 12.7-mm (0.5-in) Breda-SAFAT machine-guns in nose (some aircraft with two extra 12.7-mm/0.5-in machine-guns under lower wing), plus provision for two 220-lb (100-kg) bombs

A Fiat CR.42 Falco of the 97ª Squadriglia CT, 9° Gruppo, 4° Stormo CT, based at Benina, Libya, captured by British forces in the Western Desert during 1940. The famous 'Cavallino Rampante' insignia has been cut from the rear fuselage by souvenir hunters.

# Fiat G.50 Freccia

Sporting the 'cat and mice' emblem of the 56° Stormo CT, this G.50bis was one of the Belgian-based Italian at the end of the Battle of Britain. Given the job of 'surveillance' over the Channel the Freccia squadrons seemed to have successfully evaded combat with the RAF.

## History and Notes

Representing the first design essay of the young technician Guiseppi Gabrielli with the Fiat company, the G.50 fighter was designed in 1935-6 but, although a break from the traditional biplane formula, offered much less in operational potential than the contemporary Hawker Hurricane and Messerschmitt Bf 109. The prototype G.50 first flew on 26 February 1937 and was the first all-metal monoplane with constant-speed propeller and retractable landing gear to be evaluated by the Regia Aeronautica. Named Freccia (Arrow), the G.50 was ordered into production with the CMASA company (a subsidiary of Fiat) and 12 of the first aircraft were sent to Spain for operational evaluation. Despite the superiority of the Macchi C.200, it was decided to go ahead and equip one *stormo* and one *gruppo* with the G.50, and an initial order for 200 aircraft was placed. In November 1939 the type was delivered to the 51° Stormo, and soon afterwards to the 52° Stormo, and when Italy entered the war in the following June, 118 Freccias were in service. In November 1940 48 G.50s of the 51° Stormo moved to Belgium to take part in the air attacks on the UK; however, they saw little action, being principally engaged in 'surveillance' duties. In September that year the prototype of a new version, the G.50bis, had flown, and with improved cockpit armour and increased fuel this entered production for eventual service with five *gruppi* in North Africa. With a maximum speed of only 286 mph (460 km/h) and an armament of two machine-guns, the G.50 was hardly a match for RAF fighters in the Mediterranean, yet survived in service until July 1943. Production eventually reached 245 G.50 and 421 G.50bis fighters, and 108 of a dual-control two-seat trainer, the G.50B. G.50s were also supplied to the Croatian and Finnish air forces.

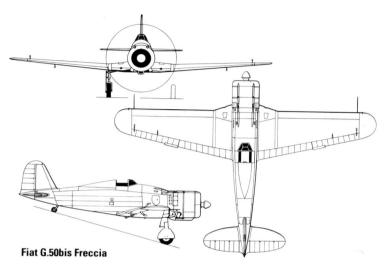

**Fiat G.50bis Freccia**

## Specification: Fiat G.50 Freccia

**Origin:** Italy
**Type:** single-seat fighter
**Powerplant:** one 840-hp (627-kW) Fiat A.74RC 38 radial piston engine
**Performance:** maximum speed 286 mph (460 km/h) at 13,125 ft (4000 m); climb to 13,125 ft (4000 m) in 4.6 minutes; service ceiling 35,270 ft (10750 m); range 360 miles (580 km)
**Weights:** empty 4,332 lb (1965 kg); maximum take-off 5,291 lb (2400 kg)
**Dimensions:** span 36 ft 0½ in (11.00 m); length 25 ft 7 in (7.80 m); height 10 ft 9¼ in (3.28 m); wing area 196.45 sq ft (18.25 m²)
**Armament:** two nose-mounted 12.7-mm (0.5-in) Breda-SAFAT machine-guns

Handicapped by the lack of a suitable inline engine, Italian fighters at the beginning of the war had to make do with bulky radials, the Fiat G.50 in particular having a disappointing performance. This aircraft served with the 352ª Squadriglia CT, 20° Gruppo CT, 56° Stormo CT, at Ursel, Belgium, in October 1940.

# Focke-Wulf Fw 190

Fw 190A-8 of III/JG 11 based at Gross-Ostheim in December 1944. The yellow 'Defence of the Reich' band denotes JG 11, whilst the superimposed wavy line denotes III Gruppe.

## History and Notes

Proposed in 1937, as the Bf 109 was joining the Luftwaffe, Kurt Tank's Focke-Wulf Fw 190 surprisingly featured a bulky air-cooled BMW radial engine. First flown on 1 June 1939, the prototype was followed by short- and long-span pre-production Fw 190A-0s, with BMW 801 14-cylinder radials. The long-span version was selected for production. Fw 190A-1s joined the Luftwaffe in mid-1941 and proved superior to the Spitfire Mk V. A-series variations included the Fw 190A-3 with BMW 801D-2 and two 7.92-mm (0.31-in) and four 20-mm guns, the Fw 190 A-4 with water-methanol power-boosting (with fighter-bomber, bomber-destroyer and tropicalized sub-variants). The Fw 190A-5 featured a slightly lengthened nose and sub-variants included versions with six 30-mm guns (A-5/U12) and torpedo-fighters (A-5/U14 and U15). The Fw 190A-7 and Fw 190A-8 entered production in December 1943 and featured increased armament and armour. The Fw 190A-8/U1 was a two-seat conversion trainer. The next main production version, the Fw 190D, featured a much lengthened nose and Junkers Jumo 213 inline engine in an annular cowling. The Fw 190D-9 was the main service version, which joined the Luftwaffe in the autumn of 1944, and was generally regarded as Germany's best wartime piston-engine fighter; with a top speed of 426 mph (685 km/h), it was armed with two cannon and two machine-guns, and was powered by a water-methanol boosted 2,240-hp (1671-kW) Jumo 2213A engine. Other late versions included the Fw 190F and Fw 190G specialized ground-attack fighter-bombers capable of carrying up to 2,205 lb (1000 kg) of bombs.

A development of the Fw 190D was the long-span Focke-Wulf Ta 152 with increased armament and boosted Jumo 213E/B (top speed 472 mph/760 km/h at 41,010 ft/12500 m); a small number of Ta 152H-1s reached the Luftwaffe shortly before the end of the war.

**Specification:** Focke-Wulf Fw 190A-8
**Origin:** Germany
**Type:** single-seat fighter
**Powerplant:** one 2,100-hp (1567-kW) BMW 801D-2 radial piston engine with water-methanol boosting
**Performance:** maximum speed 408 mph (654 km/h) at 19,685 ft (6000 m); initial climb rate 2,362 ft (720 m) per minute; service ceiling 37,400 ft (11400 m); normal range 500 miles (805 km)
**Weights:** empty 6,989 lb (3170 kg); maximum take-off 10,802 lb (4900 kg)
**Dimensions:** span 34 ft 5½ in (10.50 m); length 29 ft 1½ in (8.84 m); height 13 ft 0 in (3.96 m); wing area 196.98 sq ft (18.30 m²)
**Armament:** two 7.92-mm (0.31-in) guns on nose and up to four 20-mm guns in wings, plus provision for wide range of underfuselage and underwing bombs, guns and rockets

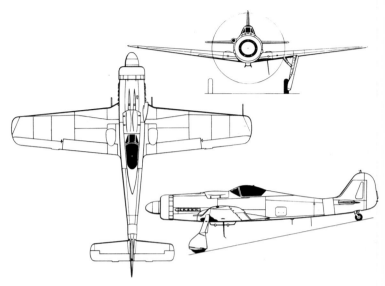

**Focke-Wulf Fw 190D-9**

A Focke-Wulf Fw 190G-2 ground attack variant equipped with a centreline ETC 250 bomb rack capable of mounting a single 551-lb (250-kg) bomb; other versions of the Fw 190G could carry bomb loads of up to 3970 lb (1800 kg).

# Focke-Wulf Fw 200 Condor

Displaying the ringed globe insignia of I/KG 40 (recalling the long-distance flights by commercial Condors), this Fw 200 of 1. Staffel was based at Bordeaux-Mérignac late in 1940 for maritime operations over Britain's Western approaches.

## History and Notes

Famous as a pre-war airliner with a number of formidable long-distance flights and records to its credit, the four-engine Focke-Wulf Fw 200 Condor was designed by Kurt Tank in 1936, and underwent military adaptation into a fairly potent anti-shipping aircraft with the Luftwaffe. Ten pre-production Fw 200C-0 maritime reconnaissance aircraft were delivered to the Luftwaffe in September 1939, some of them serving with I./KG 40 in 1940. The five-crew production Fw 200C-1 was powered by four 830-hp (619-kW) BMW 132H engines, was armed with a 20-mm gun in the nose and three 7.92-mm (0.31-in) guns in other positions, and could carry four 551-lb (250-kg) bombs. Apart from long-range maritime patrols over the Atlantic, the Fw 200C-1s also undertook extensive minelaying in British waters during 1940, each carrying two 2,205-lb (1000-kg) mines. Numerous sub-variants of the C-series appeared, of which the Fw 200C-3 with 1,000-hp (746-kW) Bramo 323R-2 radials was the most important. Later in the war the Fw 200C-6 and Fw 200C-8 were produced in an effort to enhance the Condor's operational potential by adaptation to carry two Henschel Hs 293 missiles in conjunction with FuG 203b missile control radio.

Rugged operating conditions highlighted the Fw 200's numerous structural weaknesses and there were numerous accidents in service, and for a short time in the mid-war years Fw 200s were employed as military transports, 18 aircraft being flown by Kampfgruppe zur besonderen Verwendung 200 in support of the beleaguered German forces at Stalingrad. Other Condors were used by Hitler and Himmler as personal transports. Focke-Wulf Fw 200 production for the Luftwaffe amounted to 252 aircraft between 1940 and 1944.

**Specification:** Focke-Wulf Fw 200C-3/U4
**Origin:** Germany
**Type:** seven-crew long-range maritime reconnaissance bomber
**Powerplant:** four 1,000-hp (746-kW) BMW-Bramo 323R-2 radial piston engines
**Performance:** maximum speed 224 mph (360 km/h) at 15,420 ft (4700 m); service ceiling 19,685 ft (6000 m); range 2,211 miles (3560 km)
**Weight:** empty 37,478 lb (17000 kg); maximum take-off 50,044 lb (22700 kg)
**Dimensions:** span 107 ft 9½ in (32.84 m); length 76 ft 11½ in (23.85 m); height 20 ft 8 in (6.30 m); wing area 1,290.0 sq ft (118.00 m²)
**Armament:** one 7.92-mm (0.31-in) gun in forward dorsal turret, one 13-mm (0.51-in) gun in rear dorsal position, two 13-mm (0.51-in) guns in beam positions, one 20-mm gun in forward position of ventral gondola and one 7.92-mm (0.31-in) gun in aft ventral position, plus a maximum bomb load of 4,630 lb (2100 kg)

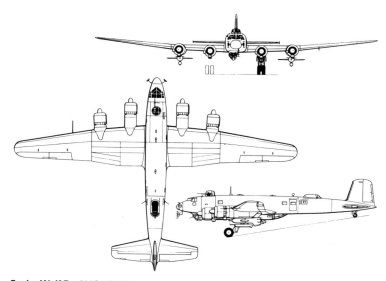

**Focke-Wulf Fw 200C-8/U-10 Condor**

The Focke-Wulf Fw 200 originated in a pre-war long-range commercial airliner. The Fw 200C-3/Us, which entered Luftwaffe service in 1941, introduced a Lofte 7D bombsight, but featured reduced gun armament.

# Fokker D.XXI

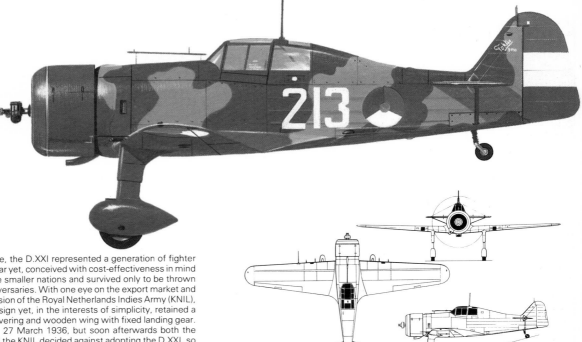

When the Germans invaded the Low Countries on 10 May 1940 fewer than 30 D.XXIs had been delivered to the Dutch air force; the aircraft depicted here was the second production aircraft to be completed and bears the pre-October 1939 national markings.

## History and Notes

Product of Dr-Ir E. Schatzki's design office, the D.XXI represented a generation of fighter aircraft that rightfully had no place in the war yet, conceived with cost-effectiveness in mind five years previously, was selected by the smaller nations and survived only to be thrown into combat with much more powerful adversaries. With one eye on the export market and the other on the likely needs of the Air Division of the Royal Netherlands Indies Army (KNIL), Schatzki produced the tidiest possible design yet, in the interests of simplicity, retained a welded steel-tube fuselage with fabric covering and wooden wing with fixed landing gear. The prototype's first flight was made on 27 March 1936, but soon afterwards both the home-based Luchtvaartafdeling (LVA) and the KNIL decided against adopting the D.XXI, so Fokker redoubled its efforts in the export market. In the event only Denmark, Finland and Spain opted to produce the aircraft under licence, and the Spanish plans came to nothing. Denmark bought two pattern aircraft and built 10 others, while Finland bought seven and herself produced 35 more, these giving excellent service against the Soviet air force in the Winter War of 1939-40. In the meantime the Dutch LVA reversed its previous decision and purchased 36 D.XXIs, and all had been delivered by the time of the German invasion of May 1940; their pilots also fought with great bravery, all but nine aircraft being destroyed in the four-day campaign. So popular had the D.XXI proved in Finland that, powered by Pratt & Whitney Twin Wasp Juniors in place of the Bristol Mercury, 50 more aircraft were built in 1941 and, together with 17 surviving Mercury D.XXIs fought at the beginning of the Continuation War. As late as 1944 five further aircraft were built from spares!

**Specification:** Fokker D.XXI
**Origin:** Netherlands
**Type:** single-seat fighter
**Powerplant:** one 840-hp (627-kW) Bristol Mercury VIII radial piston engine
**Performance:** maximum speed 286 mph (460 km/h) at 16,730 ft (5100 m); climb to

### Fokker D.XXI

16,405 ft (5000 m) in 6.6 minutes; service ceiling 33,135 ft (10100 m); range 578 miles (930 k
**Weights:** empty 3,197 lb (1450 kg); normal loaded 4,519 lb (2050 kg)
**Dimensions:** span 36 ft 1 in (11.00 m); length 26 ft 10¾ in (8.20 m); height 9 ft 8 in (2.95 m); wing area 174.38 sq ft (16.20 m²)
**Armament:** four 7.9-mm (0.31-in) FN-Browning M-36 machine-guns in wings, plus provision for light underwing bombload.

Displaying the black and orange triangle national markings adopted by the Netherlands after October 1939, this Fokker D.XXI shows the scars of battle on the rear fuselage; a photo probably taken soon after the Dutch surrender.

# Gloster Gladiator

Although it had almost disappeared from RAF service at the beginning of the war, the Gladiator continued to equip foreign air forces; the aircraft shown here was still serving with the Belgian air force when Germany invaded the country in May 1940.

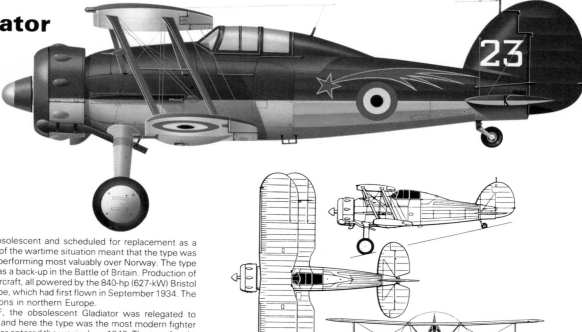

## History and Notes

By 1939 the Gladiator was decidedly obsolescent and scheduled for replacement as a front-line RAF fighter. But the exigencies of the wartime situation meant that the type was retained, serving first in France and then performing most valuably over Norway. The type was also available in very small numbers as a back-up in the Battle of Britain. Production of the Gladiator Mk I had amounted to 378 aircraft, all powered by the 840-hp (627-kW) Bristol Mercury IX radial pioneered in the prototype, which had first flown in September 1934. The Gladiator served with seven RAF squadrons in northern Europe.

As was common practice in the RAF, the obsolescent Gladiator was relegated to secondary theatres, notably North Africa, and here the type was the most modern fighter available to meet the Italians when the latter entered the war in June 1940. The type fought with considerable distinction over the Western Desert up to 1942, and was also gainfully employed in the Maltese and Greek campaigns. The principal wartime variant was the Gladiator Mk II, essentially a Gladiator Mk I with the 840-hp (627-kW) Mercury VIIA or Mercury VIIAS. The aircraft intended for operations in North Africa had tropical equipment, and six North African squadrons were equipped with the type. The other British version was the Sea Gladiator, which had catapult points, an arrester hook and dinghy stowage. Production amounted to 60 aircraft, supplemented by 38 Gladiator Mk IIs converted as Interim Sea Gladiators. A considerable number of Gladiators were exported, and 18 aircraft were operated by Sweden under the designation J8A with Nohab Mercury VIIIS.3 radials.

## Specification: Gloster Gladiator Mk II
**Origin:** UK
**Type:** single-seat interceptor fighter
**Powerplant:** one 840-hp (627-kW) Bristol Mercury VIIIA radial piston engine
**Performance:** maximum speed 255 mph (410 km/h) at 14,500 ft (4420 m); initial climb rate 2,300 ft (701 m) per minute' service ceiling 33,000 ft (10060 m); range 440 miles (708 km)
**Weights:** empty 3,480 lb (1570 kg); maximum take-off 4,810 lb (2182 kg)

## Gloster Gladiator

**Dimensions:** span 32 ft 3 in (9.83 m); length 27 ft 5 in (8.36 m); height 11 ft 9 in (3.63 m); wing area 323.0 sq ft (30.01 m²)
**Armament:** two 0.303-in (7.7-mm) Browning machine-guns in the nose and two 0.303-in (7.7-mm) Browning or Vickers machine-guns under the lower wings

At the time of Italy's entry into the war in June 1940 the defence of Malta – strategically vital to Britain in the Mediterranean – rested solely on a handful of Sea Gladiators, kept there as fleet replacements; piloted by volunteers, they sought to defend the island from half-hearted attacks by the Italian air force.

# Gotha Go 242

A Gotha Go 244B wearing the markings of 4./KGrzbV 106 early in 1943; by this time, however, the unit had almost entirely re-equipped with the Junkers Ju 52/3m.

## History and Notes

Designed by Albert Kalkert, the Gotha Go 242 transport and assault glider was the most widely used operational glider in the Luftwaffe's wartime arsenal between 1942 and 1945, and was employed in the Balkans, Sicily, North Africa and, of course, on the Eastern Front. Conceived and afforded high priority in 1940, the first prototypes (Go 242 VI and Go 242 V2) were first flown the following year; the glider was a high wing monoplane whose tail unit was carried on twin tail booms, allowing access to the central nacelle, which could accommodate 21 troops, through a hinged rear section. The first production version, the Go 242A-1, was a freight transport and had a defensive armament of up to four 7.92-mm (0.31-in) machine-guns. It was followed by the Go 242A-2 assault glider with troop accommodation. These versions entered Luftwaffe service in 1942, the towing aircraft usually being the Heinkel He 111H; they featured a twin-wheel trolley that was jettisoned after take-off.

The Go 242B followed into production in 1942 with non-jettisonable landing gear; the Go 242B-3 and Go 242B-4 were paratrooping versions, while the Go 242B-5 was a dual-control trainer. The Go 242C-1 was an interesting version capable of alighting on water and of carrying a explosive-carrying catamaran with which it was intended to attack the British fleet at Scapa Flow in 1944; a number of Go 242C-1s was delivered to 6./KG 200, but the operation was abandoned. A total of 1,528 Gotha Go 242s was produced, of which 133 were converted to the powered Go 244 version with 700-hp (522-kW) Gnome-Rhône 14M radial engines.

**Specification:** Gotha Go 242A-2
**Origin:** Germany
**Type:** medium assault glider
**Performance:** maximum towing speed 149 mph (240 km/h)
**Weights:** empty 7,055 lb (3200 kg); maximum take-off 15,656 lb (7100 kg)
**Dimensions:** span 80 ft 4⅜ in (24.50 m); length 51 ft 10¼ in (15.80 m); height 14 ft 4¼ in (4.38 m); wing area 693.2 sq ft (64.40 m²)
**Accommodation:** pilot and 21 assault troops or Kübelwagen, or alternative loads up to 8,000 lb (3630 kg); defensive armament of up to four 7.92-mm (0.31-in) MG 34 machine-guns

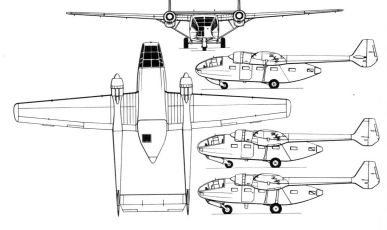

Gotha Go 244B-1 (upper view: Go 224V, lower view: Go 244B-2)

Gotha Go 244B-1 powered glider. Aircraft of this type were used by KGrzbV 104 in Greece and KGrzbV 106 in Crete during 1942, but when flown in North Africa were very vulnerable to anti-aircraft fire and were quickly withdrawn.

# Grumman F4F Wildcat

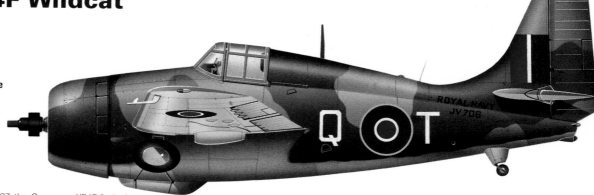

A Grumman Wildcat Mk VI of the Fleet Air Arm. This General Motors-built variant (equivalent to the US Navy's FM-2) could be identified by the taller fin found necessary to cope with the increased power of the Wright R-1820 engine.

## History and Notes

When first flown on 2 September 1937 the Grumman XF4F-2 single-seat naval fighter prototype proved to be only 10 mph (16 km/h) faster than the Brewster F2A-1, and only when a two-stage supercharged XR-1830-76 was fitted was the true potential of the design recognized, and a speed of 333.5 mph (537 km/h) was recorded during US Navy trials with the XF4F-3. Some 54 production F4F-3s were ordered in August 1939, 22 of which had been delivered by the end of 1940. These aircraft (Grumman's first monoplanes for the US Navy) served with VF-4 and VF-7 and were followed by 95 F4F-3As with single-stage supercharged R-1830-90 engines. The Wildcat was ordered by France in 1939 but the entire batch of 81 aircraft was transferred to the UK, with whose Royal Navy they served as the Martlet, being first flown in combat during 1941. US Navy and US Marine Corps F4Fs were heavily engaged during the early months of the war with the Japanese, numerous aircraft being destroyed on the ground, but also scoring a number of outstanding victories. The F4F-4 (of which 1,169 were produced), with manually-folding wings, was delivered during 1942, and an unarmed long-range reconnaissance version of this, the F4F-7, had a range of over 3,500 miles (5633 km). The F4F-4 was also built by General Motors as the FM-1, and a more powerful version, the FM-2, for operation from escort carriers. FM-1s and -2s were supplied to the UK as the Wildcat Mk V and Mk VI (the name Martlet having been dropped). F4F-4s were heavily committed in the battles of the Coral Sea and Midway. Total production of the Wildcat (excluding prototypes) was 7,885, including 5,237 FM-1s and FM-2s by General Motors, and 1,100 for the UK.

**Specification:** Grumman F4F-4 Wildcat
**Origin:** USA
**Type:** single-seat shipboard fighter
**Powerplant:** one 1,200-hp (895-kW) Pratt & Whitney R-1830-86 radial piston engine
**Performance:** maximum speed 318 mph (512 km/h) at 19,400 ft (5915 m); initial climb rate 1,950 ft (594 m) per minute; service ceiling 34,900 ft (10640 m); range 770 miles (1240 km)
**Weights:** empty 5,785 lb (2624 kg); maximum take-off 7,952 lb (3607 kg)
**Dimensions:** span 38 ft 0 in (11.58 m); length 28 ft 9 in (8.76 m); height 11 ft 10 in

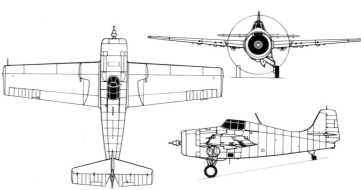

**Grumman F4F-4 Wildcat**

(3.60 m); wing area 260.0 sq ft (24.15 m²)
**Armament:** six forward-firing 0.5-in (12.7-mm) machine guns; FM-2 had four guns and provision to carry two 250-lb (113-kg) bombs or six 5-in (127-mm) rockets

A contemporary of the Japanese Zero-Sen naval fighter, the F4F Wildcat was somewhat inferior in performance, but usually held its own largely owing to its heavier armament. Though obsolete in the last two years of the war, the Wildcat, on account of its small folded size, continued to fly from small escort carriers.

# Grumman F6F Hellcat

For an aircraft that only entered service two years from the war's end, the production total of 12,275 Hellcats was a remarkable achievement, well matched by its combat prowess, for in the same period it destroyed 4,947 enemy aircraft – excluding those shot down by British pilots of the Fleet Air Arm.

## History and Notes

One of America's best wartime shipboard fighters, and second only to the F4U Corsair, the F6F Hellcat was the logical development of the F4F Wildcat, and was first flown as the XF6F-3 on 26 June 1942, production F6F-3s following only five weeks later. Deliveries to VF-9 aboard USS *Essex* started early in 1943; night-fighter versions were the F6F-3E and F6F-3N with radar in a wing pod. In 1944 the F6F-5 appeared with provision for 2,000 lb (907 kg) of bombs and two 20-mm cannon sometimes replacing the inboard wing 0.5-in (12.7-mm) guns; the radar-equipped night-fighter version was the F6F-5N; production totalled 6,435 F6F-5s and 1,189 F6F-5Ns, while 252 F6F-3s and 930 F6F-5s served with the British Fleet Air Arm as the Hellcat Mk I and Mk II respectively. Production of all F6Fs amounted to 12,275, and official figures credited the US Navy and Marine Corps aircraft with the destruction of 5,156 enemy aircraft in air combat, about 75 per cent of all the US Navy's air combat victories in the war. The Hellcat's greatest single victory was in that greatest of all carrier battles, the Battle of the Philippine Sea, in which 15 American carriers embarked 480 F6F fighters (plus 222 dive-bombers and 199 torpedo-bombers); by the end of a week's fighting Task Force 58 had destroyed more than 400 Japanese aircraft and sunk three carriers. Hellcats were still serving with the US Navy several years after the war.

**Specification:** Grumman F6F-5 Hellcat
**Origin:** USA
**Type:** single-seat shipboard fighter
**Powerplant:** one 2,000-hp (1492-kW) Pratt & Whitney R-2800-10W radial piston engine
**Performance:** maximum speed 380 mph (612 km/h) at 23,400 ft (7130 m); initial climb rate 2,980 ft (908 m) per minute; service ceiling 37,300 ft (11370 m); range 945 miles (1529 km)
**Weights:** empty 9,238 lb (4190 kg); maximum take-off 15,413 lb (6991 kg)
**Dimensions:** span 42 ft 10 in (13.05 m); length 33 ft 7 in (10.23 m); height 13 ft 1 in (3.99 m); wing area 334.0 sq ft (31.03 m²)
**Armament:** six 0.5-in (12.7-mm) machine-guns in wings, or two 20-mm cannon and four 0.5-in (12.7-mm) guns in wings, plus provision for two 1,000-lb (454-kg) bombs

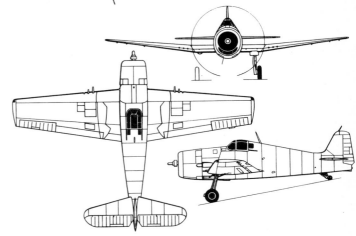

**Grumman F6F-3 Hellcat I**

A Grumman F6F-3 in the red-bordered US Navy markings used between July and September 1943. This was the first production version of the Hellcat and was first in action with US Navy Squadron VF-5 from the carrier *USS Essex* on 31 August 1943 in the Pacific.

A Hellcat recovers aboard its carrier in the Pacific. This aircraft more than any other was to turn the tide against the Japanese aggressors after the psychological and physical devastation of Pearl Harbor.

# Grumman TBF Avenger

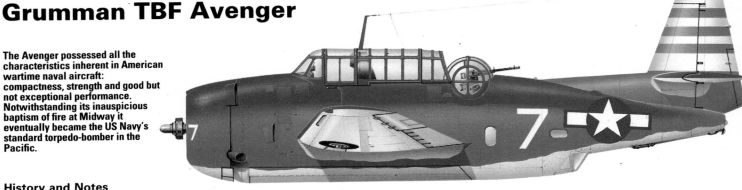

The Avenger possessed all the characteristics inherent in American wartime naval aircraft: compactness, strength and good but not exceptional performance. Notwithstanding its inauspicious baptism of fire at Midway it eventually became the US Navy's standard torpedo-bomber in the Pacific.

## History and Notes

Destined to become one of the best shipborne torpedo-bombers of the war, the TBF Avenger first saw combat during the great Battle of Midway. The XTBF-1 prototype was first flown on 1 August 1941 after an order for 286 aircraft had already been placed. The first TBF-1s appeared in January 1942 and VT-8 ('Torpedo-Eight') received its first aircraft during the following May. On 4 June six of VT-8's aircraft were launched at the height of the Battle of Midway, but only one returned – and this with one dead gunner and the other wounded. Despite this inauspicious start, production was accelerating as General Motors undertook production in addition to Grumman, producing the TBM-1 version. Sub-variants included the TBF-1C with two 20-mm cannon in the wings, the TBF-1B which was supplied to the UK under Lend-Lease, the TBF-1D and TBF-1E with ASV radar, and the TBF-1L with a searchlight in the bomb bay. Production of the TBF-1 and TBM-1, as well as sub-variants, were 2,290 and 2,882 respectively. General Motors (Eastern Division) went on to produce 4,664 TBM-3s with R-2600-20 engines, and the sub-variants corresponded with those of the TBF-1s. The UK received 395 TBF-1Bs and 526 TBM-3Bs, and New Zealand 63. The TBM-3P camera-equipped aircraft and the TBM-3H with search radar were the final wartime versions, although the Avenger went on to serve with the US Navy until 1954.

**Specification:** Grumman (General Motors) TBM-3E Avenger
**Origin:** USA
**Type:** three-crew shipborne torpedo-bomber
**Powerplant:** one 1,900-hp (1417-kW) Wright R-2600-20 radial piston engine
**Performance:** maximum speed 276 mph (444 km/h) at 16,500 ft (5030 m); initial climb rate 2,060 ft (628 m) per minute; service ceiling 30,100 ft (9175 m); range 1,010 miles (1625 km)
**Weights:** empty 10,545 lb (4783 kg); maximum take-off 17,895 lb (8117 kg)
**Dimensions:** span 54 ft 2 in (16.51 m); length 40 ft 11½ in (12.48 m); height 15 ft 5 in (4.70 m); wing area 490.0 sq ft (45.52 m²)
**Armament:** two fixed forward-firing 0.5-in (12.7-mm) guns, one 0.5-in (12.7-mm) gun in dorsal turret and one 0.3-in (7.62-mm) gun in ventral position, plus a bombload of up to 2,000 lb (907 kg) of bombs, or one torpedo, in weapons bay

**Grumman TBF Avenger**

The Grumman TBF Avenger arrived in service just in time to participate in the Battle of Midway on 4 June 1942. Pictured here is a very early TBF-1 carrying the red and white stripes on its rudder in use at the time America entered the war.

# Handley Page Halifax

Sporting the distinctive tail marking adopted by squadrons of Bomber Command's No. 4 Group, this Halifax Mk III of No. 466 Sqn, RAAF, was based at Leconfield in the mid-war years. The aircraft features the large H2S radome under the rear fuselage.

## History and Notes

Second only in importance to the Avro Lancaster in Bomber Command's great night offensive between 1941 and 1945, the four-engine Halifax was originally designed around a pair of Vulture engines, but, when first flown on 25 October 1939, the choice of four Merlins had been made. The first aircraft arrived on No. 35 Squadron in November 1940 and flew their first raid on 10-11 March 1941. Production was widely sub-contracted and quickly accelerated, the Merlin X-powered Halifax Mk I with two-gun nose turret and no dorsal turret being followed by the Mk IIA Series I with Merlin XX and two-gun dorsal turret. In the Halifax Mk II Series I (Special) the nose turret was omitted, and the Halifax Mk II Series IA a large transparent fairing improved the whole nose shape, this version also introducing a Defiant-type four-gun dorsal turret. The Halifax Mk III was powered by Bristol Hercules XVI radials, and later examples introduced a wing span increased from 98 ft 10 in (30.12 m) to 104 ft 2 in (31.75 m). The Halifax Mk V with Dowty landing gear served with Coastal and Bomber Commands; the Halifax Mk VI with Hercules 100 engines and Halifax Mk VII with Hercules XVI (both versions with increased fuel capacity) joined Bomber Command in 1944. Halifax Mk III, V and VII versions also served in paratrooping and glider towing roles with the airborne forces (being the only aircraft to tow the big Hamilcar) and were joined by the Halifax Mk VIII just before the end of the war. Production totalled 6,176 Halifaxes, the bomber versions flying a total of 75,532 sorties and dropping 227,610 tons of bombs.

**Specification:** Handley Page Halifax Mk VI
**Origin:** UK
**Type:** seven-crew night heavy bomber
**Powerplant:** four 1,800-hp (1343-kW) Bristol Hercules 100 radial piston engines
**Performance:** maximum speed 312 mph (502 km/h) at 22,000 ft (6705 m); climb to 20,000 ft (6095 m) in 50 minutes; service ceiling 24,000 ft (7315 m); range with 13,000-lb (5897-kg) bombload, 1,260 miles (2028 km)
**Weights:** empty 39,000 lb (17,690 kg); maximum take-off 68,000 lb (30845 kg)
**Dimensions:** span 104 ft 2 in (31.75 m); length 71 ft 7 in (21.82 m); height 20 ft 9 in (6.32 m); wing area 1,275.0 sq ft (118.45 m²)
**Armament:** on 0.303-in (7.7-mm) machine-gun in nose and four 0.303-in (7.7-mm) machine-guns in each of dorsal and tail turrets, plus a maximum bombload of 13,000 lb (5897 kg)

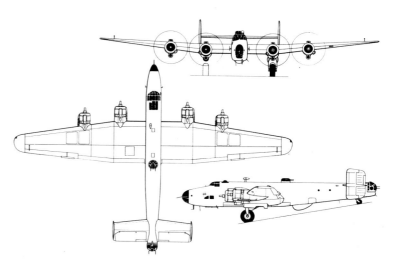

**Handley Page Halifax B.Mk VI**

Second of the RAF's four-engine heavy bombers to enter service (after the Stirling), the Halifax was originally powered by Rolls-Royce Merlin engines but, with Hercules radials, served with Bomber Command until the end of the war; a Halifax II of No. 35 Sqn is shown here.

# Handley Page Hampden

**Pictured here is a Hampden Mk I of No. 420 (Snowy Owl) Sqn, RCAF, based at Waddington, Lincs; this squadron's first operation was an attack by five aircraft on Emden on the night of 21/22 January 1942, by which time Hampdens were already being phased out of Bomber Command.**

## History and Notes

The only RAF mediu.n bomber at the beginning of the war to lack power-operated defensive gun turrets, the Hampden was nevertheless widely used by Bomber Command during the first three years. Designed to a 1932 specification, it was first flown on 21 June 1936 and joined No. 49 Squadron in August 1938. At the war's beginning the Hampden Mk I equipped eight squadrons. (A Napier Dagger-powered version, the Hereford, of which 101 were built, was used almost exclusively as an aircrew trainer.) In due course a total of 15 Bomber Command squadrons flew Hampden Mk Is, taking part in many of the epic early war raids, during which two VCs were awarded (to Flight Lieutenant R.A.B. Learoyd of No. 49 Squadron and to Sergeant J. Hannah of No. 83 Squadron). Although possessing a fairly good speed, the Hampden proved to be very vulnerable in the presence of enemy night-fighters and was withdrawn as an operational bomber after its last raid on 14-15 September 1942. Four Coastal Command squadrons were then equipped with Hampden torpedo-bombers, however, two of them (Nos 144 and 255) being based for a short time near Murmansk for protection of the North Cape convoys; the others operated against enemy shipping in the North Sea. Three other squadrons were employed for weather reconnaissance by Coastal Command. The Wright Cyclone-powered Hampden Mk II did not enter production. Hampden production totalled 1,270 in Britain and 160 in Canada.

**Specification:** Handley Page Hampden Mk I
**Origin:** UK
**Type:** four-crew medium bomber
**Powerplant:** two 1,000-hp (746-kW) Bristol Pegasus XVIII radial piston engines
**Performance:** maximum speed 254 mph (409 km/h) at 13,800 ft (4205 m); initial climb rate 980 ft (299 m) per minute; service ceiling 19,000 ft (5790 m); range with 4,000-lb (1814-kg) bombload, 1,200 miles (1931 km)
**Weights:** empty 11,780 lb (5343 kg); maximum take-off 21,000 lb (9526 kg)
**Dimensions:** span 69 ft 2 in (21.08 m); length 53 ft 7 in (16.33 m); height 14 ft 11 in (4.55 m); wing area 688.0 sq ft (63.92 m²)
**Armament:** one fixed and one flexible 0.303-in (7.7-mm) machine-guns in the nose, and twin 0.303-in (7.7-mm) machine-guns in dorsal and ventral gun positions, plus a maximum bombload of 4,000 lb (1814 kg)

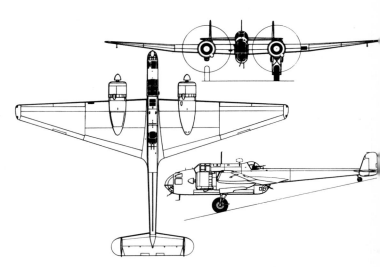

**Handley Page Hampden Mk I**

**Widely used by Bomber Command during the first two years of the war, the Hampden was the only member of the so-called heavy bombers of that period that was not equipped with any power-operated gun turret; thus with only hand-held guns for tail defence the aircraft was particularly vulnerable in the presence of night fighters.**

# Hawker Hurricane

An early production Hurricane I, without ventral fin fairing, carrying the pre-war markings of No. 111 (Fighter) Squadron, based at Northolt in 1938; this squadron was prominent in the great Battle of Britain and continued to fly Hurricanes until mid-1941.

## History and Notes

The first monoplane fighter and the first with a top speed of over 300 mph (483 km/h) to enter RAF service, the Hurricane was designed by Sydney Camm and first flown on 6 November 1935, joining the RAF in December 1937. The Hurricane Mk I with 1,030-hp (768-kW) Rolls-Royce Merlin II and an armament of eight 0.303-in (7.7-mm) machine-guns was Fighter Command's principal fighter in the Battle of Britain in 1940, and destroyed more enemy aircraft than all other defences combined. It was followed by the Hurricane Mk IIA with 1,280-hp (955-kW) Merlin XX before the end of 1940, the Hurricane Mk IIB with 12 machine-guns and the Hurricane Mk IIC with four 20-mm cannon during 1941. These versions were also able to carry up to two 500-lb (227-kg) bombs, drop tanks or other stores under the wings; they served as fighters, fighter-bombers, night-fighters, intruders and photo-reconnaissance aircraft on all fronts until 1943, and in the Far East until the end of the war. The Hurricane Mk IID introduced the 40-mm anti-tank gun in 1942. Two of these weapons were carried under the wings, and this version was particularly successful in North Africa. The Hurricane Mk IV featured a 'universal wing' which allowed carriage of up to eight 60-lb (27.2-kg) rocket projectiles or any of the external stores carried by the Mk II. More than 14,000 Hurricanes were produced, including 1,451 built in Canada (Mks X, XI and XII). This total also included many Sea Hurricanes, of which early versions were catapulted from merchant ships and flown from converted merchant aircraft carriers, and later served aboard Royal Navy fleet carriers. Always regarded as somewhat slow among RAF fighters, the Hurricane was highly manoeuvrable and capable of withstanding considerable battle damage.

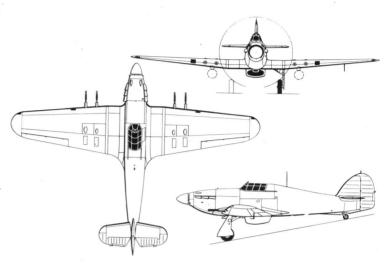

## Specification: Hawker Hurricane Mk IIC
**Origin:** UK
**Type:** single-seat fighter and fighter-bomber
**Powerplant:** one 1,280-hp (955-kW) Rolls-Royce Merlin XX inline piston engine
**Performance:** maximum speed 336 mph (541 km/h) at 12,500 ft (3810 m); climb to 20,000 ft (6095 m) in 9.1 minutes; service ceiling 35,600 ft (10850 m); range on internal fuel 460 miles (740 km)
**Weights:** empty 5,800 lb (2631 kg); loaded 8,100 lb (3674 kg)
**Dimensions:** span 40 ft 0 in (12.19 m); length 32 ft 0 in (9.75 m); height 13 ft 1 in (3.99 m); wing area 257.5 sq ft (23.92 m²)
**Armament:** four 20-mm cannon in wings, plus provision for two 500-lb (227-kg) bombs, or eight 60-lb (27.2-kg) rocket projectiles or two 90-Imp gal (409-litre) drop tanks under the wings

**Hawker Hurricane Mk IIC**

A Hurricane Mk IIC night fighter of No. 87 Sqn. Armed with four 20-mm cannon, this version performed freelance night intruder missions over France in the mid-war years and, although without the benefit of airborne radar, gained many victories in the skies over enemy bomber bases.

Like all great aircraft the Hurricane proved highly adaptable to numerous tasks. Armed with a pair of 40-mm anti-tank guns under the wings, the Mk IID was used to excellent effect against enemy armour at the Battle of Bir Hakim in the Western Desert. A later version, the Hurricane Mk IV, is seen here flying over the UK.

# Hawker Tempest

Among the squadrons equipped with Tempest Mk Vs that were deployed against the V1 flying bombs was No. 487 Sqn, RNZAF, based at Newchurch; its tally against these weapons reached 223½ destroyed before it moved to the Continent to support the Allied advance into Germany.

## History and Notes

Conscious that the Typhoon left much to be desired as an interceptor fighter as soon as it flew in 1940, Sydney Camm initiated the development of an improved version with a laminar-flow elliptical wing and a lengthened fuselage to accommodate more fuel. This aircraft, the Tempest, was first flown on 2 September 1942 and was followed by production Tempest Mk Vs which joined Nos 3 and 486 Squadrons in April 1944. The early aircraft, Tempest Mk V Series 1s, were armed with four long-barrelled 20-mm Hispano Mk II cannon, but Tempest Mk V Series 2s featured improved short-barrelled Mk V guns. Tempests were first committed to combat when the German flying-bomb offensive opened immediately after the Normandy landings, and the type shot down 638 out of the RAF's total of 1,771 bombs destroyed. Meanwhile, like the Typhoon, Tempests were being employed in the ground-attack role, being equipped to carry up to two 1,000-lb (454-kg) bombs, drop tanks or eight 60-lb (27.2-kg) rocket projectiles. However, with its top speed of 426 mph (686 km/h), the Tempest also proved an effective fighter against the new German aircraft then being introduced, and there were several instances of their shooting down Messerschmitt Me 262 jet fighters. The Tempest Mk V equipped 12 wartime RAF squadrons, 800 aircraft being completed (and 1,200 cancelled at the end of the war). The superb Bristol Centaurus-powered Tempest Mk II, although flying well before the end of hostilities, was too late to see action and was intended for service in the Far East.

**Specification:** Hawker Tempest Mk V
**Origin:** UK
**Type:** single-seat interceptor/gound attack fighter
**Powerplant:** one 2,180-hp (1626-kW) Napier Sabre II inline piston engine
**Performance:** maximum speed 426 mph (685 km/h) at 18,500 ft (5660 m); climb to 15,000 ft (4570 m) in 5.0 minutes; service ceiling, 38,000 ft (11580 m); range on internal fuel 740 miles (1190 km)
**Weights:** empty 9,000 lb (4082 kg); maximum take-off 13,540 lb (6142 kg)
**Dimensions:** span 41 ft 0 in (12.50 m); length 33 ft 8 in (10.26 m); height 16 ft 1 in (4.90 m); wing area 302.0 sq ft (28.06 m²)
**Armament:** four 20-mm cannon in wings, plus provision for two 1,000-lb (454-kg) bombs, or eight 60-lb (27.2-kg) 3-in (7.62-cm) rocket projectiles, napalm or long-range fuel tanks

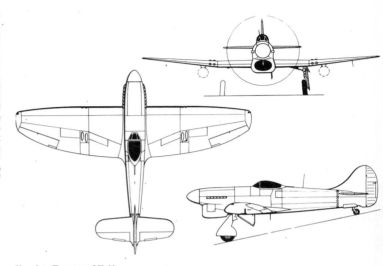

**Hawker Tempest Mk V**

Arguably the best single-seat fighter produced for the RAF during the war, the Hawker Tempest Mk V was much in evidence in the defence against the flying bombs of 1944. In the final months of the war it also served in the ground attack role on the Continent.

# Hawker Typhoon

Pictured as it appeared in the last weeks of the war, this late production Typhoon Mk IB of No. 440 Sqn, RCAF, was based at Goch during the final Allied advance into Germany; it is shown with a pair of 1,000-lb (454-kg) bombs.

## History and Notes

Conceived as a Hurricane replacement, the Typhoon entered the design process in 1937 around the new Napier Sabre 24-cylinder H-type inline engine (in parallel with the Hawker Tornado with Rolls-Royce Vulture engine). First flown on 24 February 1940, the Typhoon underwent accelerated development, as did its engine, and entered service with Nos 56 and 609 Squadrons in September 1941, the Tornado having been abandoned owing to difficulties with the Vulture. The Typhoon Mk IA was armed with 12 0.303-in (7.7-mm) machine-guns in the wings, and the Typhoon Mk IB with 20-mm cannon. Rushed development resulted in numerous accidents (caused by a structural weakness in the rear fuselage and a spate of engine failures) and after a short time the Typhoon was withdrawn from normal interception duties, being confined to the low-level interceptor role, and eventually ground attack, a duty for which the big fighter was particularly well suited. In 1943 the aircraft was being flown with two 500-lb (227-kg) bombs under the wings, and the following year its load was increased to two 1,000-lb (454-kg) bombs or drop tanks or, most successfully, to eight 60-lb (27.2-kg) rocket projectiles. During the final year of the war in Europe the rocket-firing Typhoon Mk IB proved to be one of the most effective ground-support fighters, being frequently called on to attack enemy targets, and doing so with devastating effect during the Allied advance across northern Europe from Normandy. A total of 3,330 Typhoons was built, eventually equipping 32 squadrons of the RAF.

**Specification:** Hawker Typhoon Mk IB
**Origin:** UK
**Type:** single-seat fighter-bomber
**Powerplant:** one 2,180-hp (1626-kW) Napier Sabre II inline piston engine
**Performance:** maximum speed 405 mph (652 km/h) at 18,000 ft (5485 m); climb to 15,000 ft (4570 m) in 6.2 minutes; service ceiling 34,000 ft (10365 m); range with two 1,000-lb (454-kg) bombs, 510 miles (821 km)
**Weights:** empty 8,800 lb (3992 kg); maximum take-off 13,980 lb (6341 kg)
**Dimensions:** span 41 ft 7 in (12.67 m); length 31 ft 11 in (9.74 m); height 15 ft 3½ in (4.67 m); wing area 279.0 sq ft (25.92 m²)
**Armament:** four 20-mm cannon in wings, plus provision for two 1,000-lb (454-kg) bombs or up to eight 60-lb (27.2-kg) 3-in (7.62-cm) rocket projectiles under the wings

**Hawker Typhoon Mk IB**

Rugged, powerful and fast, the Typhoon was certainly a handful for its pilots, but proved a devastating weapon in the ground attack role. Here ground crew prepare a Typhoon Mk IB of No. 175 Sqn for a bombing sortie.

# Heinkel He 59

A camouflaged Heinkel He 59D of Seenotzentrale Ägäisches Meer in May 1941. It was used for air-sea rescue duties in the Aegean Sea, and in this role the He 59 was used extensively for the first years of the war. It was superseded by the Do 18 and Do 24, and was relegated to training duties.

## History and Notes

The Heinkel He 59 originated as a 1930 design for an attack/reconnaissance biplane intended for use either as a landplane or floatplane, the first prototype being flown as a landplane in January 1932. Production of the He 59B floatplane got under way in 1933, the aircraft being powered by two 660-hp (492-kW) BMW VI 6,0 ZU inline engines and armed with a single 7.9-mm (0.31-in) MG 15 in the nose; the He 59B-2 featured a bomb-aimer's position in the nose, and ventral and dorsal gun positions each had a single 7.9-mm (0.31-in) gun. It was followed by the He 59B-3 reconnaissance aircraft and the unarmed He 59 C-2 air-sea rescue version. After some service during the Spanish Civil War (when they were used for night bombing and coastal patrols) the He 59 came to serve widely with the Luftwaffe. In September 1939 they equipped one *Staffel* on each of four *Küstenfliegergruppen* for anti-shipping and coastal reconnaissance duties. Other versions which joined the Luftwaffe were the He 59C-1 long-range reconnaissance floatplane, the He 59D-1 aircrew trainer and He 59N advanced navigation trainer. Torpedo training was undertaken in the He 59B-1, and the He 59E-2 carried three cameras for long-range reconnaissance.

Heinkel He 59s were frequently encountered performing air-sea rescue duties over the North Sea and English Channel during the first three years of the war, but their most enterprising operations were carried out during the invasion of the Netherlands in May 1940 when 12 aircraft of Staffel Schwilben landed 120 troops on the Maas to capture the large bridge at Rotterdam, four aircraft being lost to the Dutch defences.

## Specification: Heinkel He 59B-2

**Origin:** Germany
**Type:** four-crew coastal reconnaissance float biplane
**Powerplant:** two 660-hp (220-kW) BMW VI 6,0 ZU inline piston engine
**Performance:** maximum speed 137 mph (220 km/h) at sea level; initial climb rate 738 ft (225 m) per minutes; service ceiling 11,485 ft (3500 m); range 1,087 miles (1750 km)
**Weights:** empty 13,701 lb (6215 kg); maximum take-off 19,841 lb (9000 kg)
**Dimensions:** span 77 ft 9 in (23.70 m); length 57 ft 1 in (17.40 m); height 23 ft 3½ in (7.10 m); wing area 1,650.2 sq ft (153.30 m²)

**Heinkel He 59B-2**

**Armament:** single 7.92-mm (0.31-in) MG 15 machine-guns in nose, dorsal and ventral positions; some aircraft featured a single 20-mm gun in the nose

This He 59B-2 flew with 3.Staffel/Küstenfliegergruppe 106 based at List in 1936. The He 59 was originally designed under the disguise of a commercial freighter, but the Spanish Civil War saw it in the role of maritime patrol and bomber.

# Heinkel He 111

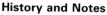

A Heinkel He 111H-3 of 1./KG 54 'Totenkopf' which operated in the opening phases of the May 1940 campaign over France, Belgium and the Netherlands. This aircraft, carrying the Death's Head unit badge, flew from Delmenhorst.

## History and Notes

Longest-serving medium bomber of the Luftwaffe, the Heinkel He 111 stemmed from a design by Siegfried and Walter Günter for a dual-purpose commercial transport/bomber produced in 1934 and flown on 24 February 1935. Early versions featured conventional stepped windscreen and elliptical wing leading edge, and a bomber version with these features (He 111B-1) served with the Legion Cóndor in the Spanish Civil War. The first production version with straight wing leading edge was the He 111F, and the He 111P incorporated a fully-glazed asymmetric nose without external windscreen step. He 111Ps with DB 601Aa engines were delivered to the Luftwaffe in 1939 before production switched to the most widely-used variant, the He 111H with Junkers Jumo 211 engines; sub-variants of this series formed the backbone of the Luftwaffe's bomber force between 1940 and 1943; they took part in numerous raids in the Battle of Britain and were flown by the pathfinder unit, KGr 100. The first version to carry torpedoes was the He 111H-6, followed by the He 111H-15; the He 111H-8 was fitted with a large and cumbersome balloon cable fender; the He 111H-11/R2 was a glider tug for the Go 242, while pathfinder versions with special radio were the He 111H-14 and He 111H-18; the He 111H-16 featured increased gun armament, and the He 111H-20 included 16-paratroop transport, night bomber and glider tug sub-variants. The He 111H-22 carried a single Fi 103 flying bomb and was used against the UK late in 1944. The most extraordinary of all was the He 111Z Zwilling (Twin) which consisted of two He 111Hs joined together with a new wing and fifth engine; it was used mainly to tow the huge Me 321 Gigant gliders. A total of about 7,300 He 111s were built.

**Specification:** Heinkel He 111H-16
**Origin:** Germany
**Type:** five-crew medium bomber
**Powerplant:** two 1,350-hp (1007-kW) Junkers Jumo 211F inline piston engines
**Performance:** maximum speed 271 km/h (436 mph) at 19,685 ft (6000 m); climb to 19,685 ft (6000 m) in 42.0 minutes; service ceiling 21,980 ft (6700 m); range 1,212 miles (1950 km)
**Weights:** empty 19,136 lb (8680 kg); maximum take-off 30,865 lb (14000 kg)
**Dimensions:** span 74 ft 1¾ in (22.60 m); length 53 ft 9½ in (16.40 m); height 13 ft 1¼ in (3.40 m); wing area 931.07 sq ft (86.50 m²)
**Armament:** one 20-mm MG FF cannon in nose, one 13-mm (0.51-in) MG 131 gun in dorsal position, two 7.2-mm (0.31-in) MG 15 guns in rear of ventral gondola and two 7.9-mm (0.31-in) MG 81 guns in each of two beam positions, plus a bombload of 4,409 lb (2000 kg) internally and 4,409 lb (2000 kg) externally

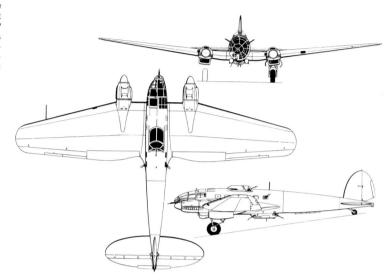

**Heinkel He 111H-16**

Among the bomber units switched from the night assault on Britain to the Eastern Front in 1941 was KG 55 'Greif' (Griffon wing), one of whose Heinkel He 111Hs is seen here being armed prior to a raid.

# Heinkel He 115

With forward-firing 20-mm MG 151 cannon, this late-series Heinkel He 115C-1 served with 1.Staffel, Küstenfliegergruppe 406; it also carried five 7.7-mm (0.303-in) MG 15 and 17 machine-guns and had provision for an auxiliary fuel tank in the bomb bay.

## History and Notes

The large twin-float Heinkel He 115 monoplane was first flown in prototype form in 1936 powered by two 960-hp (716-kW) BMW 132K radials, and quickly achieved fame by setting new world speed records with various loads. In 1938 production He 115A-1s joined the Luftwaffe as three-seat general-purpose coastal duties aircraft armed with single 7.92-mm (0.31-in) guns in the nose and rear cockpit, and was followed by the He 115A-3 with revised bomb bay and radio equipment. The He 115B-1 with increased fuel capacity was delivered in 1939, and the He 115B-2 soon after with load capability of one 2,205-lb (1000-kg) parachute mine and a 1,102-lb (500-kg) bombload, the latter also featured strengthened floats which allowed operation from ice and snow surfaces. On these aircraft fell the task of minelaying in British waters during the first two years of the war, serving in particular with Küstenfliegergruppen 106, 506 and 906. The He 115C series introduced a modified nose mounting a single 20-mm MG 151 cannon, the He 115C-2 also having the reinforced floats of the He 115B-2, and being followed by the He 115C-3 minelayer and the He 115C-4 torpedo-bomber. He 115s of KüFlGr 406 were prominent in their attacks on the North Cape PQ convoys in 1942. Very few of the four-crew He 115D series were produced.

Production of the He 115 ceased in 1942 but, surprisingly in view of Germany's heavy production priorities elsewhere, it was re-started in 1943 with the Heinkel He 115E-1 multi-purpose aircraft, which was similar to the He 115C series but mounted twin 7.92-mm (0.31-in) guns in the nose and rear positions; some aircraft also featured the 20-mm MG 151 cannon. Total production of the He 115 was about 500 aircraft.

### Specification: Heinkel He 115B-1
**Origin:** Germany
**Type:** three-crew torpedo-bomber and minelayer
**Powerplant:** two 970-hp (724-kW) BMW 132K radial piston engines
**Performance:** maximum speed 220 mph (355 km/h) at 11,155 ft (3400 m); initial climb rate 771 ft (235 m) per minute; service ceiling 18,045 ft (5500 m); range 1,243 miles (2000 km)
**Weights:** empty 11,684 lb (5300 kg); maximum take-off 22,928 lb (10400 kg)
**Dimensions:** span 72 ft 2⅛ in (22.20 m); length 56 ft 9⅛ in (17.30 m); height 21 ft 7⅞ in

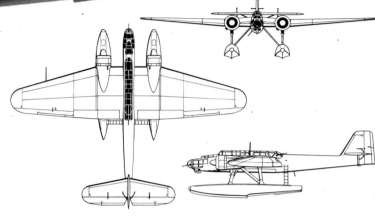

**Heinkel He 115B-1**

(6.60 m); wing area 933.3 sq ft (86.70 $^2$)
**Armament:** single flexible 7.92-mm (0.31-in MG 15 guns in nose and rear cockpit, plus one 1,764-lb (800-kg) torpedo or one 2,205-lb (1000-lb) parachute mine plus two 551-lb (250-kg) bombs

The Heinkel He 115 was one of the most efficient of all floatplanes used in Europe during the war, production being phased out in 1940 but reinstated in 1943-4; early aircraft were employed mainly for minelaying and coastal reconnaissance.

# Heinkel He 177 Greif

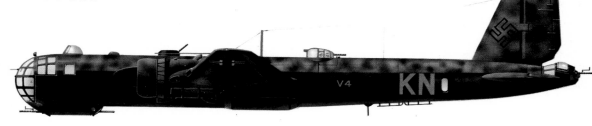

Heinkel He 177A-5 of II Gruppe, Kampfgeschwader 1 'Hindenburg' based at Prowenhren, East Prussia, mid-1944. Led by Oberstleutnant Horst von Riesen, KG 1 assembled about 90 of these bombers for attacks on Russian communications and military installations.

## History and Notes

After the scrapping of German plans for a strategic bombing force in 1936, the Luftwaffe abandoned plans to develop a heavy bomber until in 1938 the RLM approached the Heinkel company with a requirement for such an aircraft, resulting in the He 177 Greif (Griffon), a four-engine mid-wing aircraft in which the 1,000-hp (746-kW) DB 601 engines were coupled in pairs (termed DB 606s) to drive single propellers. The first aircraft, the He 177 V1, was flown on 19 November 1939. Continuing engine overheating problems as well as persistent structural failures delayed production, the first He 177A-1s not reaching I./KG 40 for operational trials until July 1942; in the course of these He 177s took part in raids on the UK, but generally they proved disappointing in service. Several sub-variants of the He 177A-3 were produced, including the He 177A-3/R3 which could carry three Hs 293 anti-shipping weapons, the He 177A-3/R5 with 75-mm gun in the ventral gondola and the He 177A-3/R7 torpedo-bomber. He 177A-3s were used by FKGr 2 to fly supply missions to the beleaguered German forces at Stalingrad in January 1943. The He 177A-5 incorporated a stronger wing to carry heavier external loads, and a small number were converted to the Zerstörer role with 33 upward-firing rocket tubes in the space normally occupied by the bomb bays. Small number of He 177A-5s returned to the night attack on the UK early in 1944; this version proved to be the last to serve with the Luftwaffe (bombers being afforded low priority during the last year of the war), but many interesting projects continued to be pursued, including the conversion of He 177 V38 as a carrier of Germany's atomic bomb, which in the event did not materialize. About 1,160 production and 30 prototype He 177s were built.

**Specification:** Heinkel He 177A-5/R2 Greif
**Origin:** Germany
**Type:** six-crew heavy bomber
**Powerplant:** two 2,950-hp (2200-kW) Daimler-Benz DB610A-1/B-1 paired inline piston engines
**Performance:** maximum speed 303 mph (488 km/h) at 19,685 ft (6000 m); initial climb rate 623 ft (190 m) per minute; service ceiling 26,245 ft (8000 m); range with two Hs 293 weapons, 3,418 miles (5500 km)
**Weights:** empty 37,257 lb (16900 kg); maximum take-off 68,342 lb (31000 kg)
**Dimensions:** span 103 ft 1¾ in (31.44 m); length 66 ft 11¼ in (20.40 m); height 20 ft 11¾ in (6.40 m); wing area 1,098.0 sq ft (102.00 m²)

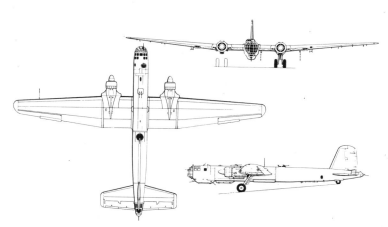

**Heinkel He 177A-5/R-6**

**Armament:** one 7.92-mm (0.31-in) MG 81 gun in nose, one 13-mm (0.51-in) MG 131 gun in forward dorsal turret, one 13-mm (0.51-in) MG 131 gun in rear dorsal turret, one 13-mm (0.51-in) MG 131 gun in rear of ventral gondola, one 20-mm MG FF cannon in front of ventral gondola and one 20-mm MG FF in tail, plus a maximum internal bombload of 13,228 lb (6000 kg) or two Hs 293 weapons

**Heinkel He 177A-0 pre-production aircraft.** These big bombers, originally intended to provide the Luftwaffe with a strategic bombing force, encountered so many development problems that they only entered service in numbers during the last 18 months of the war.

# Heinkel He 219 Uhu

Heinkel He 219A of 1. Staffel, Nachtjagdgeschwader 1 based at Munster-Handorf in the autumn of 1944. 1./NJG 1 had been the first unit to fly the He 219 in combat. The Roman IV on the nose identifies the type of radar as *Lichtenstein* SN-2.

## History and Notes

Without doubt the best German night-fighter of the war, the He 219 possessed in abundance all three attributes essential for such combat – high speed, heavy gun armament and efficient radar. The He 219 V1 was flown on 15 November 1942 and production examples would have followed quickly thereafter had an RAF raid on Rostock not destroyed more than three-quarters of the design drawings. Pre-production He 219A-Os were delivered to NJG 1 at Venlo in April 1943, and on the first combat sortie Major Werner Streib destroyed five Lancasters within 30 minutes on 11-12 June. The first version to be produced in quantity was the He 219A-5 with two 30-mm and two 20-mm cannon. At the end of 1943 the He 219 was officially abandoned on the grounds that the Ju 88G was capable of catching the Lancaster and Halifax, but as the He 219 was the only night-fighter able to deal with the Mosquito, production continued at a reduced rate. The major variant, the He 219A-7, was introduced in 1944, the He 219A-7/R1 armed with no fewer than eight cannon – four forward-firing 30-mm and two of 20-mm, plus two upward-firing 30-mm guns in a *schräge Musik* installation. Fastest of all the He 219A series versions was the He 219A-7/R6 with 2,500-hp (1865-kW) Jumo 222A/B engines and a top speed of 435 mph (700 km/h). Most aircraft were equipped with FuG 220 *Lichtenstein* SN-2 radar. It has been estimated that of all RAF Mosquitoes lost during night operations more than 60 per cent fell to He 219s – this despite the fact that production of the Uhu (Owl) amounted to no more than 268 aircraft.

**Specification:** Heinkel He 219A-7/R1 Uhu
**Origin:** Germany
**Type:** two-seat high-altitude night-fighter
**Powerplant:** two 1,800-hp (1343-kW) Daimler Benz DB 603E inline piston engines
**Performance:** maximum speed 416 mph (670 km/h) at 22,965 ft (7000 m); initial climb rate 1,805 ft (550 m) per minutes; absolute ceiling 41,665 ft (12700 m); range 1,243 miles (2000 km)
**Weights:** empty 24,691 lb (11200 kg); loaded 33,730 lb (15300 kg)
**Dimensions:** span 60 ft 8½ in (18.50 m); length 50 ft 11¾ in (15.54 m); height 13 ft 5½ in (4.10 m); wing area 479.0 sq ft (44.50 m²)
**Armament:** two 30-mm MK 108 cannon in wing roots, two 30-mm MK 103 and two 20-mm MG 151/20 in ventral gun tray, and two upward-firing 30-mm MK 108 cannon in rear cockpit

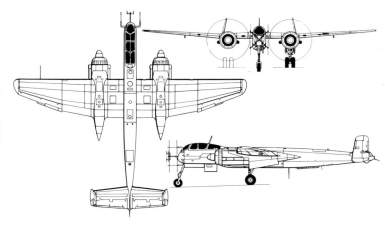

**Heinkel He 219A-5/R-1**

The Heinkel He 219A-053 was used as a prototype for the He 219A-5/R1 (the first production version); it carried an armament of two 20-mm and two 30-mm cannon, and proved easily capable of knocking down RAF bombers in large numbers.

# Henschel Hs 123

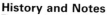

A Henschel Hs 123A-1 bearing the markings of II(Schlacht)/ Lehrgeschwader 2, a unit which, given specific cover by the Bf 109Es of I/JG 21, took an active part in close support operations during the Battle of France in 1940. Only six aircraft were lost in five weeks of hard fighting.

## History and Notes

The attractive Henschel Hs 123 single-seat ground-support biplane stemmed from one of the first requirements prepared for the new Luftwaffe in 1933. Of all-metal construction, the prototype Hs 123 was powered by the 650-hp (485-kW) BMW 132A-3 radial and first flew in the spring of 1935. Production Hs 123A-1s appeared in mid-1936 with 880-hp (656-kW) BMW 132Dc engines and were armed with two 7.92-mm (0.31-in) MG 17 guns in the nose; a single 551-lb (250-kg) bomb could be carried between the landing gear legs. They soon joined the Luftwaffe's first dive-bomber *Geschwader*, but when some aircraft were sent to fight in the Spanish Civil War they came to be employed as ground support aircraft rather than dive-bombers, and after the introduction of the Junkers Ju 87 it was in the latter role that the Hs 123 survived in Luftwaffe service.

By the outbreak of war in September 1939 production was already being brought to an end and only II.(S)/LG 2 was still equipped with the aircraft. This unit continued to fly the old biplane in combat, however, participating in the Polish campaign and in the *Blitzkrieg* attack in the West of May 1940, and was still flying them during the invasion of the Balkans in April 1941. During the early stages of the attack on the Soviet Union some Hs 123s were armed with a pair of 20-mm cannon and were adapted to carry 92 4.4-lb (2-kg) anti-personnel bombs; so effective were they that suggestions were put forward for the aircraft to re-enter production, but the plan proved impractical. II.(S)/LG 2 (redesignated II./SG 2) retained the veteran biplanes until, in mid-1944, they were finally withdrawn from service.

## Specification: Henschel Hs 123A-1
**Origin:** Germany
**Type:** single-seat close support biplane
**Powerplant:** one 880-hp (656-kW) BMW 132Dc radial piston engine
**Performance:** maximum speed 212 mph (341 km/h) at 3,940 ft (1200 m); initial climb rate 2,953 ft (900 m) per minute; service ceiling 29,530 ft (9000 m); range 534 miles (860 km)
**Weights:** empty 3,307 lb (1500 kg); maximum take-off 4,883 lb (2215 kg)
**Dimensions:** span 34 ft 5½ in (10.50 m); length 27 ft 4 in (8.33 m); height 10 ft 6⅜ in

**Henschel Hs 123A-1**

(3.21 m); wing area 267.5 sq ft (24.86 m²)
**Armament:** two synchronized 7.92-mm (0.31-in) MG 17 machine-guns in the nose, plus up to 992 lb (450 kg) of bombs

Like obsolete biplanes elsewhere (such as Britain's Gladiator and Italy's Fiat CR.42) the Henschel Hs 123 gave surprisingly good service well into the war. This Hs 123B wears the Sturmabzeichen (close combat medal insignia) and is carrying four 50-kg (110-lb) bombs under the wings.

# Henschel Hs 126

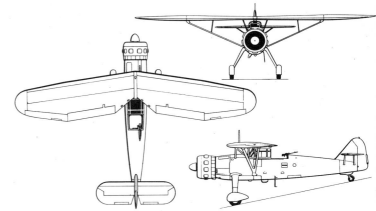

Bearing the markings of 2.(H)/31, this Hs 126 has had its wheel spats removed for ease of operating from rough fields. Conceived on exactly the same lines as the British Lysander, the Hs 126 was a common sight over the advancing German armoured columns during the Battle of France in 1940.

## History and Notes

Designed to meet much the same type of requirement as the Westland Lysander in British service, the Henschel Hs 126 battlefield reconnaissance aircraft first flew in Hs 126 V1 form (a conversion of the Hs 122B-0) towards the end of 1936, the powerplant being a Junkers Jumo 210C inline. This aircraft was generally deemed unsuitable for service use, and was followed by the Hs 126 V2 and Hs 126 V3 prototypes with redesigned vertical tails and radial powerplant, in the form of the Bramo Fafnir 323 radial. Service tests followed with the generally similar Hs 126A-0 series, of which 10 were built, before the Hs 126A-1 entered service during late 1938 with Aufklärungsgruppe 35 in Germany and Aufklärungs-staffel 88 in Spain. The Hs 126A-1 was powered by the 880-hp (656-kW) BMW 132Dc radial.

By the outbreak of war in September 1939 the production version was the definitive Hs 126B-1, which was powered by the 900-hp (671-kW) Bramo 323A and had superior radio equipment. It was this model which played a prominent part in the Polish and French campaigns of 1939 and 1940 respectively, spotting and reconnoitring for the rapid-moving Panzer forces of the German army. By the time of the German invasion of Russia in June 1941, no fewer than 48 *Staffeln* were equipped with He 126B-1 aircraft. These played their normal part in the early days of the campaign, but soon had to be provided with fighter cover as Russian fighter strength grew, and had finally to be withdrawn from daylight operations. By 1944 they were restricted to nocturnal harassing raids with the *Nachtschlachtgruppen* over the Eastern Front. Production totalled about 800.

**Specification:** Henschel Hs 126B-1
**Origin:** Germany
**Type:** two-crew battlefield reconnaissance aircraft
**Powerplant:** one 900-hp (671-kW) Bramo 323A-2 radial piston engine
**Performance:** maximum speed 221 mph (356 km/h) at 9,845 ft (3000 m); climb to 13,125 ft (4000 m) in 7.2 minutes; service ceiling 27,000 ft (8230 m); range 360 miles (560 km)
**Weights:** empty 4,475 lb (2030 kg); maximum take-off 7,209 lb (3270 kg)

**Henschel Hs 126A**

**Dimensions:** span 47 ft 6¾ in (14.50 m); length 35 ft 7 in (10.84 m); height 12 ft 3½ in (3.74 m); wing area 340.14 sq ft (31.60 m²)
**Armament:** one forward-firing 7.92-mm (0.31-in) MG 17 machine-gun and one flexible 7.92-mm (0.31-in) MG 15 machine-gun in the rear cockpit, plus 331 lb (150 kg) of bombs

Vital but least spectacular component of the *Blitzkrieg* concept, the Henschel Hs 126 undertook battlefield surveillance, spotting for artillery and providing short-range photo reconnaissance. It was flown in almost every German campaign until replaced by the Fw 189 from 1942 onwards.

# Henschel Hs 129

Henschel Hs 129B-1 of 8./Staffel, Schlachtgeschwader 1 which, formed at Lippstadt, was operational over Kursk Salient in the summer of 1943. In October the unit was redesignated 11.(Pz)/SG 9.

## History and Notes

The single-seat ground-support Henschel Hs 129 was the outcome of an imaginative though somewhat speculative requirement issued by the German air ministry in 1937 for a heavily armoured twin-engine aircraft to perform an anti-tank role. Designed by Friedrich Nicolaus, the Hs 129 V1 prototype was first flown in 1938 with two 465-hp (347-kW) Argus As 410 inline engines; it proved to be underpowered, cramped for the pilot and sluggish on the controls. These severe criticisms resulted in re-engining some of the pre-production Hs 129A-0s with captured French 700-hp (522-kW) Gnome-Rhône 14M radials.

Development Hs 129B-0s with these engines, increased cockpit space and electrically-operated trim tabs, were delivered in December 1941, followed by production Hs 129B-1s in 1942. The majority of Hs 129s served with units on the Eastern Front, playing an outstanding part in destroying Russian armour in the great battle of Kursk of July 1943, but also in North Africa where they met with less success. A large number of armament variations were developed, including the Hs 129B-1/R2 with a 30-mm MK 101 cannon under the nose with 30 rounds, the Hs 129B-3 with a 75-mm BK 7,5 anti-tank gun with 12 rounds, and numerous *Rüstsatz* variations combining light anti-personnel and fragmentation bombs with 7.92-mm (0.31-in), 13-mm (0.51-in), 15-mm (0.59-in), 20-mm and 30-mm guns. A total of 858 Hs 129s were built between 1942 and 1944 and, provided they were not opposed by defending fighters, their pilots did considerable damage amongst Russian armoured vehicles in the East, the 75-mm gun proving capable of penetrating the frontal armour of KV-1 and T-34 tanks.

## Specification: Henschel Hs 129B-1/R2
**Origin:** Germany
**Type:** single-seat anti-tank ground-support aircraft
**Powerplant:** two 700-hp (522-kW) Gnome-Rhône 14M radial piston engines
**Performance:** maximum speed 253 mph (407 km/h) at 12,750 ft (3830 m); time to 9,845 ft (3000 m) 7.0 minutes; service ceiling 29,530 ft (9000 m); range 348 miles (560 km)
**Weights:** empty 8,783 lb (3984 kg); maximum take-off 11,263 lb (5109 kg)
**Dimensions:** span 46 ft 7 in (14.20 m); length 31 ft 11¾ in (9.75 m); height 10 ft 8 in (3.25 m); wing area 312.16 sq ft (29.00 m²)
**Armament:** two 20-mm MG 151/20 and two 7.92-mm (0.31-in) MG 17 guns in nose, and one 30-mm MK 101 cannon with 30 rounds in fairing under the nose, plus a bombload of up to 772 lb (350 kg)

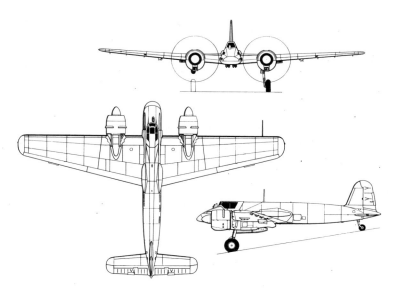

**Henschel Hs 219B-1/R4**

An Hs 129B-2/R2 of 4./Schlachtgeschwader 1 on the Eastern Front, summer 1943. The aircraft eventually proved fairly successful for ground attack, being heavily armed and armoured, though the engines were somewhat underpowered and unreliable.

# Ilyushin Il-2

Daubed with the inscription *mstitel* (avenger), this Il-2m3 lacks its rear cockpit canopy – often removed in the field so as to afford the rear gunner better visibility and field of fire. The lines inscribed on the fuselage forward of the windscreen were to assist judging gravity drop when firing air-to-ground rockets.

## History and Notes

Widely referred to as the 'Stormovik' (although the Russian *Shturmovik* applied to all ground attack aircraft), Sergei Ilyushin's rugged Il-2 came to be feared by the German soldier on the Eastern Front as the *Schwarz Tod* (Black Death). The first prototype, a single-seater known as the TsKB-57, made its maiden flight late in 1939 flown by V. Kokkinaki. With a heavily armoured front fuselage and later powered by a 1,680-hp (1253-kW) AM-38 inline engine, the prototype underwent state trials in March 1941 and entered production as the Il-2, 249 aircraft being completed before the German attack of June that year. Early experience showed the necessity of providing a gunner for rear defence, however, and with a lengthened armoured 'bath', the Il-2m3 two-seater appeared in August 1942. A further improved version, the Il-2m3(mod) was introduced soon afterwards with the 23-mm VYa cannon in the wings replaced by 37-mm Il-P-37 guns, and this version fought in large numbers during the great tank battles around Kursk in July 1943, proving capable of destroying the German Pzkpfw VI Tiger tank; these aircraft were later armed with RS-132 13.2-cm (5.2-in) rockets with hollow-charge warheads. Some Il-2m3(mod) aircraft of the Soviet Naval Aviation, designated Il-2T, carried fittings for a single 53.3-cm (21-in) torpedo, while a trainer version, the Il-2U, was also produced in Naval Aviation workshops. Huge numbers of Il-2s were produced during the war (and large numbers were destroyed by *flak* and German fighters), some sources putting the number at over 35,000 although this most likely included some aircraft with the 2,000-hp (1492-kW) AM-42 engine and later designated Il-10.

**Specification:** Ilyushin Il-2m3(mod)
**Origin:** USSR
**Type:** two-seat ground-attack aircraft
**Powerplant:** one 1,770-hp (1320-kW) AM-38F inline piston engine
**Performance:** maximum speed 251 mph (404 km/h) at 4,920 ft (1500 m) service ceiling 19,685 ft (6000 m); range 373 miles (600 km)
**Weights:** empty 9,590 lb (4350 kg); maximum take-off 14,021 lb (6360 kg)
**Dimensions:** span 48 ft 0½ in (14.60 m); length 38 ft 0½ in (11.60 m); height 11 ft 1½ in (3.40 m); wing area 414.4 sq ft (38.50 m²)
**Armament:** two forward-firing 23-mm VYa cannon and two 7.62-mm (0.3-in) ShKAS machine-guns, and one 12.7-mm (0.5-in) UBT machine-gun in rear cockpit, plus a bombload of 1,321 lb (600 kg), or various loads of rocket projectiles

Ilyushin Il-2m3

The importance attached by the Russians to the Il-2 may be judged by the terms of a telegram from Stalin to a factory that had fallen behind with deliveries: 'The Red Army needs the Il-2 as it needs air or bread. I demand more. This is my last warning.'

# Ilyushin Il-4

Used by both the Soviet air force and navy, the Il-4 was a rugged medium bomber of which more than 10,000 were produced between 1940 and 1944. During the latter part of this period it was being built with many wooden components.

## History and Notes

One of the great bombers of the war, the Russian Il-4 has not unnaturally been over-shadowed in Western thinking by the great British and American aircraft, yet well over 10,000 Il-4s were produced between 1937 and 1944, the vast majority in the last three years. The original prototype of this low-wing twin-engine bomber, designated the TsKB-26, flew in 1935, was developed through the TsKB-30, and entered production in 1937 as the DB-3 (DB being a Russian contraction denoting long-range bomber). Early examples were powered by 765-hp (571-kW) M-85 engines, but these were replaced by 960-hp (716-kW) M-86s in 1938. Although a tough and relatively simple design, the aircraft suffered from a poor defensive armament of single nose, dorsal and ventral 7.62-mm (0.3-in) guns, and lost heavily to such aircraft as the Bulldog, Gladiator and Fokker D.XXI during the Winter War against Finland in 1939-40. In 1939 a modified version with lengthened nose (the DB-3F) appeared, and in 1940, in conformity with changed Russian practice, the designation became Il-4 (denoting the designer, Sergei Ilyushin). Soon after the German attack on Russia opened in 1941 it was decided to withdraw Il-4 production to newly opening plants in Siberia, at the same time replacing a large proportion of the metal structure by less strategically critical wood. Il-4s also entered service with Soviet Naval Aviation, and it was a naval-manned force of these bombers that first raided Berlin from the east on 8 August 1941. Thereafter the Il-4 paid frequent visits to the German capital and other targets in Eastern Europe. In 1944 production ended although the Il-4 served until the end of the war and afterwards. Apart from increasing the calibre of its guns and giving it a torpedo-carrying ability, the Il-4 remained virtually unchanged between 1941 and 1944.

**Specification:** Ilyushin Il-4
**Origin:** USSR
**Type:** four-crew bomber/torpedo bomber
**Powerplant:** two 1,100-hp (821-kW) M-88B radial piston engines
**Performance:** maximum speed 255 mph (411 km/h) at 15,500 ft (4725 m); initial climb rate 886 ft (270 m) per minute; service ceiling 32,810 ft (10000 m); range with bomb load 1,616 miles (2600 km)
**Weights:** empty 13,228 lb (6000 kg); maximum take-off 22,046 lb (10000 kg)
**Dimensions:** span 70 ft 4¼ in (21.44 m); length 48 ft 6½ in (14.80 m); height 13 ft 5½ in (4.10 m); wing area 718.0 sq ft (66.7 m²)
**Armament:** single 12.7-mm (0.5-in) UBT machine-gun in nose, dorsal turret and ventral positions, plus a maximum bombload of 2,205 lb (1000 kg) or three 1,102-lb (500-kg) torpedoes

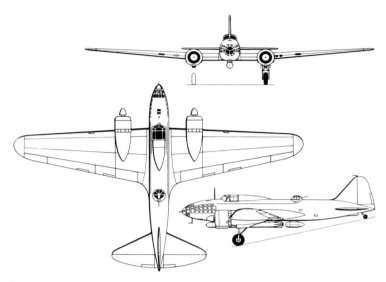

**Ilyushin Il-4**

As well as being employed as a bomber (it raided Berlin many times), the Il-4 was flown as a reconnaissance aircraft and glider tug; it was however characterized by poor defensive armament and suffered fairly heavy losses, particularly to German night fighters on the Eastern Front.

# Ilyushin Il-10

The Il-10 was greatly cleaned up compared with the Il-2, and also differed greatly in airframe shape, structure and systems. The fuselage was deeper and better streamlined, the armoured cockpits closer together and the gunner had a 20-mm gun in a better mounting with a glazed cupola fairing. Though heavier, the Il-10 had simpler main landing gears, with single legs and wheels that rotated to lie flat inside the wing. This Il-10, operated by the Soviet tactical air force in Germany in 1945, was armed with four 23-mm wing guns, a choice often associated with a single or twin UB at the rear.

# Junkers Ju 52/3m

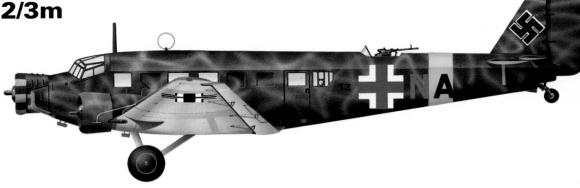

Junkers Ju 52/3mg7e of Stab IV/
Transportgeschwader 1 on the
Courland Front, winter 1944-5.
Versions of the Ju 52 were the major
transport aircraft for the Luftwaffe in
all theatres throughout the war.

## History and Notes

Affectionately known throughout the German forces as *Tante Ju* (Auntie Junkers) the three-engine Ju 52/3m with characteristic corrugated metal skin was widely used as a pre-war commercial airliner before being employed, first as a bomber and later as a troop transport, by the Luftwaffe. The Ju 52/3mg3e was flown in both roles by the Legion Cóndor in Spain from 1936 onwards. On the eve of the invasion of Poland the Luftwaffe fielded 552 transports, of which no fewer than 547 were Ju 52/3ms (the Ju 52/3mg4e and Ju 52/3mg5e versions, these aircraft having provision for alternative wheel, float or ski landing gear). Improved radio identified the Ju 52/3mg6e, and one of the main production versions, the Ju 52/3mg7e, featured automatic pilot, wider loading doors and accommodation for 18 assault troops. The Ju 52/3mg8e introduced increased cabin windows and a 13-mm (0.51-in) machine-gun in a dorsal position, and the Ju 52/3mg9e glider tug was stressed for increased take-off weight. The Ju 52/3mg10e was powered by BMW 132L radials. The final version, introduced late in 1943 when Allied fighters posed a greatly increased threat in all theatres, featured a 7.92-mm (0.31-in) gun over the cockpit. Estimates of total Ju 52/3m production (in Germany and elsewhere) vary between 5,600 and 5,900. Famous battles and campaigns in which the sturdy old workhorse participated included Norway, Crete, Demyansk (where some 200 Ju 52/3ms airlifted 24,000 tons of relief supplies, 15,000 troops and 20,000 casualties in three months), Stalingrad and Tunisia.

## Specification: Junkers Ju 52/3mg4e

**Origin:** Germany
**Type:** two/three-crew 18-seat military transport
**Powerplant:** three 830-hp (619-kW) BMW 132T radial piston engines
**Performance:** maximum speed 168 mph (270 km/h) at sea level; initial climb rate 689 ft (210 m) per minute; service ceiling 18,045 ft (5500 m); range 570 miles (917 km)
**Weights:** empty 14,352 lb (6510 kg); maximum take-off 23,148 lb (10500 kg)
**Dimensions:** span 95 ft 11½ in (29.25 m); length 62 ft 0 in (18.90 m); height 11 ft 9¾ in (3.60 m); wing area 1,189.5 sq ft (110.50 m$^2$)
**Armament:** 16 fully-equipped assault troops or 18 parachute troops; when specially adapted as air ambulance, twelve stretcher cases

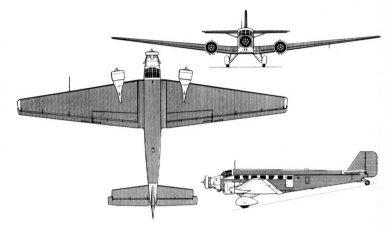

**Junkers Ju 52/3mge**

Constantly derided by Allied observers early in the war on account of its austere appearance and corrugated metal skinning, the Junkers Ju 52/3m proved robust and reliable in Luftwaffe service. More important, it was readily available.

# Junkers Ju 87

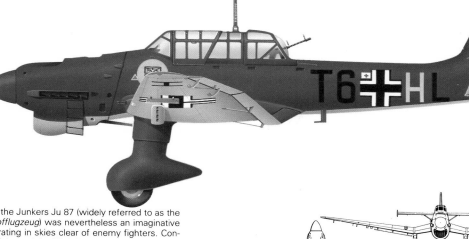

A Junkers Ju 87B-2 of 3./ Stukageschwader 2 'Immelmann' during the Battle of Britain. This aircraft crash-landed at Selsey in August 1940 following a raid on RAF Tangmere.

## History and Notes

Forever deprecated as a Nazi terror weapon, the Junkers Ju 87 (widely referred to as the Stuka – a contraction of the word *Sturzkampfflugzeug*) was nevertheless an imaginative weapon of considerable accuracy when operating in skies clear of enemy fighters. Conceived as a form of support artillery for the Wehrmacht's *Blitzkrieg* tactics, the Ju 87 was first flown in 1935, a small number of Ju 87A-1s and Ju 87B-1s being flown by the Legion Cóndor in Spain in 1938-9. To support the invasion of Poland the Luftwaffe fielded all five *Stukageschwader* thus far equipped with Ju 87s, and it was in this campaign that, with little effective opposition in the air, the Stuka's legend was born. With sirens screaming, the cranked-wing dive-bombers wrought havoc among Poland's helpless troops and civilians, effectively destroying the country's lines of communication, bridges, railways and airfields. During the difficult Norwegian campaign the Ju 87R with underwing fuel tanks was introduced to cope with the great distances involved, and in the Battle of Britain this version and the Ju 87B were heavily committed until withdrawn temporarily as a result of losses suffered at the hands of British fighter pilots. At the end of 1941 the Ju 87D, a much cleaned-up version with Jumo 211 engine, entered service on the Russian front, and appeared in North Africa the following year. The Ju 87G, a specialist anti-tank aircraft, featured a pair of 37-mm guns under the wings and achieved spectacular success, particularly in the East. Unquestionably the greatest exponent of the Stuka was Hans-Ulrich Rudel whose personal tally of a battleship, a cruiser and a destroyer sunk, and 519 tanks destroyed, far exceeded any other. Total Ju 87 production was said to be 5,709.

**Specification:** Junkers Ju 87D-7
**Origin:** Germany
**Type:** two-seat dive bomber
**Powerplant:** one 1,500-hp (1119-kW) Junkers Jumo 211P inline piston engine
**Performance:** maximum speed 248 mph (400 km/h) at 15,750 ft (4800 m); service ceiling 27,885 ft (8500 m); range 410 miles (660 km)
**Weights:** empty 8,686 lb (3940 kg); maximum take-off 14,550 lb (6600 kg)
**Dimensions:** span 49 ft 2½ in (15.00 m); length 37 ft 8¾ in (11.50 m); height 12 ft 9½ in (3.90 m); wing area 362.7 sq ft (33.60 m²)

**Junkers Ju 87B-2**

**Armament:** two forward-firing 20-mm MG 151/20 cannon and two 7.92-mm (0.31-in) MG 81 machine guns in the rear cockpit, plus a bombload of one 3,968-lb (1800-kg) bomb under the fuselage and two 1,102-lb (500-kg) bombs under the wings

A flight of three Junkers Ju 87B 'Stukas' heads for the front during the Polish campaign. With no opposing fighters, tight formations of Ju 87s could deliver devastating tactical firepower, paving the way for tanks and infantry.

# Junkers Ju 88

Ju 88A-5 of III/Lehrgeschwader 1, based at Catania for operations by X Fliegerkorps against Malta. The Ju 88A-5 proved more suitable for Sicilian airfields than previous variants due to its stronger landing gear.

## History and Notes

Designed by W.H. Evers and Alfred Gasner in 1935-6, the Ju 88 was one of the greatest aircraft of all time, its adaptability easily rivalling that of the Mosquito, and permitting the use of the type as low- medium- and high-level bomber, night-fighter and intruder, torpedo-bomber, anti-tank fighter and pilotless missile. The prototype Ju 88 V1 flew on 21 December 1936 and by the end of 1939 60 Ju 88A-1s had been completed, this being the Luftwaffe's standard version during the Battle of France and the Battle of Britain. By the end of 1940 the Ju 88A-4 was entering service with increased span and armament, while the first Ju 88C Zerstörer had already seen combat in the Battle of Britain. The Ju 88C-6b night-fighter was introduced in 1942 with *Lichtenstein* airborne radar, and from this stemmed the Ju 88R, with BMW 801 engines in place of the customary Jumo 211s, and the Ju 88G, similarly powered and with revised tail and increased armament; night-fighter Ju 88Gs constituted a major part of Germany's night defence force during the last three years of the war. Meanwhile development of the Ju 88A had continued, the Ju 88A-4/Trop being employed in North Africa the Ju 88A-6/U as a three-seat maritime bomber with search radar, the Ju 88A-7 and Ju 88A-12 as dual-control trainers, the Ju 88A-13 as a heavily-armoured ground attack bomber and the Ju 88A-17 as an anti-shiping strike aircraft capable of carrying two torpedoes. The Ju 88D was powered by Jumo 211D engines and the Ju 88P was a specialist ground-attack version with the 'solid' nose of the Ju 88C but with a variety of heavy guns, including 75-mm, 50-mm and 37-mm cannon; there were even plans to fit an 88-mm Duka gun, and a flame-thrower! The high-altitude Ju 88S fast bomber was powered by nitrous oxide-boosted BMW 801Gs, and the Ju 88H and Ju 88T were photo-reconnaissance series. Various versions of the Ju 88 were employed as the explosive-packed lower component of the *Mistel* pilotless missile in the last year of the war. Production of the Ju 88 totalled at least 14,980

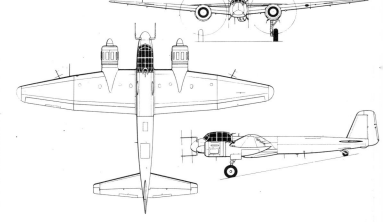

**Junkers Ju 88G-1**

**Armament:** two 7.92-mm (0.31-in) MG 81 guns firing forward, two 7.92-mm (0.31-in MG 81s in dorsal position and two 7.62-mm (0.31-in) MG 81s in rear of ventral gondola, plus a maximum bombload (internal and external) of 6,614 lb (3000 kg)

## Specification: Junkers Ju 88A-4

**Origin:** Germany

**Type:** four-crew attack bomber

**Powerplant:** two 1,340-hp (1000-kW) Junkers Jumo 211J-2 inline piston engines

**Performance:** maximum speed 292 mph (470 km/h) at 17,390 ft (5300 m); climb to 17,715 ft (5400 m) in 23 minutes; service ceiling 26,900 ft (8200 m); range 1,106 miles (1780 km)

**Weights:** empty 21,737 lb (9860 kg); maximum take-off 30,864 lb (14000 kg)

**Dimensions:** span 65 ft 7½ in (20.00 m); length 47 ft 2¾ in (14.40 m); height 15 ft 11 in (4.85 m); wing area 586.7 sq ft (54.50 m²)

A Junkers Ju 88A-5 medium bomber, with a pair of 551-lb (250-kg) bombs under the wings, prepares to take off. The Ju 88 soon proved itself a magnificently versatile aircraft, with a structure able to absorb massive combat damage and widely differing combat loads.

# Junkers Ju 188

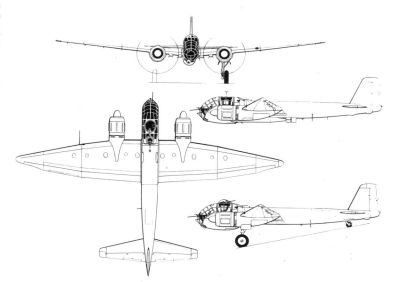

A reconnaissance Junkers Ju 188D-2 of 1.Staffel, Fernaufklärungsgruppe 124, based at Kirkenes, Norway. Equipped with FuG 200 search radar, these aircraft provided information on North Cape convoys for attacks by the torpedo-bombers of KG 26.

## History and Notes

Delays with a radical development of the superb Ju 88, the Junkers Ju 288, prompted the German air ministry to recognise the need to pursue an interim version, the Ju 188, late in 1942, pre-production Ju 188B-0s being completed in February 1943. Powered by 1,600-hp (1194-kW) BMW 801 radials, the new version featured the revised tail unit of the Ju 88G and, apart from sharply pointed wingtips, was a generally cleaned-up version of the older aircraft, although early versions produced little marked improvement in load-carrying and performance; the Ju 188E-2 was a torpedo-bomber. First operations by the Ju 188 over the UK were flown in August 1943, soon afterwards the aircraft were employed as pathfinders. Produced in parallel were the photo-reconnaissance Ju 188F series with 1,700-hp (1268-kW) BMW 801Ds. The Ju 188A-1, with water methanol-boosted 2,240-hp (1671-kW) Jumo 213A-1 engines, did not appear until January 1944, the Ju 188A-3 being a torpedo-bomber sub-variant; the Ju 188D was a widely-used photo-reconnaissance version of the Ju 188A. The Ju 188 was one of the principal bombers used by the Luftwaffe during Operation 'Steinbock', the resumption of air attacks on London early in 1944, but it was at this time that Germany's priorities were being weighted in favour of fighter production, and the Ju 188 production was terminated in the spring of 1944 after only 1,076 had been completed. Photo-reconnaissance versions however continued in service until the end of the war. The fastest version was the Ju 188T which, with three-speed two-stage supercharged and nitrous oxide-boosted 2,168-hp (1617-kW) Jumo 213E-1 engines, could achieve 435 mph (700 km/h).

## Specification: Junkers Ju 188E-1
**Origin:** Germany
**Type:** five-crew medium bomber
**Powerplant:** two 1,600-hp (1194-kW) BMW 801ML radial piston engines
**Performance:** maximum speed 311 mph (500 km/h) at 19,685 ft (6000 m); climb to 19,685 ft (6000 m) in 17.6 minutes; service ceiling 31,510 ft (9300 m); range 1,211 miles (195 km)
**Weights:** empty 2,737 lb (9860 kg); loaded 31,989 lb (14510 kg)
**Dimensions:** span 72 ft 2 in (22.00 m); length 49 ft 0½ in (14.95 m); height 14 ft 6¾ in (4.44 m); wing area 602.8 sq ft (56.00 m²)
**Armament:** one 20-mm MG 151/20 cannon in nose, one 20-mm MG 151/20 cannon in dorsal turret, one 13-mm (0.51-in) MG 131 machine-gun in rear dorsal position and one 13-mm (0.51-in) MG 131 machine-gun in rear ventral position, plus a maximum bombload of 6,614 lb (3000 kg)

**Junkers Ju 188E-1 (upper view: Ju 188E-2)**

A line-up of Junkers Ju 188D-2s as they were captured intact by Allied forces in the last weeks of the war, almost certainly grounded through lack of fuel. The style of camouflage seen here was found to be particularly effective over the sea.

# Kawanishi H6K 'Mavis'

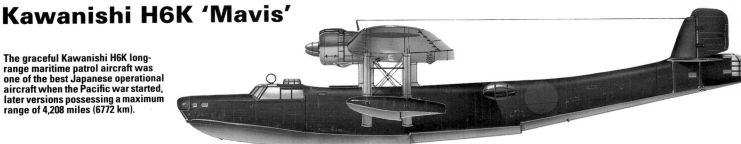

The graceful Kawanishi H6K long-range maritime patrol aircraft was one of the best Japanese operational aircraft when the Pacific war started, later versions possessing a maximum range of 4,208 miles (6772 km).

## History and Notes

The graceful H6K long-range maritime reconnaissance flying-boat owed something of its design to the work of Short Bros in the early 1930s, although its parasol wing layout was more akin to contemporary American designs. Powered by four 840-hp (627-kW) Nakajima Hikari 2 radials, the first of four H6K1 prototypes flew on 14 July 1936. Production H6K2s followed in 1939 with 1,000-hp (746-kW) Mitsubishi Kinsei 43 radials, together with a staff transport version, the H6K3. The principal production aircraft was the H6K4, of which a total of 127 was produced between 1939 and 1942; this featured considerably increased fuel capacity which bestowed a maximum range 3,780 miles (6083 km) — compared, for example, with 2,350 miles (3782 km) for the American PBY-5A Catalina. At the time of the attack on Pearl Harbor the Japanese navy possessed 64 H6K4s, some of which were employed as long-range bombers for attacks on the East Indies; however, as Allied fighter opposition improved the aircraft returned to the maritime reconnaissance role, a task for which they were well suited over the vast distances of the Pacific. A new version appeared in 1942, the H6K5, with more powerful engines and further increased fuel capacity, 36 examples being produced. A number of transports, the H6K2-L and H6K4-L versions, were also produced, bringing the total production of the H6K to 211, excluding prototypes. (The Allied reporting names were 'Mavis' for the maritime reconnaissance versions, and 'Tillie' for the transports.)

**Specification:** Kawanishi H6K5 'Mavis'
**Origin:** Japan
**Type:** nine-crew maritime reconnaissance flying-boat
**Powerplant:** four 1,300-hp (970-kW) Mitsubishi Kinsei 53 radial piston engines
**Performance:** maximum speed 239 mph (385 km/h) at 19,685 ft (6000 m); climb to 16,405 ft (5000 m) in 13.38 minutes; service ceiling 31,365 ft (9560 m); range 4,208 miles (6772 km)
**Weights:** empty 27,117 lb (12380 kg); maximum take-off 50,706 lb (23000 kg)
**Dimensions:** span 131 ft 2¾ in (40.00 m); length 84 ft 0⅞ in (25.63 m); height 20 ft 6⅞ in (6.27 m); wing area 1,829.9 sq ft (170.00 m²)
**Armament:** one 7.7-mm (0.303-in) Type 92 machine-gun in bow turret, one 7.7-mm (0.303-in) Type 92 machine-gun in open dorsal position, one 7.7-mm (0.303-in) Type 92 machine-gun in each beam blister and one 20-mm Type 99 cannon in tail turret, plus a bombload of up to 2,205 lb (1000 kg) or two 1,764-lb (800-kg) torpedoes

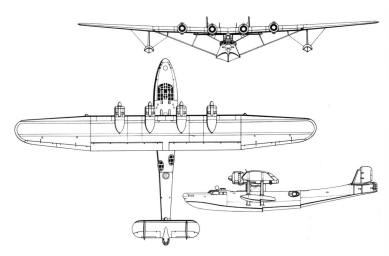

**Kawanishi H6K5 'Mavis'**

A total of 215 H6K flying-boats was produced between 1936 and 1943; the type was later used as a transport as well as occasionally for torpedo-bombing, being capable of carrying two torpedoes under the wing struts.

# Kawanishi N1K 'George'

A Kawanishi N1K2-J of the 343rd Kokutai; it was Warrant Officer Kinsuke Muot of this unit who, single-handed, engaged 12 US Navy Hellcats in February 1945, shot down four and forced the others to break off combat.

## History and Notes

In 1941 Kawanishi was still engaged in design of an attractive float-equipped fighter, the N1K1, intended as a naval fighter to support an island-hopping conquest in the Pacific without dependence on carriers or shore bases; in due course 98 of these fighters (Allied reporting name 'Rex') were produced. However, while their design was still in progress Kawanishi undertook a wheel-landing gear version, designated the N1K1-J Shiden (Violet Lightning). The prototype of the new fighter was flown on 27 December 1942 powered by the new 18-cylinder Nakajima Homare radial. Production got under way in 1943 of the N1K1-J with Homare 21 radial and an armament of two 7.7-mm (0.303-in) nose guns and four 20-mm wing cannon (two of which were carried in underwing fairings). Despite being plagued by constant engine troubles and an inherently weak landing gear, the Shiden was an excellent aircraft in combat, proving an equal match for the American F6F Hellcat; given the reporting name 'George' by the Allies, it was widely considered to be one of Japan's best wartime fighters. Three other main production versions were produced: the H1K1-Ja with nose guns deleted and all cannon mounted inside the wings; the N1K1-Jb with underwing racks for two 250-kg (551-lb) bombs; and the N1K1-Jc with racks for four 250-kg (551-lb) bombs. A new version, the N1K2-J, with improved landing gear, redesigned vertical tail surfaces and cleaner engine cowling, appeared during the last year of the war and proved even better than the N1K1; an instance occurred when a single Japanese pilot, Warrant Officer Kinsuke Muto, fought off 12 Hellcats, shooting down four. A total of 1,435 N1K Shiden landplane fighters was produced.

**Specification:** Kawanishi N1K1-J 'George'
**Origin:** Japan
**Type:** single-seat fighter
**Powerplant:** one 1,990-hp (1485-kW) Nakajima NK9H Homare 21 radial piston engine
**Performance:** maximum speed 363 mph (584 km/h) at 19,355 ft (5900 m); climb to 19,685 ft (6000 m) in 7.8 minutes; service ceiling 41,010 ft (12500 m); range 890 miles (1432 km)
**Weights:** empty 6,387 lb (2897 kg); maximum take-off 9,526 lb (4321 kg)
**Dimensions:** span 39 ft 4¼ in (12.00 m); length 29 ft 1¾ in (8.89 m); height 13 ft 3⅞ in (4.06 m); wing area 252.95 sq ft (23.50 m²)
**Armament:** two 7.7-mm (0.303-in) Type 97 machine-guns in nose and four wing-mounted 20-mm Type 99 cannon

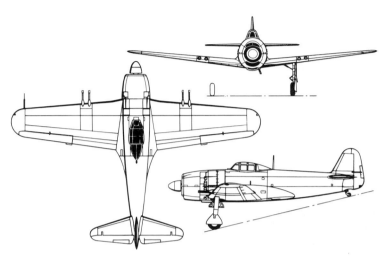

**Kawanishi N1K2-J 'George'**

The N1K2-J proved to be one of the best Japanese bomber-destroyers, being armed with four 20-mm cannon in the wings but, like so many of that nation's best aircraft, there were too few of them too late.

# Kawasaki Ki-45 'Nick'

The Ki-45 KAlc Toryu flown by the commanding officer of the 1st Chutai, 53rd Sentai, based at Matsudo in the Chiba Prefecture of Japan during the low-level B-29 raids of the winter of 1944-5. Apart from the upward-firing guns this bomber-destroyer was armed with a nose-mounted 37-mm Ho-203 cannon.

## History and Notes

Emulating the German heavy-fighter (*Zerstörer*) concept, the Japanese issued a similar requirement in 1937 for a twin-engine aircraft, to which the Nakajima Ki-37, Kawasaki Ki-38 and Mitsubishi Ki-39 were submitted. The Japanese army seemed unable to agree specification priorities, but eventually Kawasaki was instructed to start work on a development of the Ki-38, to be termed the Ki-45. A twin-Bristol Mercury-powered prototype was flown in January 1939, but subsequent development aircraft had 1,000-hp (746-kW) Nakajima Ha-25 radials. Meanwhile the designer, Takeo Doi, was working on a modified design to facilitate production, and in May 1941 the first Ki-45 KAI was completed, this being identifiable mainly by its straight-tapered wings and fin, and smooth-cowled engines. Named the Toryu (Dragon Killer), the Ki-45 KAI entered service in August 1942 in China, and was first flown in action in Burma by the 16th Sentai during October. Popular with its crews on account of its heavy armour protection and armament, it was a fairly fast aircraft and was used both to intercept USAAF B-24 bombers (of the US 5th Air Force) and to attack ground targets, being capable of carrying two 250-kg (551-lb) bombs. A night-fighter version, the Ki-45 KAlc, was introduced in 1944 with a semi-automatic 37-mm cannon in a ventral tunnel and two upward-firing 20-mm cannon; 477 of these aircraft were produced, but a radar-equipped version failed to reach service. They were widely used in defence against the American B-29 raids, claiming the destruction of eight of the big bombers on their first sortie. Production of the Ki-45 amounted to 14 prototypes, 12 pre-production aircraft and 1,675 production aircraft.

**Specification:** Kawasaki Ki-45 KAla 'Nick'
**Origin:** Japan
**Type:** two-seat heavy fighter/fighter-bomber
**Powerplant:** two 1,050-hp (783-kW) Nakajima Ha-25 radial piston engines
**Performance:** maximum speed 340 mph (547 km/h) at 22,965 ft (7000 m); climb to 16,405 ft (5000 m) in 6.30 minutes; service ceiling 35,200 ft (10730 m); range 1,404 miles (2260 km)
**Weights:** empty 8,146 lb (3695 kg); normal loaded 11,632 lb (5276 kg)
**Dimensions:** span 49 ft 3¼ in (15.02 m); length 34 ft 9¼ in (10.60 m); height 12 ft 1¾ in (3.70 m); wing area 344.44 sq ft (32.00 m²)
**Armament:** two forward-firing 12.7-mm (0.5-in) Type 9 machine-guns and one 20-mm Ho-3 cannon in ventral tunnel, and one flexible 7.92-mm (0.31-in) Type 98 machine-gun in rear dorsal position, plus provision for two 250-kg (551-lb) bombs

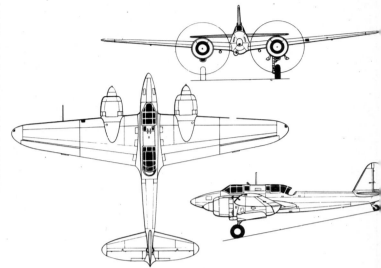

**Kawasaki Ki-45 (KAI-hei 'Nick')**

These Ki-45 KAlc (Army Type 2 Two-seat Fighter Model 2) heavy fighters belonged to the 53rd Sentai, a home-defence night fighter unit deployed to meet the low-level night operations by American B-29 bombers in the last winter of the war. Note the two Ho-5 20-mm upward-firing cannon aft of the cockpit.

# Kawasaki Ki-61 'Tony'

By the end of the war 13 Sentais were flying the Ki-61, the majority in defence of the Japanese homeland; a total of 3,159 were produced, more than 2,300 of them in the last 18 months of the war.

## History and Notes

Sometimes described as a cross between a Messerschmitt Bf 109 and a P-51 Mustang, the Kawasaki Ki-61 certainly had the distinctive nose shape associated with an inverted-Vee inline engine, the Kawasaki Ha-40 being in effect a Daimler-Benz DB 601A built under licence. The Ki-61's designers, Takeo Doi and Shin Owada, had moreover worked under the German Richard Vogt. In December 1940 they were instructed to go ahead with the Ki-61, and one year later the prototype was flown. The first production Ki-61-Is were deployed operationally in April 1943 when the 68th and 78th Sentais arrived in New Guinea. Named Hien (Swallow) in service (and codenamed 'Tony' by the Allies), the new aircraft proved popular with its pilots, being unusually well armed and armoured, and the type was at least a match for opposing American fighters. Its armament (of four 12.7-mm/0.5-in machine-guns) proved inadequate to knock down enemy bombers, however, and the Ki-61-I KAIc was introduced with a pair of 20-mm cannon in the nose, these being replaced in a small number of Ki-61-I KAId fighters by two 30-mm cannon. The Ki-61-I and Ki-61-I KAI remained in production until 1945, but in 1944 they were joined in service by the Ki-61-II with more powerful Kawasaki Ha-140 inline (producing 1,500 hp/1120 kW); with a top speed of 379 mph (610 km/h) this would have been an excellent fighter but for constant engine problems; yet when fully serviceable the Ki-61-II was the only Japanese fighter fully able to combat the B-29 at its normal operating altitude, particularly when armed with four 20-mm cannon. Excluding prototypes and development aircraft, production totalled 1,380 Ki-61-Is, 1,274 Ki-61-I KAIs and 374 Ki-61-IIs.

## Specification: Kawasaki Ki-61-I KAIc 'Tony'
**Origin:** Japan
**Type:** single-seat fighter
**Powerplant:** one 1,180-hp (880-kW) Kawasaki Ha-40 inline piston engine
**Performance:** maximum speed 366 mph (590 km/h) at 13,980 ft (4260 m); climb to 16,405 ft (5000 m) in 7.0 minutes; service ceiling 32,810 ft (1000 m); range 1,120 miles (1800 km)
**Weights:** empty 5,798 lb (2630 kg); normal loaded 7,650 lb (3470 kg)
**Dimensions:** span 39 ft 4½ in (12.00 m); length 29 ft 4 in (8.94 m); height 12 ft 1¾ in (3.70 m); wing area 215.3 sq ft (20.00 m²)
**Armament:** two 20-mm Ho-5 cannon in nose and two 12.7-mm (0.5-in) Type 1 machine-guns in wings

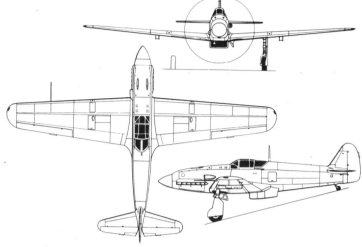

**Kawasaki Ki-61-1 'Tony'**

This Ki-61 Hien bears the markings of the 244th Sentai, one of the most famous units established at Chofu in the Tokyo Prefecture for home defence in October 1944; it was commanded by Major Tembico Kobayashi who personally shot down about a dozen American B-29s.

# Lavochkin LaGG-3

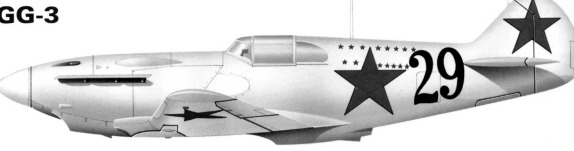

Shown in winter colour scheme (upper surfaces covered in soluble white paint), this LaGG-3 was flown by Captain Grigoryev, deputy commander of 178 IAP, 6 IAK, Moscow, winter 1942-3. Bearing in mind the general inferiority of Soviet pilots and aircraft in the first two years of the Russian campaign, the tally of 15 victories on this aircraft testifies to a creditable achievement.

## History and Notes

Designed by a committee headed by Semyon Lavochkin and including V. Gorbunov and M. Gudkov, the LaGG-3 stemmed from the LaGG-1, whose prototype (the I-22) was first flown on 30 March 1939. These aircraft were unusual in retaining an all-wood structure; only the control surfaces – and later the landing flaps – were metal. This excellent little fighter was ordered into production in 1940 as the LaGG-1 with a 1,050-hp (783-kW) Klimov M-105 inline engine, but was too late to see service during the Winter War with Finland in 1939-40. With a top speed of 373 mph (600 km/h) and an armament of one 20-mm and two 12.7-mm (0.5-in) guns, the LaGG-1 was certainly one of the world's best fighters early in 1941, but pilots complained of poor climb performance and heavy controls, and a new version, the LaGG-3, was introduced by way of the I-301 prototype after several hundred LaGG-1s had been delivered. At the time of the German attack two air regiments still flew the older aircraft, but within a year four regiments had received the LaGG-3, their task being to provide escort for the Il-2 close support aircraft; they carried a variety of armament combinations, including wing attachments for six 8.2-cm (3.23-in) rockets or light bombs. The LaGG-3 featured a constant-speed propeller and improved rudder balancing, and was popular in service; it proved very robust and was capable of sustaining considerable battle damage. Difficulties arose with maintenance of the liquid-cooled M-105PF engines in the field and this led the Russians to opt for radial engines, and in 1942 the LaGG-3 went out of production after about 1,200 had been built.

## Specification: Lavochkin LaGG-3
**Origin:** USSR
**Type:** single-seat fighter
**Powerplant:** one 1,240-hp (925-kW) M-105PF inline piston engine
**Performance:** maximum speed 348 mph (560 km/h) at 11,975 ft (3650 m); initial climb rate 2,950 ft (900 m) per minute; service ceiling 29,530 ft (9000 m); range 404 miles (650 km)
**Weights:** empty 5,776 lb (2620 kg); maximum take-off 7,275 lb (3300 kg)
**Dimensions:** span 32 ft 1¾ in (9.80 m); length 29 ft 1¼ in (8.87 m); height 8 ft 10 in (2.70 m); wing area 188.4 sq ft (17.5 m²)
**Armament:** one 20-mm ShVAK hub-firing cannon, two 12.7-mm (0.5-in) UBS machine-guns and two 7.62-mm (0.3-in) ShKAS machine-guns, plus provision for six underwing 8.2-cm (3.23-in) rockets or four 110-lb (50-kg) bombs

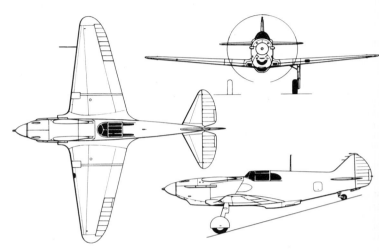

Lavochkin LaGG-3

Seen here in typical snow camouflage is a LaGG-3 serving in the Lake Ladoga region during the winter of 1943. By this time production of the aircraft had stopped, preference being given to the radial-engine La-5 and La-7.

# Lavochkin La-5/-7

A Lavochkin La-7 of the Soviet 18th Guards Fighter Regiment. Essentially a low-altitude fighter (its engine rated to give maximum power at about 6,000 ft/1828 m), the Lavochkins were ideal as escorts for the huge numbers of vulnerable Il-2 ground support aircraft.

## History and Notes

As the Soviet armies reeled back after the initial assault by Germany in the East during 1941, frantic demands were made for modern equipment to be supplied to the Russian air force. In October 1941 Semyon Lavochkin started work on the LaG-5 fighter with 1,600-hp (1194-kW) M-82 radial, passing on almost immediately to a development, the La-5, with cut-down rear fuselage which gave improved visibility for the pilot. The prototype completed its acceptance trials in May 1942 and entered production two months later; by the end of the year no fewer than 1,182 examples had been completed. In March 1943 the next and principal version, the La-5FN, entered production, a total of 21,975 aircraft including the later La-7 being produced before the end of the war; the La-5FN featured the 1,650-hp (1231-kW) M-82FN engine, but its two 20-mm cannon were supplemented by four 82-mm RS 82 rocket projectiles or two PTAB anti-tank weapons. A two-seat trainer version, the La-5UTI, was also produced. Later aircraft were armed with two 23-mm guns in place of the 20-mm weapons. In 1944 the La-7 appeared with an armament of three 20- or 23-mm cannon, an M-82FNU or FNV engine and a top speed of 423 mph (680 km/h). The first large-scale use of the La-5 was during the fighting around Stalingrad in November 1942; it was essentially a low-to-medium altitude fighter, and during the great armour battles at Kursk in July 1943 La-5s were employed in a tank-busting role, and after having discharged their hollow-charge missiles against ground targets they would climb to give fighter cover to the slower Il-2 support aircraft. The highest-scoring of all Allied fighter pilots of the war, Ivan Kojedub, achieved all his 62 combat victories while flying LaG-5s, La-5FNs and La-7s between 26 March 1943 and 19 April 1945.

**Specification:** Lavochkin La-5FN
**Origin:** USSR
**Type:** single-seat fighter/fighter-bomber
**Powerplant:** one 1,650-hp (1231-kW) M-82FN radial piston engine
**Performance:** maximum speed 402 mph (647 km/h) at 16,405 ft (5000 m); climb to 3,280 ft (1000 m) in 0.35 minutes; service ceiling 32,810 ft (10000 m); range 435 miles (700 km)
**Weights:** empty 6,173 lb (2800 kg); normal loaded 7,408 lb (3360 kg)
**Dimensions:** span 32 ft 5¾ in (9.90 m); length 27 ft 10¾ in (8.50 m); height 8 ft 4 in (2.54 m); wing area 201.8 sq ft (18.75 m²)
**Armament:** two nose-mounted 20-mm ShVAK cannon (on later aircraft 23-mm NS cannon), plus provision for four 8.2-mm (3.23-in) RS 82 rockets or 331 lb (150 kg) of bombs

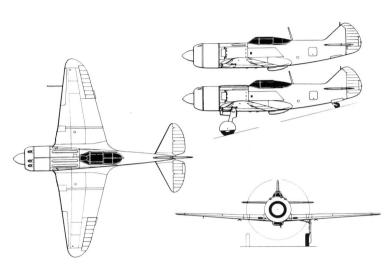

**Lavochkin La-7 (Yaroslavl – 3 guns) (top view: Moskva – 2 guns)**

Flown from the Tri Duby airfield complex in September 1944 in support of the Slovak National uprising, the La-5FNs (carrying Soviet markings) of the 1st Czech Regiment took the Germans completely by surprise; this unit was commanded by Colonel Frank Fajtl, an ex-RAF Fighter Command Battle of Britain veteran.

# Lioré et Olivier LeO 451

Lioré et Olivier 451, no. 426, of the 1ère Escadrille, Groupe de Bombardement I/II based at Orn-La Sénia, Morocco, in mid-1941; this unit had suffered heavy losses among its LeO 45s during the Battle of France before moving to North Africa.

## History and Notes

After the French air force became an independent service on 1 April 1933 a number of 'Plans' were conceived for its progressive expansion and modernization. Plan I demanded that about 1,000 modern aircraft be built immediately and called for proposals for follow-up designs. Among the latter was the LeO 45, conceived as a 'fast heavy bomber capable of being operated by day or night at medium altitude'. Powered by Hispano-Suiza 14 radials, the prototype LeO 45-01 first flew on 16 January 1937, but these engines gave constant trouble during trials and it was decided to switch to Gnome-Rhône 14N radials in production aircraft. At the outbreak of war 749 LeO 451s (and derivatives) were on order but only 10 were on Armée de l'Air charge. First unit to equip with the new bomber was GB I/31, followed soon after by GB I/12 and II/12, and these were still the only units that had completely re-equipped when the Germans launched their major attack on 10 May 1940. From the outset the LeO 451s were called upon to operate in a manner for which they were quite unsuited, namely low-level ground support in the presence of enemy air opposition. In consequence the LeO 451 suffered heavy losses, although new units were hurriedly formed and replacements quickly delivered. Indeed by the end of the Battle of France 373 LeO 451s and derivatives had been delivered to the Armée de l'Air and Aéronavale, which had lost some 150. Production continued in unoccupied France, and the LeO 451 served in North Africa and Syria with the Vichy forces. Some were flown against the Allies in these theatres. After the 'Torch' landings of November 1942 the Germans invaded the Unoccupied Zone of France, seizing 94 LeO 451s, many of which were impressed into service as transports with the Luftwaffe.

## Specification: Lioré et Olivier LeO 451

**Origin:** France
**Type:** four-crew medium bomber
**Powerplant:** two 1,060-hp (791-KW) Gnome-Rhône 14 N 48/49 radial piston engines
**Performance:** maximum speed 298 mph (480 km/h) at 15,750 ft (4800 m); service ceiling 29,530 ft (9000 m); range 1,802 miles (2900 km)
**Weights:** empty 16,600 lb (7530 kgj); maximum take-off 25,132 lb (11400 kg)
**Dimensions:** span 73 ft 10½ in (22.52 m); length 56 ft 4 in (17.17 m); height 17 ft 2¼ in (5.24 m); wing area 710.4 sq ft (66.00 m²)
**Armament:** one fixed forward-firing 7.5-mm (0.295-in) MAC 1934 M39 machine-gun, two rearward-firing 7.5-mm (0.295-in) MAC 1934 M39 machine-guns in retractable gondola, and one 20-mm H5404 cannon in dorsal position, plus a maximum bombload (with reduced fuel) of 3,086 lb (1400 kg)

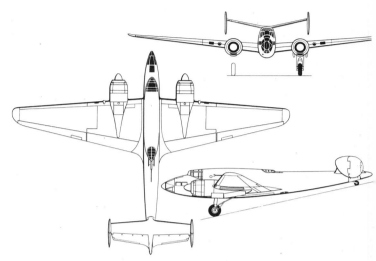

**Lioré et Olivier LeO 451**

A flight of LeO 451s, probably over North Africa in 1941-2. During 1941 all survivors of the previous year's Battle of France were modified with smooth-contoured fins and rudders, as seen here.

# Lockheed P-38 Lightning

Neutral air forces in Europe reaped a worthwhile harvest of the belligerents' aircraft which landed by design or accident in their territory. This USAAF P-38 was one that landed at Lisbon, Portugal, while flying from Britain to North Africa in 1943, and was impressed into service by the Portuguese.

## History and Notes

Representing Lockheed's first military aircraft project, the twin-engine, twin-boom P-38 was designed to meet a 1937 requirement for a high-altitude interceptor. First flown on 27 January 1939, the XP-38 was followed by production P-38s with nose armament of one 37-mm and four 0.5-in (12.7-mm) guns and powered by Allison V-1710-27/29 engines; their top speed of 390 mph (628 km/h) was greater than any other American fighter in 1941. The first version to be considered fully operational was the P-38D, however, and this was reaching squadrons at the time of Pearl Harbor. The first of an order for 143 aircraft for the RAF arrived in the UK in December 1941, but after evaluation the Lightning was rejected (on account of a ban imposed on the export of turbochargers) and the contract cancelled. In the USAAF the P-38D was followed by the P-38E, in which the 37-mm cannon was replaced by a 20-mm weapon. The P-38F, with provision for up to a 2,000-lb (907-kg) bombload under the wings, was followed by the P-38G with minor equipment changes; the P-38H could carry up to 3,200 lb (1452 kg) of bombs. In the P-38J (of which 2,970 were produced) the radiators were located in deep 'chin' fairings immediately aft of the propellers; with maximum external fuel load this version had an endurance of about 12 hours, and it was in this model of the P-38 that America's top scoring fighter pilot of the war, Major Richard I. Bong, gained the majority of his 40 victories. The P-38L was the most-built version (a total of 3,923) and differed from the P-38J only in having -111/113 engines in place of the -89/91s previously used. Photo-reconnaissance conversions, the F-4 and F-5, were also widely used in Europe and the Far East. Production of all Lightnings totalled 9,394.

**Specification:** Lockheed P-38L Lightning
**Origin:** USA
**Type:** single-seat fighter/fighter-bomber
**Powerplant:** two 1,475-hp (1100-kW) Allison V-1710-111/113 inline piston engines
**Performance:** maximum speed 414 mph (666 km/h) at 25,000 ft (7620 m); climb to 20,000 ft (6095 m) in 7.0 minutes; service ceiling 44,000 ft (13410 m); range 450 miles (724 km)
**Weights:** empty 12,800 lb (5806 kg); maximum take-off 21,600 lb (9798 kg)
**Dimensions:** span 52 ft 0 in (15.85 m); length 37 ft 10 in (11.52 m); height 9 ft 10 in (2.99 m); wing area 327.5 sq ft (30.42 m²)
**Armament:** one 20-mm and four 0.5-in (12.7-mm) guns in the nose, plus a bombload of up to two 1,600-lb (726-kg) bombs under the wings

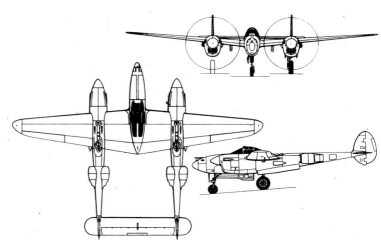

**Lockheed P-38J Lightning**

Last version of the classic P-38 to enter service during the war was the P-38M, a radar-equipped two-seat night fighter that reached squadrons in the Pacific in mid-1945; they were intended largely as a stopgap pending a build-up of deliveries of the P-61 Black Widow.

Although the Lockheed P-38 gave excellent service in the European theatre both as a long-range fighter and photo reconnaissance aircraft, the vast distances involved in the Pacific war and the increasing inferiority of Japanese aircraft represented the ideal scenario for this fast, hard-hitting twin-engine fighter.

# Lockheed 14 (A-28/-29)

A Pratt & Whitney Twin Wasp-powered Lockheed Hudson Mk V in mid-war RAF markings; 409 Mk Vs were delivered to the RAF, starting in 1941, and the aircraft shown, AM579, was one of those flown direct from California to Auckland, New Zealand.

## History and Notes

Originating in 1938, when the UK was spending considerably more money on contracts with the American aircraft industry than the US air forces themselves, the Lockheed Hudson was the outcome of a request that the Lockheed 14 transport be developed as a maritime reconnaissance aircraft. The first such aircraft was flown on 10 December 1938, and the first to arrive in the UK was disembarked at Liverpool on 15 February 1939. After the initiation of the Lend-Lease programme the aircraft was given the US designation A-28 and A-28A, some of the British aircraft being repossessed as A-29s and A-29As by the USAAF after Pearl Harbor. The first U-boat to be sunk by American forces was attacked by an A-29 of the 13th Bomb Group. An attack trainer version was produced as the AT-18 (or, with dorsal turret removed, the AT-18B). It was however in the RAF that the aircraft, as the Hudson, saw most service. The original order for 200 (soon increased to 350) aircraft were designated Hudson Mk Is; hydromatic propellers identified the Hudson Mk II, and the Hudson Mk III was powered by 1,200-hp (985-kW) Wright GR-1820 G205A radials. Hudsons entered service with the RAF's No. 224 Squadron in mid-1939, replacing Avro Ansons, and thereafter flew constant patrols over the North Sea; later, with the arrival of the Hudson Mk III with extra fuel tanks, the aircraft participated in the Battle of the Atlantic. It was the crew of a No. 269 Squadron Hudson to whom the U-boat U-570 surrendered after a determined attack on 27 August 1941. A total of 2,487 Hudsons was purchased on British contracts, of which 423 were supplied to Canada, South Africa, China, New Zealand, Australia and Portugal. Final versions were the Hudson Mks IV, V and VI with Pratt & Whitney radials. Hudsons equipped 31 RAF squadrons, serving as transports in the final years of the war.

**Specification:** Lockheed A-29 (Hudson Mk IIIA)
**Origin:** USA
**Type:** four-crew light bomber
**Powerplant:** two 1,200-hp (895-kW) Wright R-1820-87 radial piston engines
**Performance:** maximum speed 253 mph (407 km/h) at 15,000 ft (4570 m); climb to 10,000 ft (3050 m) in 6.3 minutes; service ceiling 26,500 ft (8075 m); range 1,550 miles (2494 km)
**Weights:** empty 12,825 lb (5817 kg); maximum take-off 20,500 lb (9299 kg)
**Dimensions:** span 65 ft 6 in (19.96 m); length 44 ft 4 in (13.51 m); height 11 ft 11 in (3.63 m); wing area 551.0 sq ft (51.19 m²)

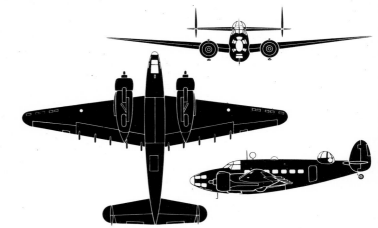

**Lockheed Hudson**

**Armament:** two fixed forward-firing 0.3-in (7.62-mm) guns in nose, one 0.3-in (7.68-mm) gun in ventral position and one 0.3-in (7.62-mm) gun in dorsal turret, plus a bombload of 1,600 lb (726 kg)

**In American service the Lockheed A-28 and A-29 were used for a variety of duties, ranging from anti-submarine patrol, photo reconnaissance and troop-carrying to crew training and target-towing.**

# Macchi C.200 Saetta

An early C.200 Saetta of the 371ª Squadriglia CT, 22° Gruppo CT, based in Albania in March 1941; note the 'Cucaracha' (cockroach) emblem on the rear fuselage. This unit later took its Saettas to the Eastern Front with the CSIR to support the Italian offensive on the Dnieper.

## History and Notes

Handicapped by Italy's pre-war lack of an inline engine suitable for fighters, Mario Castoldi's Fiat radial-powered C.200 was so underpowered and undergunned that when it arrived in service in 1939 it was already outclassed by the Hurricane which had joined the RAF two years earlier. Indeed the first C.200 unit, the 4° Stormo, expressed a preference for the CR.42 and accordingly reverted to the biplane in 1940. First flown on 24 December 1937 by Guiseppe Burei, the C.200, named the Saetta (Lightning), went on to equip the 1°, 2°, 3°, 4° (in mid-1941) and 54° Stormi, and the 8°, 12°, 13°, 21° and 22° Gruppi, a total of about 1,200 aircraft being produced by Macchi, Breda and SAI Ambrosini. On the date that Italy entered the war, 10 June 1940, two home-based *stormi* were combat-ready with the C.200, being first flown in action over Malta in September that year, and it was largely the losses suffered by the Italian fighter arm at this time and during the Greek campaign that prompted the Luftwaffe to deploy X Fliegerkorps in the Mediterranean to bolster the Regia Aeronautica's flagging resources. C.200s were heavily committed in North Africa, and were fairly evenly matched with the early Hurricane Mk Is, weighed down by tropical air filters, but the attrition suffered by all Italian air force units (principally through poor serviceability and air attacks on their airfields) quickly reduced the number of C.200s. Some 51 Saettas of the 22° Gruppo operated in the Odessa Zone of the Russian front from August 1941 onwards, proving capable of matching almost any Russian fighter in the early stages of that campaign. By the time of the Italian armistice in September 1943, however, the Regia Aeronautica's total inventory of serviceable C.200s stood at only 33.

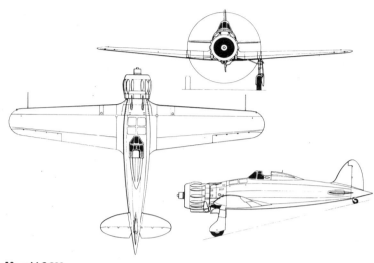

**Macchi C.200**

## Specification:
Macchi C.200 Saetta (Breda-built Series 6)
**Origin:** Italy
**Type:** single-seat fighter/fighter-bomber
**Powerplant:** one 870-hp (649-kW) Fiat A.74 RC 38 radial piston engine
**Performance:** maximum speed 313 mph (504 km/h) at 14,765 ft (4500 m); climb to 13,125 ft (4000 m) in 4.55 minutes; service ceiling 29,200 ft (8900 m); range 354 miles (570 km)
**Weights:** empty 4,321 lb (1960 kg); maximum take-off 5,280 lb (2395 kg)
**Dimensions:** span 34 ft 8½ in (10.58 m); length 27 ft 0¾ in (8.25 m); ; height 10 ft 0⅛ in (3.05 m); wing area 180.8 sq ft (16.80 m²)
**Armament:** two 12.7-mm (0.5-in) Breda-SAFAT machine-guns in nose, plus provision for up to two 331-lb (50-kg) bombs

A late-series Macchi-built Saetta. Generally regarded as marginally better than the Fiat G.50, the C.200 survived in front-line service until 1943, although by then it was wholly outclassed by mid-war Allied fighters in the Mediterranean theatre, while its gun armament was quite inadequate to combat bombers.

# Macchi C.202 Folgore

Identified as an aircraft of the 22°
Gruppo by the *Spauracchio*
(scarecrow) device on the fuselage
band, and by the numerals as
belonging to the 369ª Squadriglia,
this mid-series C.202 was based at
Capodichino, Naples as part of the
53° Stormo CT at the time of the
invasion of Sicily in July 1943.
Although its maximum speed of 373
mph (600 km/h) was adequate to
match Allied fighters of the Spitfire
Mk V's generation, the purpose of
deploying aircraft such as the C.202
to defend Italian cities from attacks
by Allied bombers was questionable
as their light armament was quite
inadequate for the role of bomber-
destroyer.

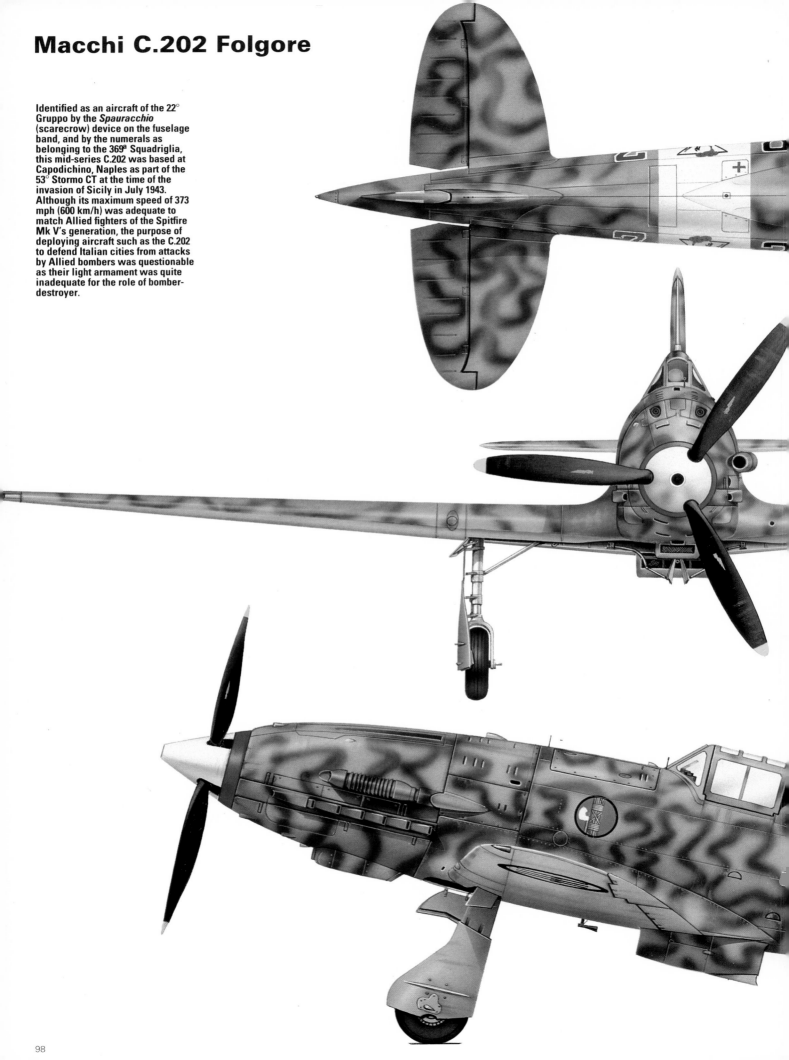

# Macchi C.202 Folgore/C.205

Following the Italian Armistice of September 1943 a relatively small number of Macchi C.205V Veltro fighters joined the Co-Belligerent Air Force, and due mainly to a lack of spares for their German engine their service was not prolonged; this C.205V served with the 155° Gruppo, 51° Stormo at Lecce late in 1944.

## History and Notes

One of the best Italian fighters of the mid-war years, Mario Castoldi's Macchi C.202 Folgore (Thunderbolt) was developed from the radial-powered C.200, but was powered by a Daimler-Benz DB 601 produced under licence as the Alfa Romeo RA 1000 RC 411. First flown by Carestiato on 10 August 1940, the C.202 Series I production version entered service with the 1° Stormo at Udine in the summer of 1941, this unit arriving in Libya in the following November. The Folgore was a low-wing monoplane with inwards retracting landing gear and an armament of two 12.7-mm (0.5-in) Breda-SAFAT machine-guns in the nose; there was also provision for two 7.7-mm (0.303-in) guns in the wings. Engine production was slow and severely delayed the build-up of the Folgore in service.

The aircraft underwent very little change and development during its life span, and was produced in 11 series. It eventually served with 45 *squadriglie* of the 1°, 2°, 3°, 4°, 51°, 52°, 53° and 54° Stormi in North Africa, Sicily, Italy, the Aegean and Russia. Production amounted to about 1,500, of which 392 were produced by the parent company and the remainder by Breda. In combat the Folgore proved to be well-matched with the Spitfire Mk V in performance, but was badly undergunned and, although certainly superior to American fighters such as the P-39 Airacobra, this armament deficiency prevented Folgore pilots from knocking down many Allied bombers.

**Specification:** Macchi C.202 Series IX Folgore
**Origin:** Italy
**Type:** single-seat fighter
**Powerplant:** one 1,075-hp (802-kW) Alfa Romeo RA 1000 RC 411 inline piston engine
**Performance:** maximum speed 373 mph (600 km/h) at 18,375 ft (5600 m); climb to 16,405 ft (5000 m) in 4.6 minutes; service ceiling 37,730 ft (11500 m); range 379 miles (610 km)
**Weights:** empty 5,489 lb (2490 kg); maximum take-off 6,459 lb (2930 kg)
**Dimensions:** span 34 ft 8½ in (10.58 m); length 29 ft 0½ in (8.85 m); height 11 ft 5½ in (3.50 m); wing area 180.8 sq ft (16.80 m²)
**Armament:** two 12.7-mm (0.5-in) Breda-SAFAT machine-guns in the nose, plus provision to mount two 7.7-mm (0.303-in) guns in the wings

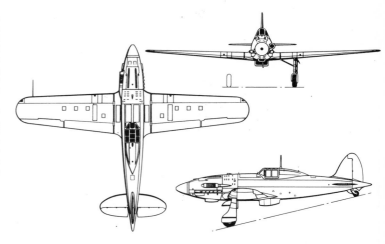

Macchi C.202

Ultimate wartime development of the C.200/202 series of Italian fighters was the Daimler Benz-powered C.205; shown here is the prototype of the C.205N Orione variant in Regia Aeronautica markings during the winter of 1942-3.

# Martin 167 Maryland

Apart from six squadrons of the Royal Air Force, a small number of Commonwealth squadrons also flew the Maryland; the aircraft shown here belonged to No. 24 Sqn, South African Air Force, based at Fuka, Egypt, at the time of the Crete campaign in May 1941.

## History and Notes

Developed as the US Army Air Corps' XA-22 attack bomber, the Martin 167 failed to gain acceptance by the Americans after its first flight on 14 March 1938. Promises of quick delivery attracted the French, who ordered 175 aircraft (the Martin 167F) for delivery by the end of 1940. About 75 of these had been delivered before France surrendered to the Germans in June that year, two units (GB I/62 and I/63) having flown the aircraft during the brief Battle of France; about 60 of these subsequently served with Vichy forces in North Africa and Syria, and in due course were flown in action against the Allies. Some of the survivors from the debacle in France were flown to the UK and served with the RAF, while the UK itself ordered a further 150 aircraft as Maryland Mk IIs with two-stage supercharged engines, to join 75 Maryland Mk Is (Martin 167Fs with single-stage supercharged engines diverted from the French order). Most of these 225 aircraft were flown or shipped to the Middle East, first serving on No. 431 General Reconnaissance Flight at Malta in October 1940. It was one of these aircraft that made the famous reconnaissance flight over Taranto harbour before the brilliant attack by Swordfish that temporarily crippled the Italian battle fleet. In due course Marylands equipped three RAF bomber squadrons and four of the South African Air Force all in the Mediterranean theatre.

**Specification:** Martin 167 Maryland Mk II
**Origin:** USA
**Type:** three-crew reconnaissance bomber
**Powerplant:** two 1,200-hp (895-kW) Pratt & Whitney S3C4-G radial piston engines
**Performance:** maximum speed 278 mph (448 km/h) at 11,800 ft (3595 m); initial climb rate 1,790 ft (546 m) per minute; service ceiling 26,000 ft (7925 m); range with bombload 1,210 miles (1947 km)
**Weights:** empty 11,213 lb (5086 kg); maximum take-off 16,809 lb (7631 kg)
**Dimensions:** span 61 ft 4 in (18.69 m); length 46 ft 8 in (14.22 m); height 14 ft 11¾ in (4.55 m); wing area 538.5 sq ft (50.03 $^2$)
**Armament:** four 0.303-in (7.7-mm) machine-guns in the wings, and single 0.303-in (7.7-mm) flexible guns in dorsal turret and ventral positions, plus a bombload of up to 2,000 lb (901 kg)

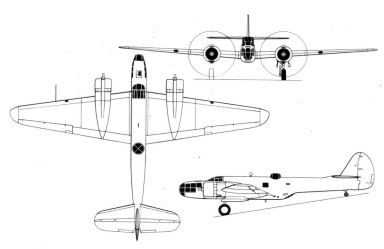

**Martin Maryland I**

Originating in a French rather than a British order, the Martin Maryland entered service with the RAF in 1940, one of its memorable exploits being a low-level reconnaissance of Taranto harbour prior to the devastating attack by Fleet Air Arm Swordfish torpedo bombers.

# Martin 187 Baltimore

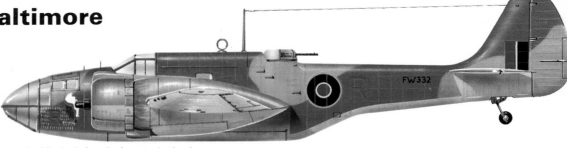

An ex-USAAF Martin A-30A-10-MA Baltimore Mk V, FW332, of No. 232 Wing, North-west African Tactical Air Force; comprising Nos 55 and 223 Sqns, the wing flew the Baltimore Mk V during the Italian campaign of 1944.

## History and Notes

One of the reasons given by the British Purchasing Mission in America for not selecting the Martin 167 bomber for the RAF was the lack of direct communication between the two front crew members and the rear gunner. In 1940, however, otherwise impressed by the performance of the aircraft purchased by France, the British requested the company to produce a new version of the Martin 167 with deeper fuselage allowing direct access between all crew members, who were to be increased to four. The prototype Martin 187 was flown on 14 June 1941, and although later designated the A-30 by the USAAF none were in fact delivered for American use. Apart from the prototype, which arrived in the UK during October of that year, deliveries started with 50 Baltimore Mk Is in 1942 with 1,600-hp (1194-kW) Wright R-2600-A5B radials and a single machine-gun in the dorsal position; 100 Baltimore Mk IIs followed with twin dorsal guns but were otherwise similar; 250 Baltimore Mk IIIs, with power-operated Boulton Paul dorsal turret and R-2600-19 engines, completed the initial order for 400 aircraft. After the negotiation of Lend-Lease, 281 further Baltimore Mk IIIs were supplied as Baltimore Mk IIIAs, followed by 294 Baltimore Mk IVs with a Martin dorsal turret. Finally 600 Baltimore Mk Vs with 1,700-hp (1268-kW) R-2600-29 engines brought the total of RAF deliveries to 1,575. The type's service was exclusively in the Mediterranean theatre, equipping seven RAF squadrons and two of the South African Air Force. From March 1942 until the end of the war these aircraft gave magnificent service in North Africa, Sicily and Italy; some were passed to the Italian Co-Belligerent Forces and were used by the *Stormo Baltimore* in operations over the Balkans in 1945.

**Specification:** Martin 187 Baltimore Mk III
**Origin:** USA
**Type:** four-crew light bomber
**Powerplant:** two 1,660-hp (1238-kW) Wright GR-2600-A5B radial piston engines
**Performance:** maximum speed 302 mph (486 km/h) at 11,000 ft (3355 m); climb to 15,000 ft (4570 m) in 12.0 minutes; service ceiling 24,000 ft (7315 m); range 950 miles (1530 km)
**Weights:** empty 15,200 lb (6895 kg); maximum take-off 23,000 lb (10433 kg)
**Dimensions:** span 61 ft 4 in (18.69 m); length 48 ft 5¾ in (14.77 m); height 17 ft 9 in (5.41 m); wing area 538.5 sq ft (50.93 m²)
**Armament:** four 0.303-in (7.7-mm) machine-guns in wings, two or four 0.303-in (7.7-mm) guns in dorsal turret and two 0.303-in (7.7-mm) guns in ventral position, and provision to fit four or six guns to fire obliquely downwards and rearwards, plus a bombload of up to 2,000 lb (907 kg)

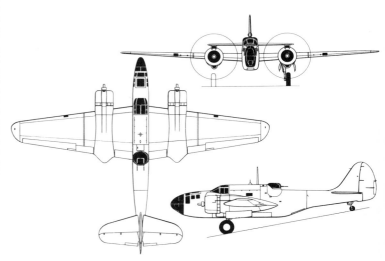

Martin Baltimore IV

Baltimore Mk III, AG837, in RAF markings; this version introduced a Boulton Paul dorsal turret in place of the manually-operated guns of the Mk I and II. All RAF Baltimores (of which 1,575 were delivered) were employed in the Mediterranean theatre.

# Martin B-26 Marauder

Marauders served on only two RAF squadrons, both in the Mediterranean theatre; the short-span Marauder Mk I depicted here flew with No. 14 Sqn in North Africa from August 1942 to September 1944. Later the long-span Marauder Mk III served on No. 39 Sqn.

Frequently associated with dangerous low-speed handling characteristics (a reflection more on inadequate training than upon faulty design), the B-26 was certainly one of the outstanding medium/light bombers of the war. Under the design leadership of Peyton M. Magruder, the Martin 179 was submitted to the US Army Board on 5 July 1939, and 1,100 aircraft were ordered just two months later. The first development B-26 was flown on 25 November 1940. Deliveries to the USAAF began in 1941, accompanied by a spate of accidents during pilot conversion. B-26As first equipped the 22nd Bomb Group, which took its new aircraft to Australia on the day that Japan attacked Pearl Harbor; the aircraft were first flown into action over New Guinea in April 1942. The B-26B introduced increased armour and improved gun armament, while later sub-variants featured increased wing span in an attempt to reduce the landing approach speed, but this was largely offset by an increase in the gross weight. A total of 1,883 B-26Bs was produced at Martin's Baltimore plant and 1,235 B-26C (similar to the B-26B) at Omaha, Nebraska. The first B-26s arrived in the UK in February 1943 but suffered heavy losses in early raids. Subsequent versions included the B-26F and B-26G with wing incidence increased by 3.5° in an attempt to improve take-off performance. Total production reached 5,157 aircraft, including some 522 which served in the RAF and SAAF in the Mediterranean. For all the difficulties encountered with its take-off and landing characteristics, the B-26 performed many outstanding daylight raids over Europe and went on to establish the lowest loss rate of any American bomber in Europe.

**Specification:** Martin B-26C Marauder
**Origin:** USA
**Type:** seven-crew medium/light bomber
**Powerplant:** two 2,000-hp (1492-kW) Pratt & Whitney R-2800-43 radial piston engines
**Performance:** maximum speed 282 mph (454 km/h) at 15,000 ft (4570 m); climb to 15,000 ft (4570 m) in 24.5 minutes; service ceiling 21,700 ft (6615 m); range 1,150 miles (1850 km)
**Weights:** empty 22,380 lb (10152 kg); maximum take-off 34,200 lb (15513 kg)
**Dimensions:** span 71 ft 0 in (21.64 m); length 58 ft 3 in (17.75 m); height 20 ft 4 in (6.20 m); wing area 658.0 sq ft (61.13 m²)
**Armament:** 12 0.5-in (12.7-mm) machine-guns disposed two in extreme nose, four forward-firing on sides of fuselage, two in dorsal turret, two in ventral position and two in tail, plus a bombload of up to 3,000 lb (1361 kg)

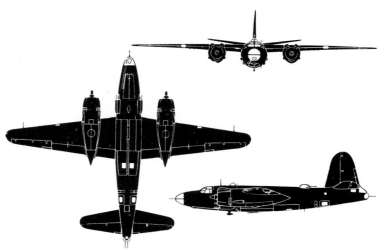

**Martin B-26 Marauder**

Though frequently criticized on account of its tricky handling qualities, the B-26 packed a heavy punch and was widely used by the USAAF in Europe. This B-26B of the 598th Bomb Squadron, 397th Bomb Wing, has had its 'invasion stripes' deliberately toned down in the interests of camouflage.

# Messerschmitt Bf 109

**Messerschmitt Bf 109E-3 flown by Hauptmann Henschel, Gruppenkommandeur, II/JG 77, which was based at Aalborg, Norway in July 1940. JG 77 at Aalborg was also involved with night-fighting using Bf 109Cs.**

## History and Notes

First flown in September 1935, Willy Messerschmitt's single-seat Bf 109 fighter saw action during the Spanish Civil War in the Bf 109B series version (Junkers Jumo 210 engine), joining the Luftwaffe in 1937 and being followed by the Bf 109C with armament increased from three to four rifle-calibre machine-guns. The Bf 109D introduced the Daimler-Benz DB 600 engine and hub-firing cannon, and was produced in 1938-9.

First major production variant was the Bf 109E with DB 601D engine and direct fuel-injection, and variations of armament between two machine-guns, and four machine-guns and one hub-cannon. Fighter-bomber and reconnaissance versions were produced during 1940. The Bf 109E was the Luftwaffe's principal fighter during 1939-40. It was followed by the Bf 109F, powered initially by the DB 601N and later the DB 601E, and introduced such equipment as nitrous-oxide power boosting, faster-firing guns (15-mm MG 151) and optional underwing gun pods. Both the Bf 109E and Bf 109F existed in tropicalized form for service in North Africa during 1941-2.

The Bf 109G, with DB 605 engine, served from 1942 until 1945 on all fronts, being built in the largest numbers and introducing armament variations which included 30-mm guns. Fastest of all was the Bf 109G-10 (429 mph/690 km/h). Final main production version was the Bf 109K with boosted versions of the DB 605. Other versions included the Bf 109H high-altitude fighter and Bf 109T shipboard fighter.

More than 33,000 Bf 109s were built between 1937 and 1945.

## Specification: Messerschmitt Bf 109G-6
**Origin:** Germany
**Type:** single-seat interceptor fighter
**Powerplant:** one 1,475-hp (1100 kW) Daimler-Benz DB 605A inline piston engine
**Performance:** maximum speed 387 mph (623 km/h) at 22,965 ft (7000 m); climb to 19,685 ft (6000 m) in 6.0 minutes; service ceiling 38,550 ft (11750 m); normal range 450 miles (725 km)
**Weights:** empty 5,952 lb (2700 kg); maximum take-off 6,944 lb (3150 kg)
**Dimensions:** span 32 ft 6½ in (9.92 m); length 29 ft 7 in (9.02 m); height 11 ft 2 in (3.40 m); wing area 172.8 sq ft (16.05 m²)
**Armament:** two nose-mounted 7.92-mm (0.31-in) MG 17 machine guns, one 30-mm Mk 108 cannon firing through propeller hub and two 20-mm MG 151/20 cannon mounted under the wings

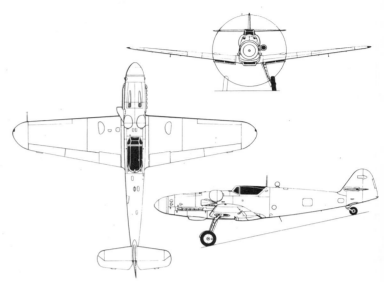

**Messerschmitt Bf 109G-14**

**The Messerschmitt Bf 109E-4 Trop fighters of 1./Jagdgeschwader 27 brought a new tactical dimension to air operations over North Africa, as they clearly outclassed all available British fighters in that theatre in spring 1941.**

# Messerschmitt Bf 110

**Messerschmitt Bf 110C of the Stabsschwarm (staff flight) of I/Zerstörergeschwader 2, based at Amiens during July 1940. The type proved itself a failure against the RAF's Spitfires and Hurricanes during the Battle of Britain.**

## History and Notes

Germany's first essay in the twin-engine two-seat 'heavy fighter' (or *Zerstörer*, destroyer) category was the Messerschmitt Bf 110, conceived in 1934 and first flown on 12 May 1936; pre-production Bf 110A-Os followed in 1937-8 with Junkers Jumo 210B engines. Production started with the Bf 110B in 1938 with Jumo 210Gs and forward armament of two 20-mm and four 7.92-mm (0.31-in) guns plus one 7.92-mm (0.31-in) gun in the rear cockpit. Daimler-Benz DB 601A-powered Bf 110Cs joined the Luftwaffe in 1939 in time for the attack on Poland, and were employed as fighters and fighter-bombers throughout 1940; the Bf 110C-5 was a reconnaissance version.

The long-range Bf 110D entered service in 1940, and sub-variants were the first Bf 110 to be employed as night-fighters; there were also tropicalized and fighter-bomber versions. The Bf 110E fighter-bomber was powered by BD 601Ns and the Bf 110F by DB 601Es.

Despite its high top speed, the Bf 110 was quickly shown to be no match for opposing single-engine fighters, and from 1941 development was confined mainly to ground-attack and night-fighter versions. The Bf 110F-4 introduced two 30-mm guns under the fuselage, and the Bf 110F-4/U1 featured twin upward-firing 20-mm guns (*schräge Musik* installation). The Bf 110G with DB 605Bs was produced in *Zerstörer*, fighter-bomber, reconnaissance and night-fighter versions, and sub-variants introduced the 37-mm gun under the fuselage. Radar-equipped Bf 110Gs formed the principal night-fighter equipment of the Luftwaffe between 1943 and 1945, as well as participating in the daylight air defence battles over Germany during this period.

**Specification:** Messerschmitt Bf 110C-4
**Origin:** Germany
**Type:** two-seat heavy fighter
**Powerplant:** two 1,100-hp (821-kW) Daimler-Benz DB 601A inline piston engines
**Performance:** maximum speed 349 mph (560 km/h) at 22,965 ft (7000 m); initial climb rate 2,165 ft (660 m) per minute; service ceiling 32,810 ft (10000 m); normal range 482 miles (775 km)
**Weights:** empty 11,464 lb (5200 kg); maximum take-off 14,881 lb (6750 kg)
**Dimensions:** span 53 ft 4¾ in (16.27 m); length 41 ft 6¾ in (12.65 m); height 11 ft 6 in (3.50 m); wing area 413.3 sq ft (38.40 m)
**Armament:** two 20-mm MG 151 cannon and four 7.92-mm (0.31-in) MG 17 guns in the nose, firing forward, and one 7.92-mm (0.31-in) MG 81Z twin gun on flexible mounting in the rear cockpit firing aft

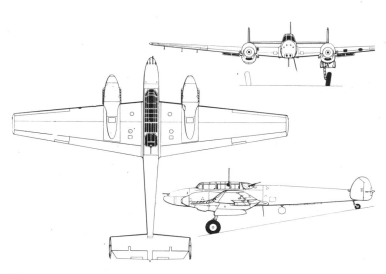

**Messerschmitt Bf 110C-3**

**Messerschmitt Bf 110F-1s (in this instance of SKG 210, wearing yellow theatre bands) were of great use to the Luftwaffe in the Mediterranean, where the type's great range and tactical flexibility proved a decided advantage.**

# Messerschmitt Bf 110

Messerschmitt Bf 110C-4/B of 9. Staffel, Zerstörergeschwader 26 'Horst Wessel', shown carrying two 551-lb (250-kg) and four 220-lb (100-kg) bombs. This unit was among the first German units to be sent to the Mediterranean, being based at Palermo at the end of 1940.

Keith Fretwell

# Messerschmitt Me 163 Komet

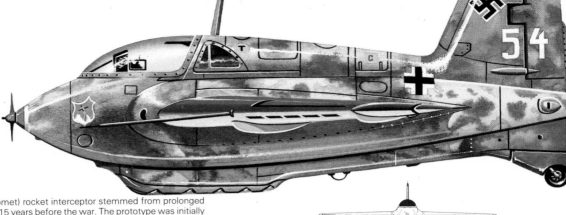

This Me 163B-1 wears the unit badge of JG 400, a rocket-powered flea. The two letter stencils on the aircraft's back denote the fuelling points for the two separate fuels (C-Stoff and T-Stoff), contact between which could result in fatal accidents.

## History and Notes

The Messerschmitt Me 163 Komet (Comet) rocket interceptor stemmed from prolonged research by Dr Alexander Lippisch over 15 years before the war. The prototype was initially test flown as a glider during the spring of 1941 before being fitted with a Walter RII-203 rocket using *T-Stoff* and *Z-Stoff* propellants. Powered flights by the Me 163 V1 started in the late summer of 1941, and on 2 October the aircraft reached 623.8 mph (1004.5 km/h); two months later the Me 163B Komet was ordered into production.

Production Me 163Bs were powered by Walter 109-509A rocket motors using *T-Stoff* (hydrogen peroxide) and *C-Stoff* (hydrazine hydrate, methyl alcohol and water) to give a thrust of 3,748 lb (1700 kg). Early Me 163B-0s were armed with a pair of 20-mm guns, but Me 163B-1s carried two 30-mm weapons. The aircraft possessed no conventional landing gear, but took off from a trolley which was jettisoned immediately after take-off.

Introduction to Luftwaffe service was a protracted and hazardous process owing to difficulties in handling the fuels and a number of fatal accidents, and only very experienced pilots were selected. Production Me 163B-1a fighters equipped I./JG 400 at Brandis, near Leipzig, in June 1944 and first intercepted B-17 Fortress daylight bombers on 16 August that year. All manner of difficulties faced the pilots, apart from the hazards already mentioned, and it was found difficult to aim and fire the guns with the result that upward-firing 50-mm shells and underwing rockets came to be developed.

Although some 300 Me 163Bs were produced (as well as a few Me 163Cs with increased fuel) and JG 400's other two *Gruppen* re-equipped by the end of 1944, only nine confirmed air victories were achieved by the *Geschwader*.

## Specification: Messerschmitt Me 163B-1a Komet

**Origin:** Germany
**Type:** single-seat interceptor fighter
**Powerplant:** one 3,748-lb (1700-kg) thrust Walter 109-509A-2 rocket motor
**Performance:** maximum speed 596 mph (960 km/h) at 9,845 ft (3000 m); initial climb rate

### Messerschmitt Me 163B Komet

11,810 ft (3600 m) per minute; service ceiling 39,700 ft (12100 m); normal range 50 miles (80 km)
**Weights:** empty 4,200 lb (1905 kg); maximum take-off 9,061 lb (4110 kg)
**Dimensions:** span 30 ft 7¼ in (9.33 m); length 18 ft 8 in (5.69 m); height 9 ft 0½ in (2.76 m); wing area 211.2 sq ft (19.62 m²)
**Armament:** two 30-mm MK 108 cannon

Operational Me 163B-1 Komets of JG 400, the only unit to fly the extraordinary little fighter. The two-wheel trolley on which the aircraft stands would be jettisoned on take-off, the Komet alighting on its skid after its short sortie.

# Messerschmitt Me 210/Me 410 Hornisse

One of the first units to receive the Messerschmitt Me 410A Hornisse (Hornet) was III Gruppe, Zerstörergeschwader 1, in May 1943. This Me 410A-1 was flown by 9. Staffel from Gerbini.

## History and Notes

Originally conceived in 1937 to replace the Bf 110, the Messerschmitt Me 210V1 prototype was first flown on 2 September 1939 with twin fins and rudders like its predecessor, and was powered by two Daimler-Benz DB 601Aa engines. Production Me 210A-1s joined the Luftwaffe in 1941 and were armed with two 20-mm forward-firing guns and two 7.92-mm (0.31-in) guns in remotely-controlled barbettes on the sides of the fuselage, firing aft. Variants included the Me 210A-2 fighter-bomber, the Me 210B-1 photo-reconnaissance aircraft and the Me 210C and Me 210D series with 1,475-hp (1100-kW) DB 605B engines.

As a result of continuing handling difficulties, development of the Me 210 was halted in 1942 and design effort was concentrated on the Me 410 Hornisse (Hornet), powered by two DB 603A engines. A prototype flew at the end of the year and was followed by Me 410A-1 light bombers armed with two 20-mm and two 7.92-mm (0.31-in) guns in the nose and two guns in the barbettes; it could also carry two 2,205-lb (1000-kg) bombs internally. Variants included the Me 410A-1/U1 photo-reconnaissance aircraft and the Me 410A-1/U4 bomber-destroyer with a single 50-mm gun (with 21 rounds) under the fuselage. The light bombers were widely used against the British Isles from 1943 onwards. The Me 410B appeared in 1944 powered by two 1,900-hp (1417-kW) DB 603G engines, and sub-variants included a torpedo fighter (the Me 410B-5) and an anti-shipping fighter (the Me 410B-6) with a forward armament of two 30-mm, and two 20-mm and two 13-mm guns as well as FuG 200 *Hohentweil* radar. Production of this excellent aircraft ceased in September 1944 after 1,160 had been produced, but the type remained in service with the Luftwaffe until the end of the war.

**Specification:** Messerschmitt Me 410A-1/U2
**Origin:** Germany
**Type:** two-seat heavy fighter
**Powerplant:** two 1,750-hp (1305-KW) Daimler-Benz DB 603A inline engines
**Performance:** maximum speed 388 mph (625 km/h) at 21,980 ft (6700 m); climb to 21,980 ft (6700 m) in 10.7 minutes; service ceiling 32,810 ft (10000 m); range 1,448 miles (2330 km)
**Weights:** empty 13,558 lb (6150 kg); maximum take-off 23,483 lb (10650 kg)
**Dimensions:** span 53 ft 7¾ in (16.35 m); length 40 ft 8½ in (12.40 m); height 14 ft 0½ in (4.28 m); wing area 389.7 sq ft (36.20 m²)
**Armament:** four 20-mm MG 151/20 and two 7.92-mm (0.31-in) MG 17 forward-firing guns, and two 13-mm (0.51-in) MG 131 machine-guns in rear remotely-controlled barbettes

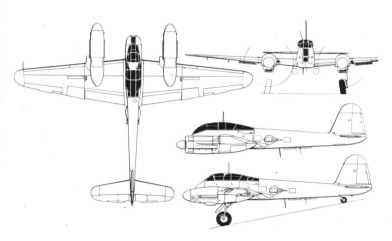

**Messerschmitt Me 410A-1 (upper view: Me 410D)**

The excellent Messerschmitt Me 410 was produced to perform a number of different duties. This Me 410A-3 of 2. Staffel, Aufklärungsgruppe 122, was based at Trapani in May 1943 for specialist photo-reconnaissance.

# Messerschmitt Me 262

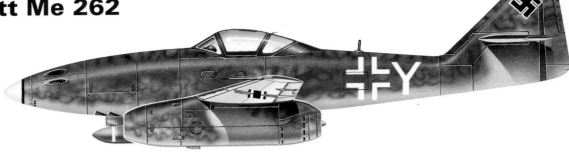

A Messerschmitt Me 262A-2a bomber. By persisting with bomber development on Hitler's direction, the Luftwaffe was deprived of this remarkable fighter until late 1944. This example served with I/KG 51 at Achmer in spring 1945.

## History and Notes

The Messerschmitt Me 262 was the world's first turbojet-powered aircraft to achieve combat status, and was the result of pre-war research with gas turbines in Germany. Design of the aircraft started in 1938 and prototype airframes were ready in 1941 but, as the Junkers jet engines were not then ready, the first flight on 18 April was made using a single Jumo 210G piston engine; it was not until 18 July 1942 that the Me 262 V3 first made an all-jet flight powered by two 1,852-lb (840-kg) thrust Junkers 109-004A-0 turbojets. Early prototypes featured tailwheel landing gear, but when production started in 1944 a tricycle arrangement had been standardized. As Hitler persisted in demanding development of the Me 262 as a bomber for reprisal raids on the UK, development of the fighter was badly delayed and it was not until late in 1944 that the aircraft entered Luftwaffe service. The Me 262A-1a Schwalbe (Swallow) fighter was armed with four 30-mm guns in the nose and joined Kommando Nowotny in October; it was followed by the Me 262A-1a/U1 with two additional 20-mm guns, the Me 262A-1a/U2 bad-weather fighter and the Me 262A-1a/U3 unarmed reconnaissance aircraft. The Me 262A-2a Sturmvogel (Stormy Petrel) bomber could carry up to 2,205 lb (1000 kg) of bombs in addition to the four 30-mm guns, and a two-seat version (with prone bomb aimer), the Me 262A-2a/U2, was also produced.

Before the end of the war Me 262s were being flown with some success against Allied bombers both as day and night fighters (the latter were radar-equipped Me 262B-1a/U1s), and air-to-air rockets were being developed. Dogged by difficulties brought on by Allied raids on factories and airfields, the Luftwaffe's jet fighter units nevertheless posed a formidable threat to Allied air superiority during the last few months of the war.

**Specification:** Messerschmitt Me 626A-1a
**Origin:** Germany
**Type:** single-seat interceptor fighter
**Powerplant:** two 1,984-lb (900-kg) thrust Junkers Jumo 109-004B-4 turbojets
**Performance:** maximum speed 541 mph (870 km/h) at 22,965 ft (7000 m); initial climb rate 3,937 ft (1200 m) per minute; service ceiling 36,090 ft (11000 m); normal range 525 miles (845 km)
**Weights:** empty 8,818 lb (4000 kg); maximum take-off 14,936 lb (6775 kg)
**Dimensions:** span 41 ft 0⅛ in (12.50 m); length 34 ft 9½ in (10.61 m); height 12 ft 6¾ in (3.83 m); wing area 233.3 sq ft (21.68 m²)
**Armament:** four 30-mm MK 108 cannon in nose

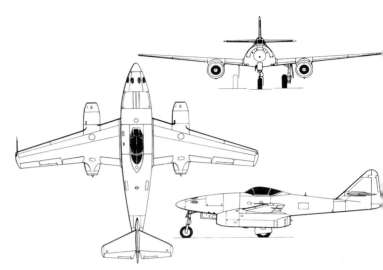

**Messerschmitt Me 262A-1a**

Me 262B-1a/U1 two-seat jet night fighter with *Lichtenstein* SN-2 radar; aircraft of this type were flown by Kommando Welter in defence of Berlin during March 1945. The aircraft shown here carries markings applied after capture by the Allies.

# Messerschmitt Me 323

Owing to its obvious vulnerability, the Me 323 was not employed as an assault aircraft but for heavy lift duties behind the front line. This Me 323E of I/TG 5 served behind the Southern Sector of the Russian Front in late 1953.

## History and Notes

Before the Messerschmitt Me 321 Gigant glider had flown in 1941 the manufacturers started work to produce a fully-powered version, the Me 323. The first prototype Me 323 V1 was powered by four 1,140-hp (850-kW) Gnome-Rhône 14N radials when it first flew in May 1942, but proved to be so badly underpowered that the Me 323 V3 was fitted with six engines of the same type. The first production version, the Me 323D-1, appeared in September 1942 and featured defensive armament of five 7.92-mm (0.31-in) guns in the nose and up to ten 7.92-mm (0.32-in) guns in the fuselage sides. Four months later the Me 323D-5 appeared with the nose guns increased to 13-mm (0.51-in) calibre; this had a crew of five and normally carried up to 130 troops, although many more could be accommodated in emergencies. Me 323DF-1s first joined Kampfgruppe zur besonderen Verwendung 323 in Sicily in November 1942, and were later joined by Me 323D-6s; they were heavily committed during the evacuation of the German forces in North Africa but suffered heavily under the guns of Allied fighters.

Later versions included the Me 323E-1 with 1,200-hp (895-kW) Gnome-Rhône 14N engines and gun turrets (each with a 20-mm gun) in the top of each wing, and the Me 323E-3 with 1,340-hp (1000-kW) Junkers Jumo engines, a nose gun turret and four 13-mm (0.51-in) guns in the rear of the inboard and outboard engine nacelles. Early in 1944 Me 323s joined I. and II./TG 5 on the Eastern Front, part of the large German air transport fleet that was employed in supplying the German armies falling back before the advancing Russians.

The Me 323, of which 198 were produced, was a remarkable aircraft capable of carrying heavy loads, but it came to be employed in conditions of enemy air superiority with resulting heavy losses, despite ever-increasing defensive armament.

**Specification:** Messerschmitt Me 323D-6
**Origin:** Germany
**Type:** heavy military transport
**Powerplant:** six 1,600-hp (1194-kW) BMW 801A radial piston engines
**Performance:** maximum speed 177 mph (285 km/h) at sea level; initial climb rate 708 ft (216 m) per minute; range 683 miles (1100 km)
**Weights:** empty 60,251 lb (27330 kg); maximum take-off 94,797 lb (43000 kg)
**Dimensions:** span 180 ft 5½ in (55.00 m); length 92 ft 4¼ in (28.15 m); height 31 ft 6 in (9.60 m); wing area 3,229.3 sq ft (300.0 m²)
**Accommodation and armament:** crew of five and accommodation for 130 fully-armed

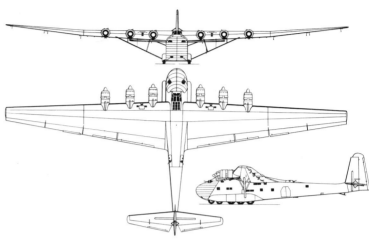

**Messerschmitt Me 323D-1**

troops or up to 35,030 lb (15890 kg) of military stores; defensive armament of five 13-mm (0.51-in) and 10 7.92-mm (0.31-in) machine-guns

**The first six-engined prototype of the Me 323 proved to have sufficient power, but performance margin was slight, necessitating still more powerful engines for production versions. Structure of this huge aircraft was steel tubing and wood, with wood and fabric covering.**

# Mikoyan-Gurevich MiG-3

A MiG-3 of the 34th Fighter Aviation Regiment, IA-PVO, based at Vnukovo, probably early in 1943. Owing to handling problems the MiG-3 was no match for German fighters such as the Bf 109G which took such a heavy toll of Soviet aircraft in the mid-war years.

## History and Notes

Gaining a reputation as a 'hot ship' in the mid-war years, Artem Mikoyan's MiG-3 was plagued by difficult handling and very poor armament, and although among the fastest of Russian fighters of that period, it proved no match for the German Bf 109G or Fw 190. Flown in prototype form as the I-61 in the spring of 1940, the initial design included the 1,200-hp (895-kW) Mikulin AM-35 inline engine, and this was retained in the production MiG-1, which started appearing in September 1940. Handicapped by the overall length of the engine which seems to have resulted in poor directional stability, and armed with only three machine-guns, the MiG-1 suffered heavily in the opening months of Operation 'Barbarossa', and the MiG-3, delivered during the second half of 1941, proved little better with a 1,350-hp (1007-kW) AM35A engine, which gave the fighter a top speed of 398 mph (640 km/h); introduced at the same time was a constant-speed propeller, increased wing dihedral and improved cockpit canopy. Handling was only marginally improved, so the MiG-3 was transferred to attack bomber escort and close support duties; in 1942 two 12.7-mm (0.5-in) machine-guns were added in underwing fairings by operational units, but gradually the aircraft was replaced by radial-engine fighters such as the La-5. Total production was said to be about 4,000, of which 2,100 were the earlier MiG-1.

**Specification:** Mikoyan MiG-3
**Origin:** USSR
**Type:** single-seat fighter
**Powerplant:** one 1,350-hp (1007-kW) Mikulin AM-35A inline piston engine
**Performance:** maximum speed 398 mph (640 km/h) at 12,880 ft (3925 m); initial climb rate 3,935 ft (1200 m) per minute; service ceiling 39,370 ft (12000 m); range 777 miles (1250 km)
**Weights:** empty 5,996 lb (2720 kg); normal loaded 7,694 lb (3490 kg)
**Dimensions:** span 33 ft 9½ in (10.30 m); length 26 ft 9 in (8.15 m); height 8 ft 9 in (2.67 m); wing area 187.7 sq ft (17.44m²)
**Armament:** one 12.7-mm (0.5-in) Beresin BS and two 7.62-mm (0.3-in) ShKAS nose-mounted machine guns (later increased by two 12.7-mm/05-in underwing guns), plus provision for six 8.2-cm (3.23-in) underwing rockets or two 220-lb (100-kg) bombs

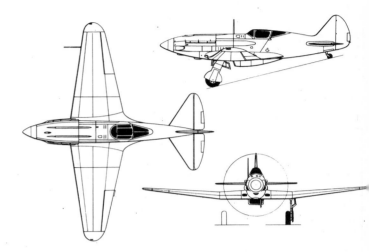

**Mikoyan-Gurevich MiG-3**

Although introduced to overcome some of the tricky handling problems in the MiG-1, the MiG-3 was always regarded as an unforgiving aeroplane, and the increased power from its Mikulin AM-35A did nothing to alleviate a vicious torque-induced swing on take-off.

# Mitsubishi J2M 'Jack'

Unusual among Japanese fighters in combining a four-cannon armament with high rate of climb, the J2M Raiden (Thunderbolt) was widely deployed for defence of the homeland against American bombing raids.

## History and Notes

Although designed to a 1939 requirement, at a time when Japanese war leaders scarcely imagined a situation requiring a home defence fighter, the Mitsubishi J2M Raiden (Thunderbolt) only came into its own while defending the Japanese homeland against American raids in the last year of the war. The Japanese navy's emphasis upon speed and climb rate, rather than its customary demands for range and manoeuvrability, prompted the designer Jiro Hirikoshi to adopt a squat single-engine design with long-chord radial engine cowling, laminar-flow wings and high-raked, curved windscreen. First flight of the prototype J2M1 took place on 20 March 1942, but the aircraft soon attracted criticism from navy pilots on numerous counts, not least that the view from the cockpit was inadequate. Modifications to rectify these shortcomings were delayed owing to Mitsubishi's preoccupation with the A6M. Production J2M2s left the factory slowly and entered service with the 381st Kokutai late in 1943, and were followed by the J2M3 with a stronger wing stressed to mount four 20-mm cannon. The heavier armament now restricted the performance of the Raiden to the extent that it no longer met the original demands, and the J2M4 was an attempt to restore the performance by including a turbocharger. The final production variant, the J2M5 (34 built), was powered by a 1,820-hp (1358-kW) Mitsubishi Kasei 26a radial. In all, 476 J2Ms were built. In acknowledgement of the fact that J2Ms could not combat the B-29s at their operating altitudes, some J2M3s were armed with two upward-firing 20-mm cannon in addition to their wing guns. (The Allies selected the reporting name 'Jack' for the J2M.)

**Specification:** Mitsubishi J2M3 'Jack'
**Origin:** Japan
**Type:** single-seat fighter
**Powerplant:** one 1,800-hp (1343-kW) Mitsubishi Kasei 23a radial piston engine
**Performance:** maximum speed 365 mph (588 km/h) at 17,390 ft (5300 m); climb to 32,810 ft (10000 m) in 19.5 minutes; service ceiling 38,385 ft (11700 m); range 575 miles (925 km)
**Weights:** empty 5,423 lb (2460 kg); normal loaded 7,573 lb (3435 kg)
**Dimensions:** span 35 ft 5¼ in (10.80 m); length 32 ft 7½ in (9.95 m); height 12 ft 11¼ in (3.95 m); wing area 215.82 sq ft (20.05 m²)
**Armament:** four wing-mounted 20-mm Type 99 cannon; some aircraft also armed with two upward-firing 20-mm Type cannon

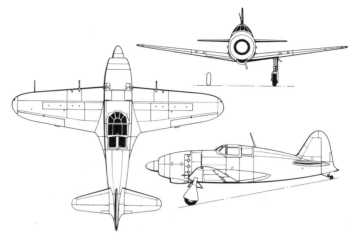

Mitsubishi J2M3 'Jack'

Shown here carrying a fuselage-mounted drop tank, the J2M3 had a useful range of 1,180 miles (1899 km), though largely superfluous in its eventual defensive role; codenamed 'Jack', it was nevertheless much respected by Allied pilots.

# Mitsubishi Ki-21 'Sally'

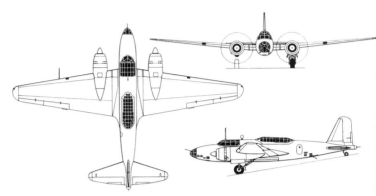

A Ki-21-IIb with 12.7-mm (0.5-in) heavy machine-gun in a dorsal turret; aircraft of this type were used on Japanese suicide commando-style attacks against American bases in the Pacific in the closing months of the war.

## History and Notes

Although acknowledged by the Japanese as approaching obsolescence at the beginning of the Pacific war, the Mitsubishi Ki-21 'heavy' bomber (or by British and American standards of the time, a light/medium bomber) remained in production until 1944 and was still in service one year later. Designed to a 1936 requirement, the first Ki-21 made its maiden flight on 18 December the same year, and when the 60th and 61st Sentais arrived in China with their Ki-21-Is late in 1938 it could be said that the first stage in the Japanese army air force's modernization programme had been completed. However, bearing in mind the lack of effective fighter opposition, the army authorities were aware that in the context of a war with the USA and UK the Ki-21 would be vulnerable to fighter attack and, late in 1939, Mitsubishi was instructed to improve the bomber's performance, with the result that by the beginning of the Pacific war the early 850-hp (634-kW) Ha-6 radials had been replaced by 1,500-hp (1119-kW) Ha-101 engines in much larger nacelles. The new version, the Ki-21-II (codenamed 'Sally' by the Allies) was produced in two forms, the Ki-21-IIa retaining the large 'greenhouse' with hand-held 7.7-mm (0.303-in) gun in the rear dorsal position, and the Ki-21-IIb having the 'greenhouse' replaced by a turret mounting a 12.7-mm (0.5-in) gun. Despite fast accelerating losses to Allied fighters from 1942 onwards, Ki-21 units remained operational almost to the end of the war, a total of 777 Ki-21-Is and 1,278 Ki-21-IIs being built by Mitsubishi and Nakajima.

**Specification:** Mitsubishi Ki-21-IIb 'Sally'
**Origin:** Japan
**Type:** five-crew heavy bomber
**Powerplant:** two 1,500-hp (1119-kW) Mitsubishi Ha-101 radial piston engines
**Performance:** maximum speed 302 mph (486 km/h) at 15,485 ft (4720 m); climb to 19,685 ft (6000 m) in 13.2 minutes; service ceiling 32,810 ft (10000 m); range 1,680 miles (2700 km)
**Weights:** empty 13,382 lb (6070 kg); maximum take-off 23,391 lb (10610 kg)
**Dimensions:** span 73 ft 9¾ in (22.50 m); length 52 ft 5⅞ in (16.00 m); height 15 ft 10⅞ in (4.85 m); wing area 749.2 sq ft (69.60 m²)
**Armament:** single flexible 7.7-mm (0.303-in) Type 89 machine-guns in nose, ventral, tail and beam positions, and one 12.7-mm (0.5-in) Type 1 machine-gun in dorsal turret, plus a normal bombload of 1,653 lb (750 kg), or a maximum bombload of 2,205 lb (1000 kg)

**Mitsubishi Ki-21 'Sally'**

Originally codenamed 'Jane' by the Allies, after General MacArthur's wife (a compliment not appreciated), the Ki-21 was hurriedly re-named 'Sally', and was employed by the Japanese throughout the Pacific war. A total of 2,064 was built by Mitsubishi and Nakajima.

# Mitsubishi A6M 'Zeke'

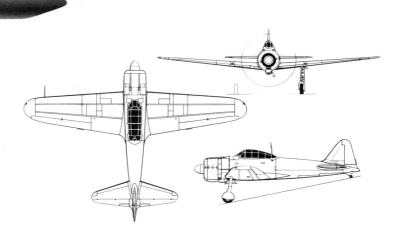

The A6M3 was powered by a two-stage supercharged Sakae 21 engine and featured reduced-span wings; the aircraft depicted here served with the 251st Kokutai on Kyushu, Japan, late in 1942 and is shown with a 330-litre (72.6 Imp gal) centreline drop tank.

## History and Notes

The famous A6M, popularly known as the 'Zero', was the first carrierborne fighter in the world capable of outperforming any contemporary land-based fighter it was likely to confront. Because of inept Allied intelligence it was able to achieve immediate air superiority over the East Indies and South East Asia from the day Japan entered the war. Designed under the leadership of Jiro Horikoshi in 1937 as a replacement for the neat but obsolescent A5M, the prototype A6M1 was first flown on 1 April 1939 with a 780-hp (582-kW) Mitsubishi Zuisei 13 radial; production A6M2s with two wing-mounted 20-mm guns and two nose-mounted 7.7-mm (0.303-in) guns were fitted with the 950-hp (709-kW) Nakajima Sakae 12 radial, and it was with this version that the Japanese navy escorted the raiding force sent against Pearl Harbor, and gained air superiority over Malaya, the Philippines and Burma. In the spring of 1942 the A6M3 with two-stage supercharged Sakae 21 entered service, later aircraft having their folding wing tips removed. The Battle of Midway represented the Zero-Sen's combat zenith; thereafter the agile Japanese fighter found itself ever more outclassed by the American F6F Hellcat and P-38 Lightning. To counter the new American fighters the A6M5 was rushed to front-line units; this version, with Sakae 21 engine and improved exhaust system, possessed a top speed of 351 mph (565 km/h), more A6M5s (and sub-variants) being produced than any other Japanese aircraft. It was five A6M5s of the Shikishima kamikaze unit that sank the carrier *St Lo* and damaged three others on 25 October 1944. Other versions were the A6M6 with water-methanol boosted Sakae 31 engine, and the A6M7 fighter/dive-bomber. Total production of all A6Ms was 10,937. (The reporting name 'Zeke' was given to the A6M, and 'Rufe' to a float version, the A6M2-N.)

**Specification:** Mitsubishi A6M5b 'Zeke'
**Origin:** Japan
**Type:** single-seat fighter
**Powerplant:** one 1,100-hp (821-kW) Nakajima NK2F Sakae 21 radial piston engine
**Performance:** maximum speed 351 mph (565 km/h) at 19,685 ft (6000 m); climb to 19,685 ft (6000 m) in 7.0 minutes; service ceiling 38,520 ft (11740 m); range 710 (1143 km)
**Weights:** empty 4,136 lb (1876 kg); normal loaded 6,025 lb (2733 kg)
**Dimensions:** span 36 ft 1 in (11.00 m); length 29 ft 11⅛ in (9.12 m); height 11 ft 6⅛ in

**Mitsubishi A6M2 'Zeke'**

(3.51 m); wing area 229.27 sq ft (21.30 m²)
**Armament:** one 7.7-mm (0.303-in) Type 97 and one 13.2-mm (0.52-in) Type 3 machine-gun in nose, and two wing-mounted 20-mm Type 99 cannon, plus underwing provision for two 132- or 551-lb (60- or 250-kg) bombs

**Fatally underestimated by the Allies at the outbreak of the Pacific war, the Zero-Sen ran circles round RAF Hurricane and Buffalo fighters in Malaya prior to the fall of Singapore. The late A6M5 version, seen here, was captured intact by the Americans in 1944.**

# Mitsubishi A6M Reisen

The subject of this illustration was one of the rare late-war stop-gap variants which tried to stem the tide of Allied air power until the A7M Reppu could be cleared for production. An A6M5c of the 210th Kokutai, it combined the non-folding rounded wingtips and thick wing skins, separate exhaust stacks and other improvements of the basic A6M5 (Model 52) with heavier firepower from two 13.2-mm (0.52-in) guns added in the wings outboard of the cannon. Most had better protection, with rear armour and self-sealing wing tanks, but the crucial fault of inadequate power was not rectified and only 93 of this model were built. Note the absence of a white border to the Hinomaru insigne.

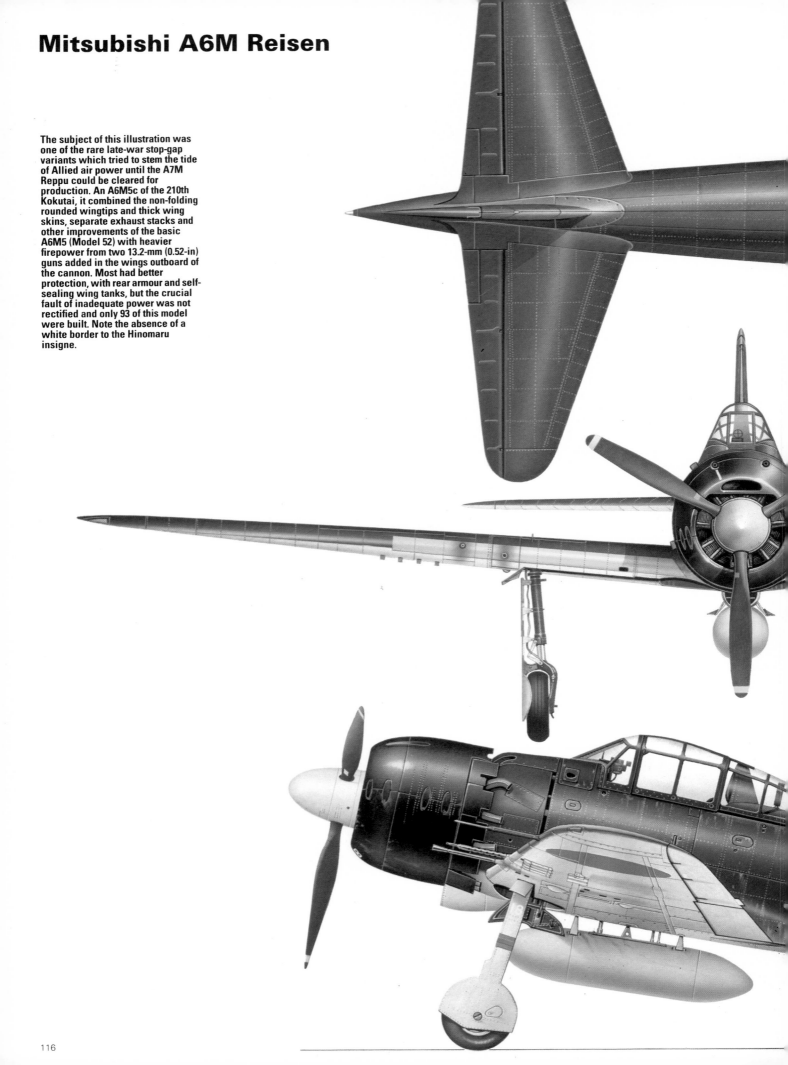

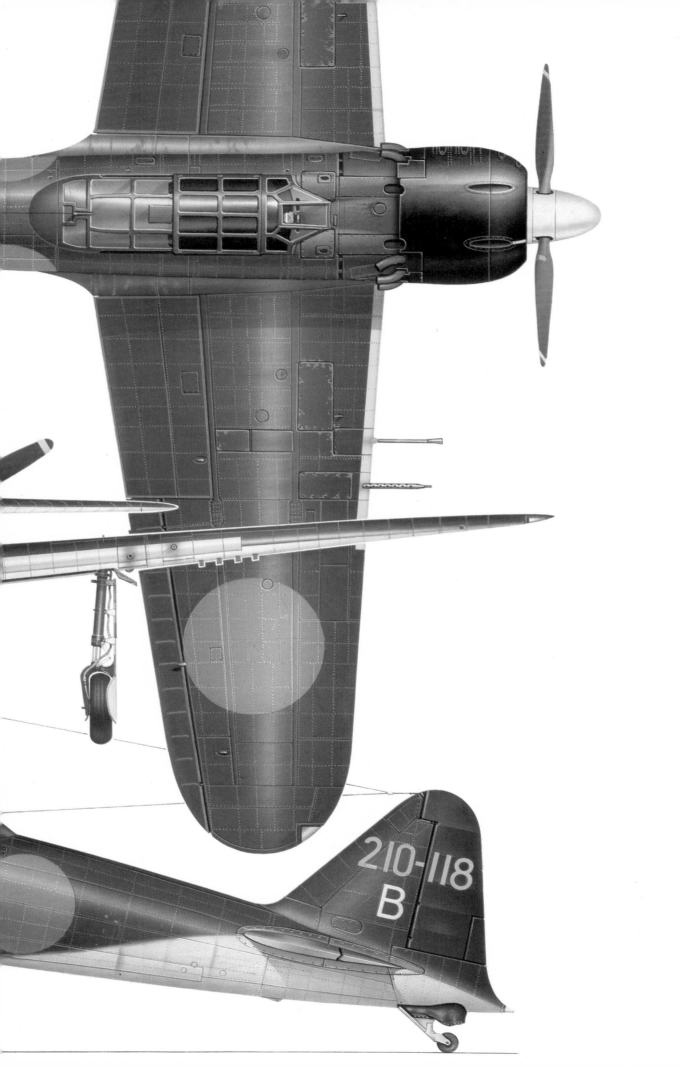

# Mitsubishi G4M 'Betty'

Identified by its dihedral tailplane, the Mitsubishi G4M3 was produced in limited numbers during the last two years of the war. Portrayed here is an aircraft of the Yokosuka Kokutai, Atsugi, as it appeared in September 1945.

## History and Notes

Codenamed 'Betty' by the Allies, the Mitsubishi G4M long-range medium bomber remained in service with the Japanese navy from the first to the last day of the war; it took part in the attack that sank the British warships HMS *Prince of Wales* and HMS *Repulse* in December 1941 – and carried the Japanese surrender delegation on 19 August 1945. Designed to a 1937 requirement for a long-range bomber, the G4M1 prototype made its first flight on 23 October 1939, and during trials recorded an extraordinary performance of 276 mph (444 km/h) top speed and 3,450-mile (5555-km) range – albeit without bombload. The first production G4M1s were initially deployed against China in mid-1941 but on the eve of the attack on Malaya the bombers moved to Indo-China and within a week had successfully attacked the *Prince of Wales* and *Repulse*. When Allied fighter opposition eventually increased to effective proportions, the G4M1 was seen to be very vulnerable, possessing little armour protection for crew and fuel tanks, and it was in a pair of G4M1s that Admiral Yamamoto and his staff were travelling when shot down by P-38s over Bougainville on 18 April 1943. The G4M2 was therefore introduced with increased armament, increased fuel and 1,800-hp (1343-kW) Mitsubishi Kasei radials, and this version remained in production until the end of the war. A further improved version, the G4M3, with increased crew protection, was also produced in small numbers. Production amounted to 1,200 G4M1s, 1,154 G4M2s and 60 G4M3s.

## Specification: Mitsubishi G4M2 'Betty'

**Origin:** Japan
**Type:** seven-crew land-based naval bomber
**Powerplant:** two 1,800-hp (1343-kW) Mitsubishi MK4P Kasei 21 radial piston engines
**Performance:** maximum speed 272 mph (438 km/h) at 15,090 ft (4600 m); climb to 26,245 ft (8000 m) in 32.4 minutes; service ceiling 29,365 ft (8950 m); range 3,765 miles (6059 km)
**Weights:** empty 17,990 lb (8160 kg); normal loaded 27,558 lb (12500 kg)
**Dimensions:** span 82 ft 0¼ in (25.00 m); length 67 ft 7⅞ in (20.00 m); height 19 ft 8¼ in (6.00 m); wing area 840.93 sq ft (78.125 m²)
**Armament:** two 7.7-mm (0.303-in) Type 92 machine-guns in nose, one 7.7-mm (0.303-in) Type 92 machine-gun in each side blister position, one 20-mm Type 99 cannon in dorsal turret and one 20-mm Type 99 in tail, plus 2,205 lb (1000 kg) of bombs or one 1,764-lb (800-kg) torpedo

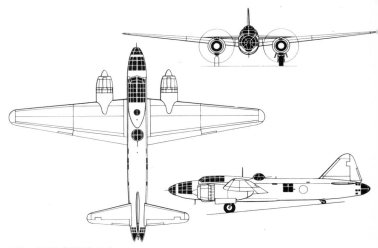

Mitsubishi G4M 'Betty'

The Mitsubishi G4M came to be widely used in the Pacific war from beginning to end. This example, believed to be a G4M2e, is seen carrying an Ohka suicide bomb, a version that saw action during the last six months of the war.

# Mitsubishi Ki-46 'Dinah'

With extensively redesigned nose and Ha-112 radials, the excellent Ki-46-III entered service late in 1943, delivery priority being given to war fronts where the Allies had gained air superiority, on account of its good performance. Shown is an aircraft of the 19th Dokuritsu Dai Shijugo Chutai which was based in Japan at the end of the war.

## History and Notes

The attractive Ki-46 two-seat reconnaissance aircraft was designed during 1938 under the direction of Tomio Kubo, who produced a twin-engine low-wing monoplane with slim fuselage and straight-tapered wings and tail surfaces. When first flown in November 1939 the prototype Ki-46, powered by Ha-26-I engines of only 900-hp (670-kW), returned a speed of 335 mph (529 km/h) – faster than the navy's new Zero-Sen fighter. With the adoption of two-stage supercharged Ha-102 radials of 1,080-hp (806-kW) the production Ki-46-II, which began coming off the production line in March 1941, was capable of a speed 375 mph (604 km/h), well beyond the capabilities of any Allied fighter when Japan entered the war. Indeed a Ki-46-II was flown on clandestine sorties without interference over Malaya before the outbreak of war to reconnoitre the proposed invasion areas. Many months later, in anticipation of the arrival of Spitfire Mk Vs and P-38s in the Pacific theatre, the Ki-46-III (codenamed 'Dinah' by the Allies) was introduced with improved nose shape, fuel injection and revised exhaust system to give some thrust augmentation, these modifications increasing the top speed to 391 mph (630 km/h). Operating at heights over 30,000 ft (9145 m), the aircraft maintained a watch over the USAAF bases for B-29s in the Marianas, but eventually suffered mounting losses with the arrival of the excellent P-47N fighter from the USA. Although by no means as adaptable as the British Mosquito or American P-38, the Ki-46 must be regarded as one of the best reconnaissance aircraft of the Pacific war. Production of the Ki-46-II reached 1,093, and that of the Ki-46-III 609.

**Specification:** Mitsubishi Ki-46-III 'Dinah'
**Origin:** Japan
**Type:** two-seat reconnaissance aircraft
**Powerplant:** two 1,500-hp (1119-kW) Mitsubishi Ha-112-II radial engines
**Performance:** maximum speed 391 mph (630 km/h) at 19,685 ft (6000 m); climb to 26,250 ft (8000 m) in 20.25 minutes; service ceiling 34,450 ft (10500 m); range 2,485 miles (4000 km)
**Weights:** empty 8,446 lb (3831 kg); maximum take-off 14,330 lb (6500 kg)
**Dimensions:** span 48 ft 2¾ in (14.70 m); length 36 ft 1 in (11.00 m); height 12 ft 8¾ in (3.88 m); wing area 344.44 sq ft (32.00 m²)
**Armament:** two 20-mm Ho-5 forward-firing cannon in nose

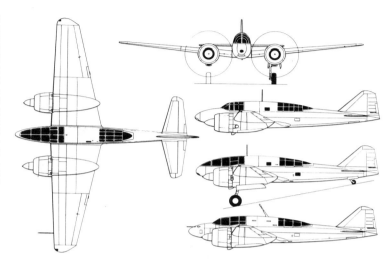

**Mitsubishi Ki-46-III 'Dinah' (upper view: Ki-46-II, lower view: Ki-46-III Kai)**

Codenamed 'Dinah' by the Allies, the Ki-46 was an attractive aircraft which was widely used by the Japanese in numerous roles. The example shown here was a Ki-46-II which served with the 81st Sentai, 2nd Chutai, probably in 1942.

# Mitsubishi Ki-67 'Peggy'

So pleased were the Japanese (particularly the army) with the Ki-67 that it was ordered into mass production at Mitsubishi, Kawasaki and Tachikawa, but only 698 aircraft were finally built – the Japanese aircraft and engine plants being heavily damaged by American B-29 raids in the last months of the war.

## History and Notes

Like the Ki-21 and G4M, the Ki-67 was classified by the Japanese as a heavy bomber, yet by Western standards would have scarcely rated the medium bomber category. It was nevertheless the best bomber to serve Japan in the war, albeit too late to influence the tide of events of the last year. By then the American air raids on the Japanese homeland were devastating aircraft plants and production was seriously affected. The Ki-67 Hirya (Flying dragon) was designed to a 1940 Specification, issued in 1941, for a strategic bomber intended for use in an anticipated war with the Soviet Union on the Siberia-Manchukuo border. By departing from established Japanese practice and including armour protection and self-sealing fuel tanks, design of the prototype Ki-67 was protracted, and it was not until 27 December 1942 that the first aircraft flew; it proved to be highly manoeuvrable and pleasant to fly, and possessed a top speed of 334 mph (538 km/h). In the same month it was decided to adapt some Ki-67s as torpedo-bombers. The army put forward such a host of suggestions for additional equipment that production suffered long delays, and it was not until October 1944 that the Ki-67 (codenamed 'Peggy' by the Allies) was first flown in combat by the 7th and 98th Sentais, and by the navy's 762nd Kokutai in the torpedo role during the battle off Formosa. Thereafter modifications were held to a minimum as production was afforded the highest priority; but by then American raids (and a devastating earthquake in December 1944) severely disrupted production, and no more than 698 Ki-67s were produced, some of them being flown in kamikaze strikes in the last months of the war.

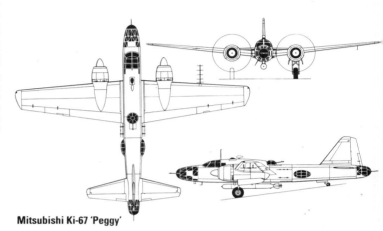

Mitsubishi Ki-67 'Peggy'

## Specification: Mitsubishi Ki-67 'Peggy'
**Origin:** Japan
**Type:** six/eight-crew heavy bomber
**Powerplant:** two 1,900-hp (1417-kW) Mitsubishi Ha-104 radial piston engines
**Performance:** maximum speed 334 mph (537 km/h) at 19,980 ft (6090 m); climb to 19,685 ft (6000 m) in 14.5 minutes; service ceiling 31,070 ft (9470 m); range 1,740 miles (2800 km)
**Weights:** empty 19,068 lb (8649 kg); normal loaded 30,347 lb (13765 kg)
**Dimensions:** span 73 ft 9¾ in (22.50 m); length 61 ft 4¼ in (18.70 m); height 25 ft 3⅛ in (7.70 m); wing area 708.8 sq ft (65.85 m²)
**Armament:** single flexible 12.7-mm (0.5-in) Type 1 machine-guns in nose, two beam positions and tail, and one 20-mm He-5 cannon in dorsal turret, plus a bombload of 1,764 lb (800 kg) or one 2,359-lb (1070-kg) torpedo, or 6,393-lb (2900-kg) of bombs for kamikaze mission

Although classified as a heavy bomber (by Japanese standards), the Ki-67 was closer to the American B-26 Marauder medium bomber in concept. It was probably the best of all army and navy bombers but arrived in service too late to influence the Pacific war. This Ki-67-Ib belonged to the 98th Sentai, 3rd Chutai.

# Morane-Saulnier MS.406

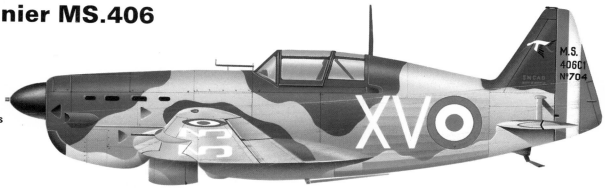

Outdated in 1940 and hopelessly outclassed by the modern Luftwaffe aircraft flown against them in the Battle of France, the MS.406 equipped 14 Groupes de Chasse at the time of the German attack on 10 May. The aircraft shown here carries the stork emblem of GC I/2 based at Toul/Ochey.

## History and Notes

Most numerous of French fighters at the time of Germany's attack in the West in 1940, the MS.406 was a curious anomaly in having been ordered into production in 1937 when its performance was already notably far below that of current British and German fighters. Moreover, its complicated development within the MS.405-411 family was as wasteful of effort as it was counterproductive. The prototype MS.406 was in fact the fourth development MS.405 and first flew on 20 May 1938 with 860-hp (642-kW) Hispano-Suiza 12Y31 and 'moteur-canon', typifying the continental practice of using a hub-firing cannon to avoid the need to synchronize its fire. By April 1938 orders totalling 955 MS.406s had been placed for completion by September 1939, but in the event only 572 had been produced by that date. At the outbreak of war these aircraft equipped five *groupes de chasse* at Chartres and Dijon, plus two in Algeria; 29 aircraft had been shipped to Tunisia and 10 to Indo-China. By 10 May 1940 the number of combat-ready MS.406s had actually dropped from 367 to 278, a situation quickly aggravated by the loss of 37 aircraft on the ground at Cambrai, Damblain, Vitry and Le Quesnoy on the first day. The MS.406 quickly proved to be outclassed in the air and during the Battle of France about 150 were lost in combat (plus some 100 on the ground). The aircraft's inferiority was acknowledged and by the time of the Armistice conversion to other aircraft was already being undertaken by 10 MS.406 *groupes*.

**Specification:** Morane-Saulnier MS.406
**Origin:** France
**Type:** single-seat fighter
**Powerplant:** one 860-hp (642-kW) Hispano-Suiza HS 12Y 31 inline piston engine
**Performance:** maximum speed 304 mph (490 km/h) at 14,765 ft (4500 m); climb to 19,685 ft (6000 m) in 9.0 minutes; service ceiling 32,810 ft (10000 m); range 684 miles (1100 km)
**Weights:** empty 4,178 lb (1895 kg); normal loaded 5,600 lb (2540 kg)
**Dimensions:** span 34 ft 9½ in (10.62 m); length 26 ft 9⅓ in (8.17 m); height 10 ft 8½ in (3.25 m); wing area 172.2 sq ft (16.00 m²)
**Armament:** one 20-mm HS404 hub-firing cannon and two 7.5-mm (0.295-in) MAC 1934 machine-guns in the wings

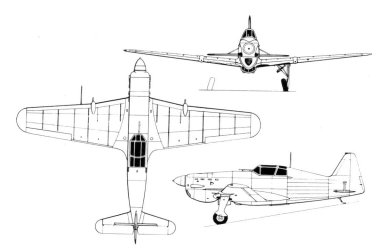

Morane-Saulnier MS.406C-1

Despite the tragedy being enacted in Metropolitan France in May 1940, numerous Armée de l'Air units remained deployed overseas in the French Empire. These MS.406s belonged to a well-trained Groupe de Chasse, GC 1/7, based at Rayack, Syria.

# Nakajima B5N 'Kate'

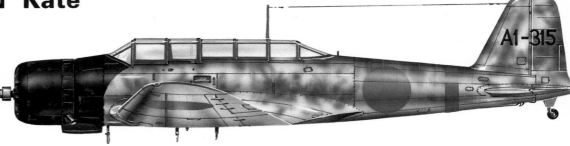

Most modern naval attack aircraft in service at the beginning of the Pacific war, the B5N delivered the attack at Pearl Harbor, carrying torpedoes specially adapted to run in shallow waters; also used as a conventional bomber, the aircraft shown here is however equipped with torpedo crutches.

## History and Notes

Designed to a 1935 requirement, and already in service for four years when Japan entered the war, the Nakajima B5N was in 1941 without question the best carrierborne torpedo-bomber in the world. Powered by a Nakajima Hikari radial engine, the low-wing three-crew monoplane with inwards-retracting, wide-track landing gear was exceptionally clean, and first flew in January 1937. The following year production B5N1s were embarking in Japan's carriers as shore-based units were deployed in China. In 1939 the improved B5N2 appeared with a more powerful Sakae 11 engine in a smaller cowling, although armament and bombload remained unchanged, and this version remained in production until 1943. When Japan attacked the USA the B5N2 had wholly replaced the B5N1 with operational units, and 144 B5N2s were involved in the fateful attack on Pearl Harbor; within the next 12 months aircraft of this type sank the American carriers USS *Hornet*, USS *Lexington* and USS *Yorktown*. Given the reporting name 'Kate' by the Allies, the B5N certainly earned the respect of the Americans, and in all the major carrier battles of the Pacific War attracted the undivided attention of defending fighters. With its puny defensive armament of a single machine-gun and laden with a large bomb or torpedo, however, the B5N began to suffer very heavily, and although they were fully committed during the Solomons campaign the survivors were withdrawn from combat after the Philippine battles of 1944. Thereafter, on account of their excellent range, they were assigned to anti-submarine and maritime reconnaissance duties in areas beyond the range of Allied fighters. Production of all B5Ns reached 1,149.

## Specification: Nakajima B5N2 'Kate'
**Origin:** Japan
**Type:** three-crew carrierborne torpedo-bomber
**Powerplant:** one 1,000-hp (746-kW) Nakajima NK1B Sadae 11 radial piston engine
**Performance:** maximum speed 235 mph (378 km/h) at 11,810 ft (3600 m); climb to 9,845 ft (3000 m) in 7.7 minutes; service ceiling 27,100 ft (8260 m); range 1,237 miles (1990 km)
**Weights:** empty 5,024 lb (2279 kg); maximum take-off 9,039 lb (4100kg)
**Dimensions:** span 50 ft 10⅞ in (15.52 m); length 33 ft 9½ in (10.30 m); height 12 ft 1⅝ in (3.70 m); wing area 405.8 sq ft (37.70 m²)
**Armament:** one 7.7-mm (0.303-in) Type 92 flexible machine-gun in rear cockpit, plus one 1,764-lb (800-kg) torpedo or an equivalent weight of bombs

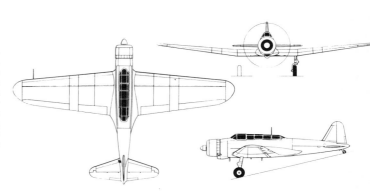

**Nakajima B5N2 'Kate'**

A pair of Sakae-powered B5N2s in flight over ships of the Imperial Japanese Navy; codenamed 'Kate' by the Allies, this was the version that delivered the fatal blows against the American carriers USS *Hornet, Lexington* and *Yorktown* in 1942.

# Nakajima Ki-43 'Oscar'

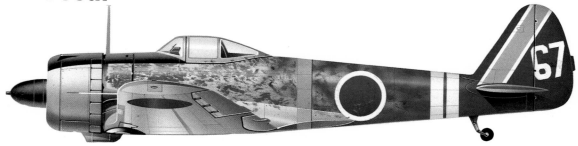

A Ki-43-IIa Hayabusa (Peregrine Falcon) of the 2nd Chutai, 25th Fighter Sentai, a unit that fought in China during 1944 and until about March 1945. First flown early in 1939 it was hopelessly outclassed by American fighters by the last two years of the war.

## History and Notes

With its relatively low-powered radial engine, two-blade propeller and twin rifle-calibre machine-gun armament, the Ki-43 Hayabusa (Peregrine falcon) was the most dangerously underestimated Japanese fighter of the early months of the Pacific war; yet flown by Japanese army air force pilots, it gained complete mastery over Brewster Buffaloes and Hawker Hurricanes in Burma. It was the result of a 1937 design which emerged as a lightweight fighter-bomber that required no more than its 950-hp (709-kW) to meet its speed demands. In common with other Japanese fighters of the time, however, its armament was puny by RAF standards, and possessed neither armour nor self-sealing fuel tanks. As the Allied air forces pulled themselves together after the first shock of defeat, the Ki-43-I's weaknesses were discovered and increasing losses suffered, resulting in the introduction of the Ki-43-II (codenamed 'Oscar' by the Allies), with pilot armour, rudimentary self-sealing fuel tanks and reflector gunsight; the engine was also changed to the 1,150-hp (858-kW) Nakajima Ha-115 radial which increased the top speed to 329 mph (530 km/h), roughly the same as that of the Hurricane Mk II. The Ki-43-IIb entered mass production in November 1942, first with Nakajima and six months later with Tachikawa. Final variant was the Ki-43-III with 1,230-hp (918-kW) engine and a top speed of 358 mph (576 km/h), but relatively few examples reached operational units. The Ki-43 was numerically the most important of all Japanese army air force aircraft, production totalling 5,886, plus 33 prototypes and trials aircraft.

**Specification:** Nakajima Ki-43-IIb 'Oscar'
**Origin:** Japan
**Type:** single-seat fighter-bomber
**Powerplant:** one 1,150-hp (858-kW) Nakajima Ha-115 radial piston engine
**Performance:** maximum speed 329 mph (530 km/h) at 13,125 ft (4000 m); climb to 16,405 ft (5000 m) in 5.8 minutes; service ceiling 36,750 ft (11200 m); range 1,095 miles (1760 km)
**Weights:** empty 4,211 lb (1910 kg); maximum take-off 6,450 lb (2925 kg)
**Dimensions:** span 35 ft 6¾ in (10.84 m); length 29 ft 3¼ in (8.92 m); height 10 ft 8¾ in (3.27 m); wing area 230.37 sq ft (21.40 m²)
**Armament:** two 12.7-mm (0.5-in) Ho-103 machine-guns in wings, plus two 250-kg (551-lb) bombs carried under the wings

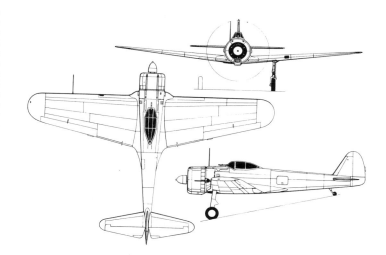

**Nakajima Ki-43-I-Ko 'Oscar'**

The yellow fin bar identifies this Ki-43-IIa as belonging to the 3rd Chutai, 25th Fighter Sentai. Despite its obvious inferiority, the Hayabusa was available in such large numbers that it continued to be widely deployed right up to the end of the war.

# Nakajima B6N 'Jill'

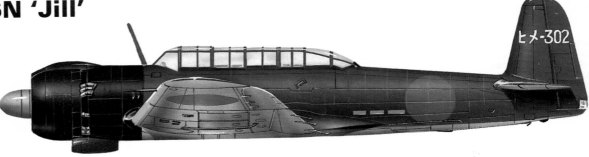

A B6N2 of the type that entered service in the last 18 months of the war, after American fighters had gained almost universal air superiority; codenamed 'Jill', they were used with limited effect for kamikaze attacks during the Okinawa campaign.

## History and Notes

At a time when the triumphs of the B5N were still almost three years in the future, the Japanese navy issued a specification for a replacement, recognizing that only limited overall design improvement of the B5N could be achieved in the B5N2. Accordingly design went ahead in 1939 of the B6N and, despite the navy's preference for the Mitsubishi Kasei radial, a Nakajima Mamoru was selected for the prototype which flew early in 1941. Superficially the B6N Tenzan (Heavenly Mountain) resembled the earlier aircraft, but the much increased power and torque of the big engine and four-blade propeller was found to impose considerable directional stability problems, demanding that the vertical tail surfaces be offset to one side. Flight trials dragged on, and were further delayed by troubles during carrier acceptance tests; then Nakajima was ordered to stop production of the Mamoru engine, so modifications had to be introduced to suit installation of the Kasei. In due course B6N1s (of which only 133 were built) were embarked in the carriers *Shokaku*, *Taiho*, *Hiyo*, *Junyo* and *Zuikaku*, and took part in the great Battle of the Philippine Sea of June 1943, many being lost when the three first-named carriers were sunk. In that month production started of the slightly improved B6N2 (of which 1,133 were produced before the end of the war), but the heavy losses among Japanese carriers resulted in the 'Jill' being largely deployed ashore, particularly after the Battle of Leyte Gulf. Thereafter many B5Ns were consigned to the kamikaze role.

**Specification:** Nakajima B6N2 'Jill'
**Origin:** Japan
**Type:** three-crew carrier-borne torpedo bomber
**Powerplant:** one 1,850-hp (1380-kW) Mitsubishi MK4T Kasei 25 radial piston engine
**Performance:** maximum speed 299 mph (481 km/h) at 16,075 ft (4900 m); climb to 16,405 ft (5000 m) in 10.4 minutes; service ceiling 29,660 ft (9040 m); range 1,085 miles (1746 km)
**Weights:** empty 6,636 lb (3010 kg); maximum take-off 12,456 lb (5650 kg)
**Dimensions:** span 48 ft 10⅜ in (14.89 m); length 35 ft 7½ in (10.87 m); height 12 ft 5⅝ in (3.80 m); wing area 400.42 sq ft (37.20 m²)
**Armament:** one flexible 13-mm (0.51-in) Type 2 machine-gun in rear cockpit and one 7.7-mm (0.303-in) Type 97 machine-gun in ventral tunnel position, plus one 1,764-lb (800-kg) torpedo or an equivalent weight of bombs

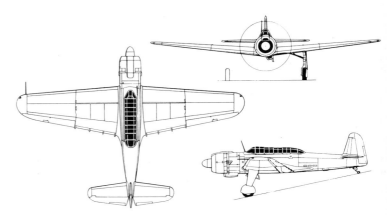

Nakajima B6N2 'Jill'

Nakajima B6N1 Tenzan (Heavenly Mountain) fitted with a Mamoru 11 radial of 1,870 hp (1394 kW); when production of this engine was prematurely suspended, Nakajima opted to switch to the 1,850-hp (1379-kW) Mitsubishi Kasei 25.

# Nakajima Ki-49 'Helen'

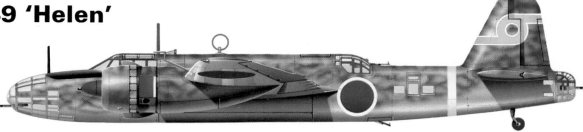

Much improved by the installation of more powerful Ha-109 engines, the Ki-49-II also featured heavier machine gun armament; the aircraft shown served with the 3rd Chutai, 62nd Sentai, in Burma, the Dutch East Indies and New Guinea during 1944.

## History and Notes

The Ki-49 was intended to replace the Ki-21, which had entered service in 1938, and although the Ki-49 certainly included modern design features it proved a disappointment in service, representing a great deal of aeroplane to carry a crew of eight and a maximum bombload of only 2,205 lb (1000 kg) over a sortie radius of not much more than 500 miles (800 km). Design started in 1938 and the first prototype made its maiden flight in August 1939 with a pair of 1,080-hp (806-kW) Ha-5 radials. Production Ki-49-I Donryu (Storm dragon) bombers started delivery to the Japanese army air force in August 1941 and by the end of the year the 61st Sentai was partially equipped. Codenamed 'Helen' by the Allies, the Ki-49-I was first flown on operations over China, and later over New Guinea, taking part in a number of raids over Australia's Northern Territory. The Ki-49 was relatively unusual among Japanese bombers early in the war in including armour protection for the crew as well as self-sealing fuel tanks, features which made the aircraft fairly popular with its crews, yet despite its top speed of around 300 mph (483 km/h) and well-distributed gun armament it proved very vulnerable to Allied fighters and losses mounted quickly from mid-1942 onwards. In the Ki-49-II, the first of which entered service at the end of 1942, most of the 7.7-mm (0.303-in) guns were replaced by 12.7-mm (05-in) weapons, and the 1,250-hp (933-kW) Ha-41 radials gave place to 1,500-hp (1119-kW) Ha-109s. Although this was the major production version it never wholly replaced the veteran Ki-21, and in the last year of the war Ki-49-IIs were diverted for use as night-fighters (operating in pairs, one aircraft with a searchlight, the other with a 75-mm cannon), as transports and in suicide attacks at Mindoro in December 1944. Production amounted to 23 prototypes and development aircraft, and 796 production examples.

**Specification:** Nakajima Ki-49-IIa 'Helen'
**Origin:** Japan
**Type:** eight-crew heavy bomber
**Powerplant:** two 1,500-hp (1119-kW) Nakajima Ha-109 radial piston engines
**Performance:** maximum speed 306 mph (492 km/h) at 16,405 ft (5000 m); climb to 16,405 ft (5000 m) in 13.6 minutes; service ceiling 30,510 ft (9300 m); range 1,243 miles (2000 km)
**Weights:** empty 14,396 lb (6530 kg); maximum take-off 25,133 lb (11400 kg)
**Dimensions:** span 67 ft 0⅛ in (20.42 m); length 54 ft 1⅝ in (16.50 m); height 13 ft 11¼ in (4.25 m); wing area 743.25 sq ft (69.05 m²)

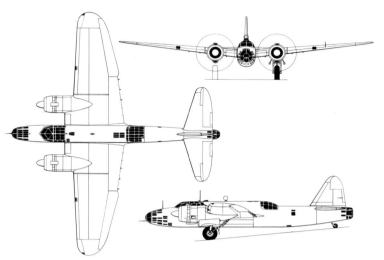

**Nakajima Ki-49 'Helen'**

**Armament:** (Ki-49-IIb) single 12.7-mm (0.5-in) Ho-103 machine-guns in nose, ventral and tail positions, single 7.7-mm (0.303-in) Type 89 machine-guns in two beam positions and one 20-mm Ho-1 cannon in dorsal position, plus a maximum bombload of 2,205 lb (1000 kg)

**The Ki-49 Donryu was just starting delivery to the Japanese army air force when the Pacific war started. The early Ki-49-I, shown here, was criticized by Service crews as being tricky to handle and possessing a disappointing performance.**

# Nakajima Ki-84 'Frank'

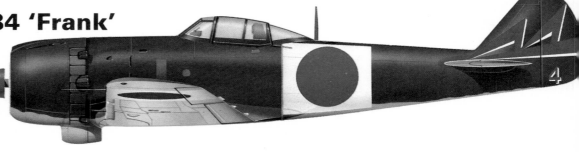

Bearing the blue spinner and tail markings of the 1st Chutai, 47th Sentai, this Ki-84-I was based at Narumatsu, Japan, for home defence in 1945. Late production aircraft such as this proved to be well-matched in performance with contemporary American escort fighters.

## History and Notes

Best of all Japanese fighters available in quantity during the last year of the war, the Ki-84 Hayate (Gale) not only possessed a reasonable performance but – unusual among Japanese aircraft – carried a powerful armament capable of knocking down the heavily armed and armoured American bombers. Not flown in prototype form until April 1943, the Ki-84 met with immediate approval by Japanese army air force pilots, but was subjected to lengthy service trials which undoubtedly delayed its introduction to combat operations. Production got underway at Nakajima's Ota plant in April 1944, pre-production aircraft having equipped the 22nd Sentai in China the previous month. Immediately afterwards 10 Sentais of the Ki-14-I, codenamed 'Frank' by the Allies, were deployed in the Philippines to confront the advancing American forces. In an effort to accelerate production of the excellent new fighter, Nakajima opened up a new line at its Otsonomiya plant, and as the American B-29 raids began to take their toll of Japanese cities a new 'bomber destroyer', the Ki-84-Ic, was produced with an armament of two nose-mounted 20-mm cannon and two wing-mounted 30-mm cannon. Some measure of the importance attached to the Ki-84 may be judged by the fact that in the last 17 months of war 3,382 aircraft were completed, this despite the tremendous havoc wrought by the B-29 raids and the fact that, owing to such damage at Musashi, Nakajima's engine plant had to be transferred elsewhere.

**Specification:** Nakajima Ki-84-Ia 'Frank'
**Origin:** Japan
**Type:** single-seat fighter and fighter-bomber
**Powerplant:** one 1,800-hp (1343-kW) Nakajima Ha-45 radial piston engine
**Performance:** maximum speed 392 mph (631 km/h) at 20,080 ft (6120 m); climb to 16,405 ft (5000 m) in 5.9 minutes; service ceiling 34,450 ft (10500 m); range 1,053 miles (1695 km)
**Weights:** empty 5,864 lb (2660 kg); maximum take-off 8,576 lb (3890 kg)
**Dimensions:** span 36 ft 10½ in (11.24 m); length 32 ft 6¼ in (9.92 m); height 11 ft 1¼ in (3.39 m); wing area 226.04 sq ft (21.00 m²)
**Armament:** two nose-mounted 12.7-mm (0.5-in) Ho-103 machine-guns and two wing-mounted 20-mm Ho-5 cannon, plus two 250-kg (551-lb) bombs under the wings

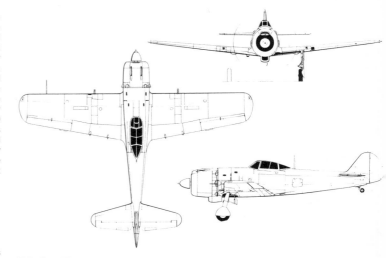

**Nakajima Ki-84 'Frank'**

A Ki-84-I of the 104th Sentai which was equipped with these fighters in November 1944 in Manchuria, and remained operational until the end of the war. American pilots spoke highly of these aircraft when subsequently evaluated in the United States.

# North American P-51 Mustang

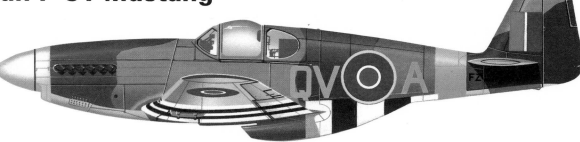

A Mustang Mk III of No. 19 (Fighter) Sqn, RAF, based at Ford at the time of the great Normandy landings of June 1944; many RAF Mustangs were fitted with a bulged sliding canopy, known as the Malcolm hood.

## History and Notes

One of the truly great fighters of the war, the P-51 was originally designed in 1940 to a British requirement which stipulated the construction of a prototype within 120 days, use of an inline engine and an armament of eight machine-guns. The prototype NA-73 was first flown in October that year with a 1,100-hp (820-kW) Allison V-1710-F3F but, although two early aircraft were evaluated by the USAAF as XP-51s, the type was not adopted by that air force. Most of the early aircraft were supplied to the RAF (620 aircraft as Mustang Mk IAs and Mk IIs), but their poor performance prevented their use as fighters, relegating them instead to use in the ground support (army co-operation) role. After the USA's entry into the war the USAAF adopted the aircraft, ordering 148 P-51s which, for the same reason as in the RAF, entered service with wing bomb shackles in the attack category as the A-36A. The British in the meantime had re-engined four Mustangs with Rolls-Royce Merlins, and this expedient transformed the aircraft. In America the armament was reduced to four 0.5-in (12.7-mm) guns and a 1,200-hp (895-kW) Allison V-1710-81 was used in the P-51A, 310 being ordered in 1942. So spectacular were the benefits of the Merlin that a Packard-built Merlin (as the V-1650) was used in the P-51B, of which 1,988 were produced at Inglewood; 1,750 of the similar P-51C were built at Dallas, Texas. Later aircraft had the armament restored to six guns, while increased fuel capacity extended the range to a maximum of 2,080 miles (3347 km), enabling Mustangs to escort American bombers to Berlin. The P-51D featured a cut-down rear fuselage and 'tear-drop' canopy. The Merlin P-51 joined the RAF as the Mustang Mk III (P-51B and P-51C) and Mustang Mk IV (P-51D). Fastest of all versions was the lightened P-51H with a top speed of 487 mph (784 km/h), 555 being built during the war. Total production of the P-51 was 15,586, including 7,956 P-51Ds and 1,337 generally similar P-51Ks with an Aeroproducts propeller.

**Specification:** North American P-51D (Mustang Mk IV)
**Origin:** USA
**Type:** single-seat long-range fighter
**Powerplant:** one 1,490-hp (1112-kW) Packard Rolls-Royce Merlin V-1650-7 inline piston engine
**Performance:** maximum speed 437 mph (704 km/h) at 25,000 ft (7620 m); climb to 30,000 ft (9145 m) in 13.0 minutes; service ceiling 41,900 ft (12770 m); maximum range 2,080 miles (3347 km)
**Weights:** empty 7,125 lb (3232 kg); maximum take-off 11,600 lb (5262 kg)

**North American P-51D (Mustang Mk IV)**

**Dimensions:** span 37 ft 0¼ in (11.28 m); length 32 ft 3¼ in (9.85 m); height 12 ft 2 in (3.71 m); wing area 233.2 sq ft (21.65 m²)
**Armament:** six 0.5-in (12.7-mm) machine-guns in the wings, plus provision for up to two 1,000-lb (454-kg) bombs or six 5-in (127-mm) rocket projectiles

**Considered by many to be the war's best escort fighter, the P-51D possessed sufficient range to enable it to accompany American heavy bombers all the way from Britain to Berlin and back. Its Packard-built Rolls-Royce Merlin transformed it from mediocrity to excellence.**

Resplendent in colourful personal liveries and black and white invasion stripes (carried by many Allied aircraft after the 1944 Normandy landings), these USAAF P-51Ds represented the pinnacle of wartime long-range fighter design and a brilliant marriage of American airframe with British engine.

# North American B-25 Mitchell

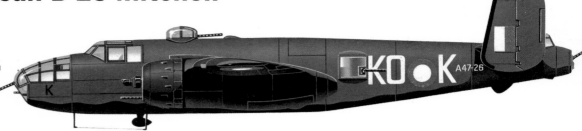

The Mitchell served with numerous Allied air forces during the war. The majority of B-25Js flew in the South-West Pacific theatre, and this 12-gun aircraft is shown in the markings of the Royal Australian Air Force.

## History and Notes

About 11,000 Mitchells were produced during the war, of which the USAAF received a total of 9,816, the RAF 700 and the Soviet Union others. Initially flown on 19 August 1940, the first B-25 was completed with full-wing dihedral but inadequate directional stability led to a reduction of dihedral outboard of the engines in later aircraft, producing the gull-wing appearance that was to characterize the Mitchell. B-25As started arriving with the 17th Bomb Group in 1941, and were followed by 120 B-25Bs with increased gun armament, this version joining the RAF as the Mitchell Mk I. It was also B-25Bs that, led by Lieutenant Colonel James H. Doolittle, made the famous raid on Tokyo having taken off from the carrier *Hornet* in April 1942. The B-26C and B-26D versions with much increased all-up weight and extra fuel capacity were produced at Inglewood, California (1,619 built), and at Dallas, Texas (2,290 built) respectively. The B-25G introduced the standard US Army 75-mm field gun, this weapon being mounted in the nose, and although 405 aircraft were produced, the version was inferior to the B-25H which featured the lighter T-13E1 75-mm gun as well as no fewer than 14 0.5-in (12.7-mm) machine-guns. A return to the previous 'bomber' nose was made in the most-produced B-25J version, although it retained the four 'package' guns on the sides of the fuselage. In the final months of the war, when B-25Js flew low-level raids with diminishing fighter opposition, the bomb aimer was discarded, and eight machine-guns mounted in a 'solid' nose, as well as eight 5-in (127-mm) rocket projectiles under the wings.

## Specification: North American B-25J Mitchell
**Origin:** USA
**Type:** six-crew medium/light bomber
**Powerplant:** two 1,700-hp (1268-kW) Wright R-2600-92 radial piston engines
**Performance:** maximum speed 272 mph (438 km/h) at 13,000 ft (3960 m); climb to 15,000 ft (4570 m) in 17.5 minutes; service ceiling 24,200 ft (7375 m); range 1,350 miles (2173 km)
**Weights:** empty 19,480 lb (8836 kg); maximum take-off 35,000 lb (15876 kg)
**Dimensions:** span 67 ft 7 in (20.60 m); length 52 ft 11 in (16.13 m); height 16 ft 4 in (4.98 m); wing area 610.0 sq ft (56.67 m²)
**Armament:** 12 0.5-in (12.7-mm) machine-guns disposed two in extreme nose, four forward-firing on sides of fuselage, two in dorsal turret, one in each beam position and two in tail, plus eight 5-in (127-mm) underwing rockets and a 3,000-lb (1361-kg) bombload

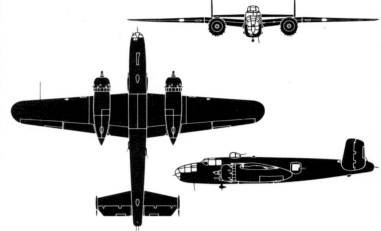

**North American B-25J Mitchell**

Famous for its brilliant raid on Tokyo led by Lieutenant-Colonel Jimmie Doolittle in 1942, the B-25 light bomber was a sound design, well liked by its crews. The B-25D, seen here, was built at a North American factory at Kansas City.

# Northrop P-61 Black Widow

A Northrop P-61B Black Widow in full warpaint. This version could carry four 1,600-lb (726-kg) bombs or two 300-gallon (1363-litre) drop tanks under the wings, and eventually replaced all the interim Douglas P-70 night fighters in service with the USAAF.

## History and Notes

Despite the advances made by the night bomber since the earliest years of military aviation, the concept of a specialist night-fighter was almost universally ignored up to 1940, and nowhere more so than in the United States. Spurred by events in Europe and encouraged by early British experiments with airborne radar, the US Army accepted proposals by Northrop in 1940 for a large twin-engine twin-boom night-fighter. The prototype of this, the XP-61, flew for the first time on 21 May 1942 and was named the Black Widow. Thirteen YP-61s were followed by 200 production P-61As; armed with four 20-mm cannon under the nose and four 0.5-in (12.7-mm) machine-guns in a remotely-controlled dorsal turret (the latter omitted after the first 37 aircraft), the P-61A featured AI radar (developed from British equipment by the Massachusetts Institute of Technology), and obtained its first 'kill' with the 18th Fighter Group in the Pacific theatre on 7 July 1944. The P-61B, strictly speaking a night intruder, started entering service that month, capable of carrying four 1,600-lb (726-kg) bombs, and the final 250 aircraft of the order for 400 had the four-gun turret reinstated. This version was in service with the USAAF night-fighter squadrons in Europe in August 1944. Final wartime version was the P-61C (of which 41 were produced), powered by two 2,800-hp (2090-kW) R-2800-73 engines. The Black Widow proved a devastating weapon in the Far East during the last year of the war, several squadrons being deployed in India and China for the defence of the newly-created B-29 bases.

## Specification: Northrop P-61B Black Widow
**Origin:** USA
**Type:** three-crew night-fighter/intruder
**Powerplant:** two 2,000-hp (1492-kW) Pratt & Whitney R-2800-65 radial piston engines
**Performance:** maximum speed 366 mph (589 km/h) at 20,000 ft (6095 m); climb to 20,000 ft (6095 m) in 12.0 minutes; service ceiling 33,100 ft (10090 m); range 1,590 miles (2559 km)
**Weights:** empty 22,000 lb (9980 kg); maximum take-off 38,000 lb (17240 kg)
**Dimensions:** span 66 ft 0 in (20.12 m); length 49 ft 7 in (15.11 m); height 14 ft 8 in (4.46 m); wing area 664.0 sq ft (61.69 m²)
**Armament:** four fixed forward-firing 20-mm cannon under the nose and four 0.5-in (12.7-mm) guns in remotely-controlled dorsal turret, plus a bombload of four 1,600-lb (726-kg) bombs or eight 5-in (127-mm) rockets under the wings

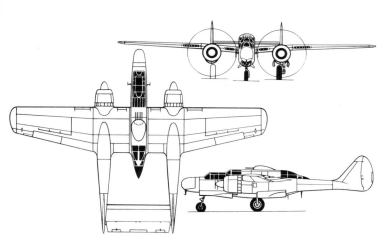

**Northrop P-61B-20 Black Widow**

The big Black Widow was the USAAF's first purpose-designed, radar-equipped night fighter and entered service in mid-1944. This P-61A was one of the early aircraft built before the dorsal turret was temporarily deleted from the production line.

# Petlyakov Pe-2

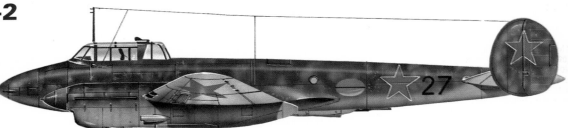

Often referred to as the 'Russian Mosquito', the Pe-2 was certainly a most versatile combat aircraft, the interceptor fighter version having a maximum speed of 408 mph (657 km/h). The bomber could carry up to 6,600 lb (2993 kg) of bombs.

## History and Notes

Regarded with some disdain by ill-informed Western observers during the war, the Pe-2 was superior to, and certainly more successfully adaptable than such aircraft as the Blenheim, Boston and Ventura. Designed by Vladimir Petlyakov's bureau, the prototype VI-100 was powered by two Klimov inline engines (developed from Hispano-Suiza designs) and flew in 1939 as a high-altitude heavy fighter. Successful negotiation of its state trials in January 1940 was followed by production of the Pe-2 in June that year, the aircraft being adapted as a shallow-dive attack bomber with dive-brakes added under the wings. With its top speed of 336 mph (540 km/h) it proved a fairly difficult adversary for the German fighters of 1941, but with the advent of the Bf 109G casualties began to increase, and in 1943, as production was rapidly extended in the Soviet Union, new versions with the 1,260-hp (940-kW) M-105PF engine, increased armament, additional armour and self-sealing fuel tanks appeared. With a top speed of 360 mph (580 km/h) this represented an effective battlefield support aircraft. Numerous air regiments were flying the Pe-2 as an attack bomber, the Pe-21 heavy fighter, the Pe-2R long-range reconnaissance aircraft, and the Pe-3bis reconnaissance fighter; final production versions were powered by 1,600-hp (1194-kW) M-107A engines which bestowed a top speed of 408 mph (657 km/h). Total production reached 11,400 before ending in 1945, although the Pe-2 derivatives remained in service for some years afterwards. A dual-control trainer, the Pe-2U, was also produced in the mid-war years.

## Specification: Petlyakov Pe-2
**Origin:** USSR
**Type:** three-crew attack bomber
**Powerplant:** two 1,260-hp (940-kW) M-105PF inline piston engines
**Performance:** maximum speed 360 mph (580 km/h) at 9,845 ft (3000 m); initial climb rate 1,410 ft (430 m) per minutes; service ceiling 28,870 ft (8800 m); range 721 miles (1160 km)
**Weights:** empty 12,952 lb (5875 kg); maximum take-off 18,728 lb (8495 kg)
**Dimensions:** span 56 ft 3½ in (17.16 m); length 41 ft 6½ in (12.66 m); height 11 ft 6 in (3.50 m); wing area 436.0 sq ft (40.5 m²)
**Armament:** two fixed forward-firing 12.7-mm (0.5-in) UBS machine-guns, one 12.7-mm (0.5-in) UBT machine-gun in dorsal turret, one 12.7-mm (0.5-in) UBT machine-gun in ventral position, and two 7.62-mm (0.3-in) ShKRS beam guns, plus a bombload of 2,205 lb (1000 kg), later increased to 6,614 lb (3000 kg)

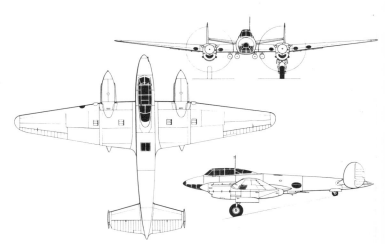

**Petlyakov Pe-2 (early production)**

High level bombing was never a forte of the Soviet air forces and in the bombing role the Pe-2 was confined largely to medium level and dive-bombing, proving to be an elusive target for German fighters when used in the ground support and attack roles.

# Potez 63

It had always been assumed that the Potez 63.11 reconnaissance aircraft would operate under fighter protection, but this seldom proved possible during the Battle of France, more than one in three of the 700 delivered being shot down in two months.

## History and Notes

The short operational history of the French Potez 63 series is one of the most dramatic of any aircraft of the war, not so much on account of its design excellence but for the magnificent courage of its crews and the magnitude of its part in the Battle of France in 1940. The type also served in far greater numbers than any other French aircraft. Conceived to a 1934 requirement for a combined fighter director/day attack and night-fighter, the prototype Potez 630-01 first flew on 25 April 1936 and immediately displayed all the shortcomings of design compromise. Disorganization, reorganization and amalgamation in the French aircraft industry delayed production of the aircraft, but by the outbreak of war 379 examples of five versions were in service, albeit already approaching obsolescence; these were the Potez 630 and Potez 631 two/three-crew day and night fighters, Potez 633 two-seat light bombers, Potez 637 three-crew reconnaissance aircraft and Potez 63.11 three-crew army co-operation aircraft. Owing to their superficial resemblance to the German Bf 110 there were numerous occasions when they were attacked by RAF and French fighters. Deliveries continued at an increasing rate after the beginning of the war, and by 10 May 1940 equipped numerous fighter, bomber, reconnaissance and army co-operation units of the Armée de l'Air, as well as fighter squadrons of the Aéronavale. In the face of superior German fighter opposition they were called on to perform all manner of operations, suffering appalling loss. By the armistice only 663 (251 of them in North Africa) survived from a total of 1,115 delivered, roughly 400 having been lost in combat. Some of the survivors served in the Vichy air force in France, North Africa and Syria, and the Germans seized 134 aircraft, of which 53 were sent to Romania as trainers. Total production of the whole Potez 63 series was 1,395, including a number of undelivered Potez 63.11 aircraft seized by the Germans and flown by the Luftwaffe.

## Specification: Potez 631
**Origin:** France
**Type:** two/three-crew day and night-fighter
**Powerplant:** two 700-hp (522-kW) Gnome-Rhône 14 M4/MS radial piston engines
**Performance:** maximum speed 275 mph (442 km/h) at 14,765 ft (4500 m); climb to 13,125 ft (4000 m) in 5.9 minutes; range 758 miles (1220 km)
**Weights:** empty 5,401 lb (2450); normal loaded 8,289 lb (3760 kg)
**Dimensions:** span 52 ft 6 in (16.00 m); length 36 ft 4 in (11.07 m); height 11 ft 10½ in (3.62 m); wing area 351.98 sq ft (32.70 m²)

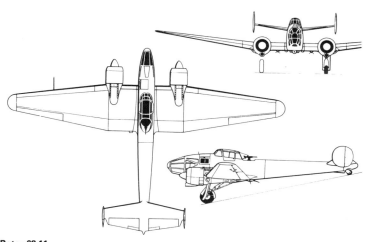

**Potez 63.11**

**Armament:** two fixed forward-firing 20-mm HS404 cannon and one flexible 7.5-mm (0.295-in) MAC 1934 machine-gun in rear cockpit, plus (optionally) four 7.5-mm (0.295-in) MAC 1934 machine-guns in underwing packs

A Potez 63.11 of the Free French Flight No. 2 in Libya; it still bears the tail insignia of 2e Escadrille, GR II/39 which had escaped after the collapse of France in June 1940.

# PZL P-11

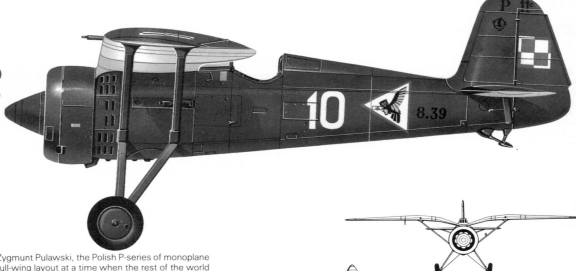

Bearing the marking of No. 113 (Owls) Sqn, this P-11C was also one of the 1st Air Regiment's aircraft during the Polish campaign of September 1939. After about a week's fighting orders were given for all unit insignia to be painted over.

## History and Notes

Initiated by the talented designer Ing. Zygmunt Pulawski, the Polish P-series of monoplane fighters was characterized by a high gull-wing layout at a time when the rest of the world was still engrossed with wringing the last performance drops out of the biplane formula. The series entered service with the Polish air force in the form of the initial P-7a during the winter of 1932-3. Production of the P-7 series amounted to 153 aircraft powered by the 485-hp (362-kW) Skoda-built Bristol Jupiter VIIF radial and typical performance included a speed of about 170 mph (274 km/h) at sea level. But by the time the P-7 was in service, Pulawski had moved on to more refined things, and the prototype P-11/I first flew in September 1931. The first production version was the P-11b and this, powered by the 525-hp (392-kW) IAR-built Gnome-Rhône 9K radial, entered service in 1935. Developments then produced the P-11F with Gnome-Rhône 9Krse radial, and the P-11a and P-11c with the Skoda-built Bristol Mercury VI or Mercury VIS.2 radials. When Germany invaded Poland in September 1939 the Polish fighter arm had 128 P-11 aircraft deployed in six regiments. The P-11 pilots fought with great gallantry, but their aircraft were totally outmoded by the Bf 109 and losses amounted to 46 PZL fighters in the first three days of the campaign. Production of the P-11 series amounted to some 330 aircraft of all versions, and about 300 of the improved P-24 series had been produced for export.

## Specification: PZL P-11c

**Origin:** Poland
**Type:** single-seat interceptor fighter
**Powerplant:** one 645-hp (481-kW) Skoda-built Bristol Mercury VIS.2 radial piston engine
**Performance:** maximum speed 242 mph (390 km/h) at 18,050 ft (5500 m); climb to 16,405 ft (5000 m) in 6.0 minutes; service ceiling 26,250 ft (8000 m); range 435 miles (700 km)
**Weights:** empty 2,529 lb (1147 kg); maximum take-off 3,968 lb (1800 kg)

### PZL P-11

**Dimensions:** span 35 ft 2 in (10.72 m); length 24 ft 9¼ in (7.55 m); height 9 ft 4½ in (2.85 m)
**Armament:** two forward-firing 7.7-mm (0.303-in) KM Wz33 machine-guns

Seen during a goodwill visit to Sweden in 1936, these PZL P-11 fighters belong to No. 114 (Fighting Cocks) Sqn. In the campaign of 1939 this squadron was assigned to the 1st Air Regiment, Defence of Warsaw. The parasol fighter, though flown bravely, was no match for the Luftwaffe's Messerschmitts.

# PZL P-23 Karas

A P-23 of No. 42 (Bomber) Sqn, Army Pomorze. Restricted by their subordination to local army command, these bomber squadrons lost much of their value while awaiting suitable targets at a time when they could have reinforced forces in hard-pressed areas elsewhere.

## History and Notes

Probably not significantly inferior to the Fairey Battle fielded by the RAF and Belgian air force, the PZL P-23 Karas (Crucian Carp) was a single-engine light bomber designed to meet the tactical requirements of the Polish army. The basic design was more than adequate, but the type's operational capabilities foundered on lack of power once the Bristol Pegasus had been specified. First flown in August 1934 as the P-23/I prototype with the 590-hp (440-kW) Pegasus IIM.2, the Karas entered service in June 1936 as the P-23a with the same engine. So low was performance with payload, however, that all 40 aircraft were soon converted to dual-control trainers. The first true operational variant was thus the P-23b, which had been evolved by way of the P-23/III third prototype re-engined with the 680-hp (507-kW) Pegasus VIII. The P-23b was the major production model, some 210 being built. The type entered service in 1937, and in September 1939 some 150 were operational in 12 squadrons of the Polish air force: five in the Bomber Brigade, and the other seven as reconnaissance units attached to the army staffs involved in trying to stem the rapid German advance. In 16 days about 112 P-23b bombers were lost, all but 22 in aerial combat. Much better capability was offered by the P-43 developed version, which was powered by the 970-hp (724-kW) Gnome-Rhône 14 NO 1. But all 54 P-43 aircraft were ordered by Bulgaria, though none were for a short period retained by Poland.

**Specification:** PZL P-23b Karas
**Origin:** Poland
**Type:** three-crew light bomber
**Powerplant:** one 680-hp (507-kW) PZL-built Bristol Pegasus VIII radial piston engine
**Performance:** maximum speed 186 mph (300 km/h) at 6,560 ft (2000 m); climb to 6,560 ft (2000 m) in 4.75 minutes; service ceiling 23,950 ft (7300 m); range 782 miles (1260 km)
**Weights:** empty 4,250 lb (1928 kg); normal loaded 7,716 lb (3400 kg)
**Dimensions:** span 45 ft 9¼ in (13.95 m); length 31 ft 9¼ in (9.68 m); height 10 ft 10 in (3.30 m); wing area 288.5 sq ft (26.80 m²)
**Armament:** one forward-firing 7.7-mm (0.303-in) KM Wz33 machine-gun and single 7.7-

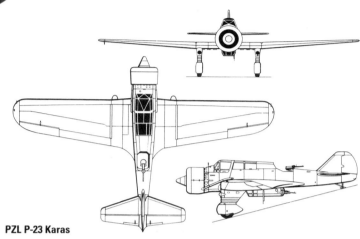

**PZL P-23 Karas**

mm (0.303-in) Vickers 'F' machine-guns in the dorsal position and ventral gondola, plus a bombload of 1,543 lb (700 kg)

A total of 118 PZL P-23 Karas reconnaissance bombers was available to the Polish air force on 1 September 1939. This aircraft flew with No. 22 (Bomber) Sqn of the Bomber Brigade, a unit which participated in the series of effective raids against the German 10th Army Group's armoured divisions between 4 and 8 September.

# Reggiane Re.2000

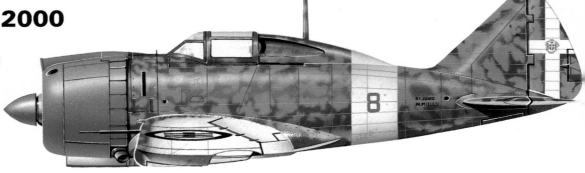

Almost all the 170 Re.2000s produced went to foreign air forces, namely those of Sweden and Hungary. Nevertheless one of those flown by the Regia Aeronautica was this Re 2000 GA Series IIIa of the 377ª Squadriglia Autonomo based at Palermo in March 1942.

## History and Notes

Desperately handicapped by the lack of an indigenous inline engine suitable for fighter aircraft, Italian aircraft designers before the war were obliged to persevere with second-rate radial engines, and the Re.2000 was ample manifestation of this handicap; indeed it represented only a marginal improvement over the Macchi C.200. The prototype Re.2000 was flown by de Bernadi on 24 May 1939. As production got under way the Italian government cancelled its order, with the result that Reggiane decided to complete the first 188 aircraft at private expense so as to offer for export an off-the-shelf fighter (and it was an astonishing fact that the UK negotiated an order for a batch in January 1940, and this was 'approved' by Germany). In the event 70 aircraft were purchased by Hungary, these aircraft being designated Re.2000 Series I. As soon as Italy entered the war the government order was reinstated, none being delivered to the UK. Being the only aircraft readily adaptable to accommodate extra fuel, the Re.2000 was selected to fly direct from Italy to East Africa to cover the Italian colonies, but swiftly changing fortunes in the theatre put paid to this plan. First deliveries to the Regia Aeronautica were to the 3° Stormo in Sicily in 1941, the Re.2000 Series I aircraft being mainly confined to home defence. Only 10 Re.2000 Series III aircraft, converted for catapult launching from Italian warships, were delivered. Elsewhere the Re.2000 enjoyed longer service; in Hungary it entered licence production by MAVAG, 192 being built under the name Heja and serving with the 1/1 and 2/4 Squadrons of the Hungarian 2nd Air Brigade at Szolnok and Kolozsvar on the Russian front. A total of 60 Re.2000s was also supplied to Sweden, where the type served as the J 20 with the Flygvapen. Total production of the Re.2000 (including those in Hungary) was 380, plus two prototypes.

## Specification: Reggiane Re.2000 Series I
**Origin:** Italy
**Type:** single-seat fighter
**Powerplant:** one 985-hp (735-kW) Piaggio PXI RC 40 radial piston engine
**Performance:** maximum speed 329 mph (530 km/h) at 16,405 ft (5000 m); climb to 13,125 ft (4000 m) in 4.5 minutes; service ceiling 30,510 ft (9300 m); range 708 miles (1140 km)
**Weights:** empty 4,563 lb (2070 kg); maximum take-off 6,349 lb (2880 kg)
**Dimensions:** span 36 ft 1 in (11.00 m); length 26 ft 2½ in (8.00 m); height 10 ft 6 in

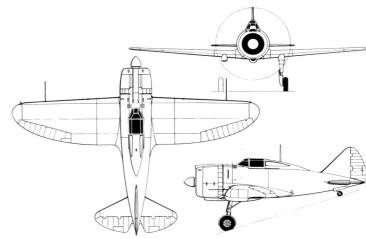

**Reggiane Re.2000**

(3.20 m); wing area 219.6 sq ft (20.40 m²)
**Armament:** two 12.7-mm (0.5-in) Breda-SAFAT machine-guns in nose

Unashamedly copied from the Sikorsky P-35, the Re.2000 was produced in relatively small numbers during 1939-40. Highly manoeuvrable, it however suffered the common Italian failing of paltry armament, possessing a pair of 0.5-in (12.7-mm) synchronized guns in the nose.

# Republic P-47 Thunderbolt

P-47s were used by many Allied air forces in World War II, notably the British, French and Russian. Another operator was the Brazilian air force, which after joining the war on 22 August 1942 sent a fighter group (1° Grupo de Caca) to Italy, with P-47D-25s, becoming part of the 12th AF. This aircraft was based at Tarquinia.

## History and Notes

Evolved from Major Alexander P. Seversky's radial-powered P-35, the big P-47 was designed under the leadership of Alexander Kartveli to become one of America's three outstanding fighters of the war, perpetuating American preference in 1939-40 for air-cooled radial engines. First flown on 6 May 1941, the XP-47B was designed around the 2,000-hp (1492-kW) Pratt & Whitney R-2800 with exhaust-driven turbocharger in the rear fuselage; armament was eight 0.5-in (12.7-mm) machine-guns in the wings. Some 171 production P-47Bs were built with minor improvements and a top speed of 429 mph (691 km/h), this version being brought to the UK in January 1943 by the 56th and 78th Fighter Groups; they were first flown in combat on 8 April that year, flying escort for B-17s. Early P-47s proved to possess poor climb and manoeuvrability, but were popular on account of their ability to survive heavy battle damage. A lengthened fuselage and provision for an under-fuselage drop tank identified the P-47C. The major version (of which no fewer than 12,602 were built) was the P-47D with water-injection power boost, and cut-down rear fuselage with 'bubble' hood on later sub-variants; P-47Ds served in the UK, the Mediterranean and the Far East; in Burma 16 RAF squadrons flew the P-47B (as the Thunderbolt Mk I) and P-47D (Thunderbolt Mk II), a total of 826 being delivered. Developed as a result of demands for a 'sprint' version, the P-47M with improved turbocharger and a top speed of 473 mph (762 km/h) at 32,000 ft (9755 m) reached Europe at the end of 1944, while the P-47N with blunt-tipped enlarged wing and increased fuel capacity was developed purely for service in the Pacific; a total of 1,816 was produced and these flew escort for B-29s in their raids on Japan in 1945. A total of 15,675 P-47s was produced.

**Specification:** Republic P-47D-25 (Thunderbolt Mk II)
**Origin:** USA
**Type:** single-seat long-range fighter
**Powerplant:** one 2,300-hp (1716-kW) Pratt & Whitney R-2800-59 radial piston engine
**Performance:** maximum speed 428 mph (689 km/h) at 30,000 ft (9145 m); climb to 20,000 ft (6095 m) in 9.0 minutes; service ceiling 42,000 ft (12800 m); maximum range 1,260 miles (2028 km)
**Weights:** empty 10,000 lb (4536 kg); maximum take-off 19,400 lb (8800 kg)
**Dimensions:** span 40 ft 9½ in (12.43 m); length 36 ft 1¾ in (11.01 m); height 14 ft 2 in (4.32 m); wing area 300.0 sq ft (27.87 m²)

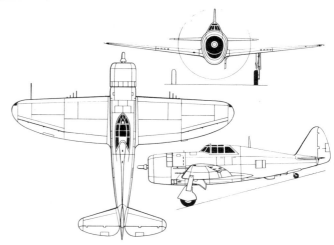

**Republic P-47C Thunderbolt**

**Armament:** eight 0.5-in (12.7-mm) machine-guns in the wings, plus up to two 1,000-lb (454-kg) bombs

A fine portrait of a P-47D (Evansville-built) on a combat mission in the Europe theatre. This unit is the 82nd Fighter Squadron, 78th Fighter Group, based at Duxford. The photograph was taken after D-Day because in addition to the famed black/white check cowl the aircraft carries black/white 'invasion stripes'.

# Republic P-47 Thunderbolt

Fighter-bomber par excellence, the P-47D is seen here with bombs of the 1,000-lb (454-kg) size hung under the wing pylons and one of the nine types of drop tank and napalm carried on the centreline. This particular aircraft, a P-47D-25-RE, served with the 527th Fighter Squadron of the 86th Fighter Group. This was one of the leading fighter groups in the Mediterranean theatre; it fought its way from North Africa through Sicily into Italy, and equipped with P-47Ds in 1944. It then operated intensively not only in ground attack on Kesselring's retreating forces in Italy but also over the Balkans and on long-range escort duties of B-24s (occasionally other bombers) as far as Berlin. The principal home base for 'Rabbit' was Pisa. Note that the stripes of the 86th FG have obliterated the USAAF tail number.

# Savoia-Marchetti SM.79 Sparviero

The 'Electric Man' device on this Sparviero identifies it as an aircraft of the 193ª Squadriglia BT, 87° Gruppo BT, 30° Stormo BT, based in Sicily during 1940 and 1941 for operations against Malta; the unit had also flown against the French in Tunisia earlier in 1940.

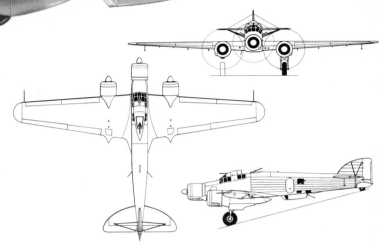

## History and Notes

Alessandro Marchetti's excellent SM.79 Sparviero (Sparrow) was in emotional terms to the Italian people what the Spitfire was to the British and the P-51 was to the Americans. The three-engine aircraft was developed from the SM.81 in 1934 as a commercial entry for the 'MacRobertson' England-Australia race, but was not completed in time to compete, making its maiden flight in October that year; the second prototype was completed as a bomber. A number of Sparvieri served in Spain while SM.79-Is entered service with the Regia Aeronautica in 1937, first as a medium bomber, and later as a torpedo-bomber. By 1939 a total of 11 *stormi* were equipped with the SM.79-I powered by Alfa Romeo radials, a total of 389 aircraft being deployed in Italy, Albania and the Aegean; by June the following year the number had increased to 14 *stormi* with 594 aircraft. Of these, three *stormi* were located in Italy, two in Sardinia, four in Libya and five in Sicily. They participated in the short-lived campaign against France and in the Balkans, as well as supporting Italian operations in the Western Desert; contrary to propaganda of the day, the Sparviero was not easy meat for British fighters in 1940-1, and had it not been for its relatively light bombload, their presence in large numbers would have presented serious problems for the British in North Africa, particularly with the arrival of the SM.79bis with 1,000-hp (746-kW) Piaggio P.XI radials. Indeed, it was these aircraft operating with torpedoes that caused the Allies most concern, with numerous British ships sunk in a series of brilliant attacks. However, the increasing attrition of war in North Africa quickly reduced the number of SM.79s available, and at the time of the 'Torch' landings no more than 112 were available. Total production of the Sparviero was 1,330, including a number of the cleaned-up SM.79ter (SM.79-III) versions produced in 1944.

**Specification:** Savoia-Marchetti SM.79-I Sparviero
**Origin:** Italy
**Type:** four/five-crew medium bomber
**Powerplant:** three 780-hp (582-kW) Alfa Romeo 126 RC 34 radial piston engines
**Performance:** maximum speed 267 mph (430 km/h) at 13,125 ft (4000 m); climb to 13,125 ft (4000 m) in 13.25 minutes; service ceiling 21,325 ft (6500 m); range 2,051 miles (3300 km)
**Weights:** empty 15,322 lb (6950 kg); maximum take-off 23,644 lb (10725 kg)
**Dimensions:** span 69 ft 6⅔ in (21.20 m); length 53 ft 1¾ in (16.20 m); height 13 ft 5½ in (4.10 m); wing area 664.2 sq ft (61.70 m²)

### Savoia-Marchetti SM.79-II

**Armament:** one fixed 12.7-mm (0.5-in) Breda-SAFAT machine-gun firing forward, one 12.7-mm (0.5-in) Breda-SAFAT machine-gun in dorsal position, one 12.7-mm (0.5-in) Breda-SAFAT machine-gun in the rear of ventral fairing and one 7.7-mm (0.303-in) Lewis gun for beam defence, plus a bombload (maximum) of five 551-lb (250-kg) bombs

The Italians achieved some outstanding success with the torpedo-carrying Sparviero. The most celebrated unit was the 132° Gruppo, comprising the 278ª (one of whose aircraft is seen here) and 281ª Squadriglie, based in Sicily during 1942. Among the ships struck by their torpedoes were the battleship HMS *Malaya* and carrier HMS *Argus*.

# Savoia-Marchetti SM.81

Italy sent a force of aircraft to Russia on 29 July 1941 to assist Germany in her invasion of that country, known as the Corpo de Spedizione Italiano in Russia. This Savoia-Marchetti SM.81 served with the 245ª Squadriglia *Hasporto*, Krivoy Rog, Ukraine, September 1941.

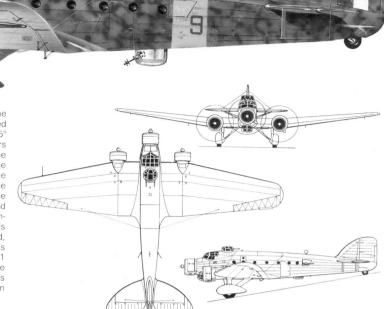

## History and Notes

Curiously similar in concept to the German Ju 52/3m, Italy's SM.81 was developed from the SM.73 transport as a medium bomber and first appeared in 1934. It quickly entered production with three 670-hp (500-kW) Piaggio P.X radials, joining the 7°, 9°, 13° and 15° Stormi in 1935. Many of these aircraft served during the Ethiopian campaign as bombers and transports, and from 1936 onwards participated in the Spanish Civil War. By the outbreak of the war in 1939, the SM.81 was widely regarded as obsolescent in view of the arrival of the excellent SM.79, yet when Italy entered the conflict the following year the Regia Aeronautica still fielded 304 serviceable SM.81s, of which 147 were based in the Mediterranean and 59 in East Africa as bombers, and the remainder as transports. Some updating of the aircraft was attempted with the installation of Alfa Romeo 125 RC 35 and 126 RC 34, and Gnome-Rhône K14 radials, but in service the aircraft remained fundamentally unchanged. In East Africa SM.81s of the 4° and 29° Gruppi were active in raids over Khartoum, Port Sudan and Aden, and in support of the Italian invasion of Somaliland, but eventually suffered losses to extinction. In the Mediterranean, Aegean-based SM.81s of the 39° Stormo made a number of attacks on the British fleet, but in the main SM.81 operations in the Western Desert were confined to transport duties. During the war the SM.81 equipped a total of 24 *squadriglie* of the 7°, 8°, 9°, 14°, 15°, 37°, 38° and 39° Stormi as bombers, and of the 18° Stormo as transports. By the time of the Italian armistice in September 1943 the aircraft had almost disappeared from service.

**Specification:** Savoia-Marchetti SM.81 Series 5
**Origin:** Italy
**Type:** five-crew medium bomber
**Powerplant:** three 780-hp (582-kW) Alfa-Romeo 126 RC 34 radial piston engines
**Performance:** maximum speed 209 mph (336 km/h) at 16,405 ft (5000 m); climb to 16,405 ft (5000 m) in 19.27 minutes; service ceiling 21,600 ft (6600 m); range 1,243 miles (2000 km)
**Weights:** empty 14,991 lb (6800 kg); maximum take-off 23,148 lb (10500 kg)
**Dimensions:** span 78 ft 8¾ in (24.00 m); length 64 ft 3 in (19.58 m); height 14 ft 4 in (4.37 m); wing area 1,001.1 sq ft (93.00 m²)
**Armament:** two 7.7-mm (0.303-in) Breda-SAFAT machine-guns in each of

**Savoia-Marchetti SM.81**

dorsal and ventral turrets, and one 7.7-mm (0.303-in) Breda-SAFAT machine-gun in either of two beam positions, plus a bombload of up to four 1,102-lb (500-kg) bombs

**Similar in design concept to the German Ju 52/3m, the big SM.81 retained its bombing capability longer, being employed in this capacity well into the war, particularly in Italian East Africa. Being sturdy and of relatively simple construction, it was indeed an ideal aircraft for 'colonial' warfare.**

# Savoia-Marchetti SM.79 Sparviero

Savoia-Marchetti SM.79-II of the 205ª Squadriglia, displaying the *Sorci Verdi* (Green Mice) emblem adopted from the pre-war SM.79 record-breaking Sparviero flight led by Colonel Attilio Biseo. Although early in the war Italian bombers tended to be deployed and operated in *gruppo* strength, battle losses during the final stages of the North African campaign resulted in many such units being disbanded. The 205ª Squadriglia was however re-formed as an autonomous unit at Milis, Sardinia, on the eve of the invasion of Sicily in July 1943, albeit with only four serviceable Sparvieri.

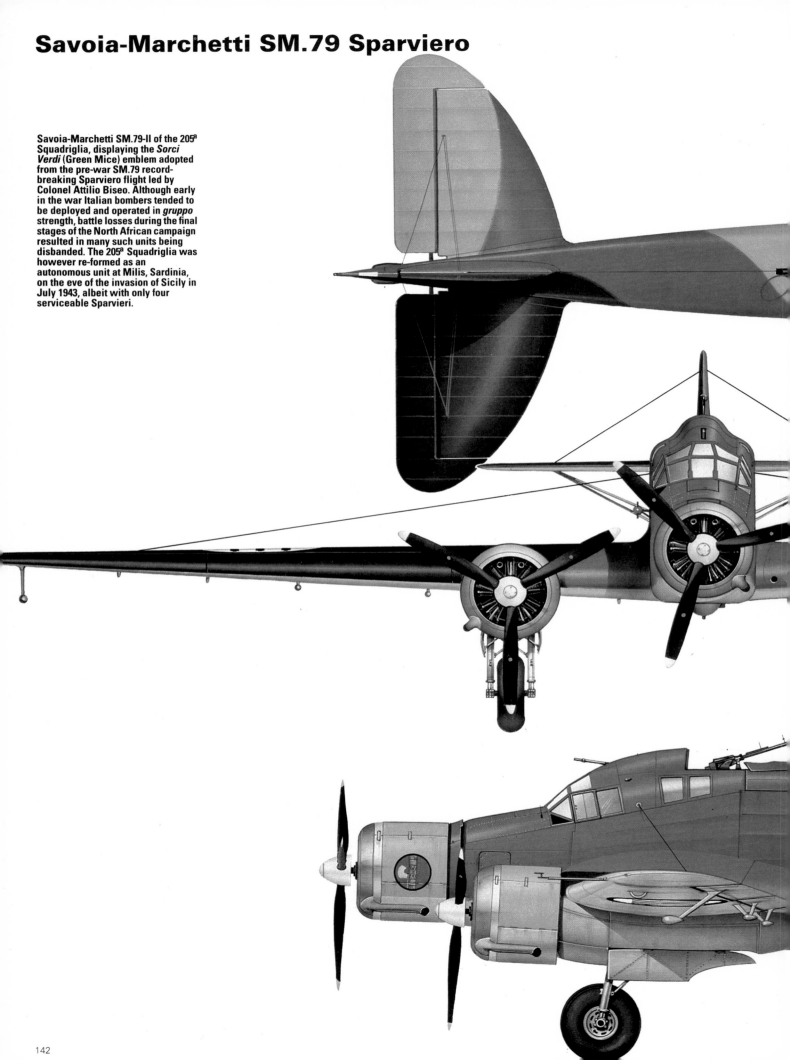

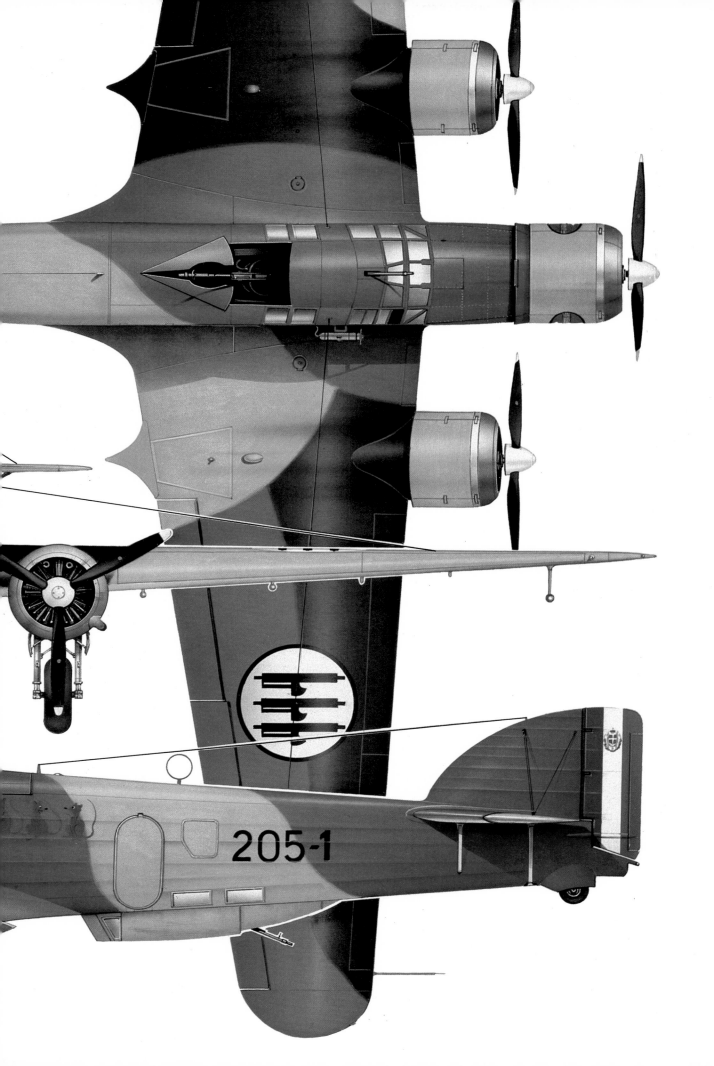

205-1

# Short Stirling

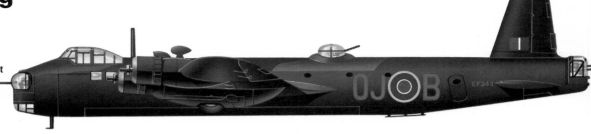

**Shown here is a Stirling Mk I of No. 149 (East India) Sqn based at Mildenhall in January 1942. This squadron flew its Stirlings in the first of the famous 1,000-bomber raids on Germany, and continued flying them until September 1942.**

## History and Notes

The Stirling was the first of Bomber Command's trio of four-engine heavy bombers that mounted the great night offensive over Europe during the last four years of the war, and the only one conceived from the outset as a four-engine aircraft. Designed to a 1936 specification, the Stirling was initially flown as a half-scale prototype in 1938, this being followed by the full-scale prototype which was destroyed on its first flight in May 1939. Production deliveries were first made to No. 7 Squadron in August 1940 (at the height of the Battle of Britain) and the Stirling flew its first operation on 10-11 February 1941. The type first bombed Berlin two months later. The Stirling Mk I, of which 756 were produced, was powered by Hercules XI radials, but the Stirling Mk II with Wright Cyclones did not progress beyond the prototype stage. The Stirling Mk III was powered by Hercules XVIs and, with 875 built (plus many Mk Is converted) constituted the main bomber variant; it also introduced the two-gun dorsal turret. Stirlings were the first operational aircraft to carry the original form of 'Oboe' radar in 1941, and in August 1942 took part in the first Pathfinder operations. Two posthumous VCs were won by Stirling pilots (Flight Sergeant R.H. Middleton of No. 149 Squadron and Flight Sergeant A.L. Aaron of No. 218 Squadron), both during raids on Northern Italy. By 1944 the Stirling Mk III was obsolescent, and flew its last raid in September that year. The Stirling Mk IV (of which 577 were built) was a transport/glider tug without nose and dorsal turrets, and was widely used on operations by the airborne forces during the last year of the war. The Stirling Mk V transport (160 built), without armament, joined the RAF in January 1945. Stirling bombers equipped 15 squadrons.

**Specification:** Short Stirling Mk III
**Origin:** UK
**Type:** seven- or eight-crew night heavy bomber
**Powerplant:** four 1,650-hp (1231-kW) Bristol Hercules XVI radial piston engines
**Performance:** maximum speed 270 mph (435 km/h) at 14,500 ft (4420 m); service ceiling 17,000 ft (5180 m); range with 14,000-lb (6350-kg) bombload, 590 miles (949 km)
**Weights:** empty 43,200 lb (19596 kg); maximum take-off 70,000 lb (31790 kg)
**Dimensions:** span 99 ft 1 in (30.20 m); length 87 ft 3 in (26.50 m); height 22 ft 9 in (6.93 m); wing area 1,460.0 sq ft (135.60 m²)
**Armament:** two 0.303-in (7.7-mm) machine-guns in each of nose and dorsal turrets, and four 0.303-in (7.7-mm) guns in tail turret, plus a maximum bombload of 14,000 (6350 kg)

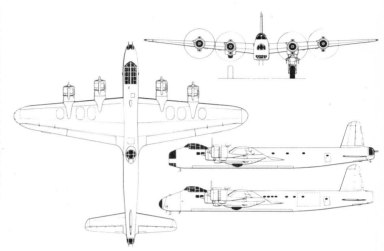

**Short Stirling Mk III (top view: Mk IV glider tug, lower view Mk V transport)**

First of the RAF's four-engine heavy bombers, the Stirling – on account of its huge undercarriage – always gave the impression of great size. Capable of carrying up to 14,000 lb (6350 kg) of bombs, its performance was however disappointing and was never as popular in service as the Halifax and Lancaster.

# Short Sunderland

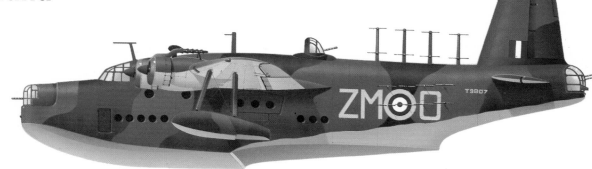

Festooned with ASV (air-to-surface vessel) radar aerials, Sunderlands ranged far and wide over the Atlantic and Indian Oceans throughout the war in their endless search for enemy submarines and surface raiders; bristling with machine-guns, they frequently gave a good account of themselves when attacked by enemy aircraft.

## History and Notes

The big, graceful Sunderland, which played such a vital part in the Battle of the Atlantic, was a military development of the famous pre-war 'C'-class Empire flying boat. It made its maiden flight in October 1937 and joined Nos 210 and 230 Squadrons during the following summer. Production continued until October 1945 by which time 721 aircraft had been produced. The Sunderland Mk I featured a prominent forward step in the planing bottom; Sunderland Mk IIs, which first flew in 1941, introduced a two-gun dorsal turret, and the Sunderland Mk III of 1942 introduced a shallower forward step in the planing bottom. All these versions were powered by four 1,065-hp (795-kW) Bristol Pegasus XVIII radials, and the first powerplant change came with the Sunderland Mk V of 1943 with Pratt & Whitney Twin Wasps. The Sunderland Mk IV (later known as the Seaford) did not enter service during the war. Affectionately known as the 'Flying Porcupine', on account of its heavy defensive armament, the Sunderland flew with 17 squadrons of the RAF based in the UK, the Middle East, the Far East, Iceland, Gibraltar and West Africa. The type flew countless hours protecting convoys in the Atlantic, rescued survivors from torpedoed ships, hunted and sank a number of U-boats (the first on 30 January 1940), and assisted in a number of transport operations, notably during the evacuations of Norway, Greece and Crete. Above all, their crews maintained a long and lonely vigil over vast areas of ocean throughout the war.

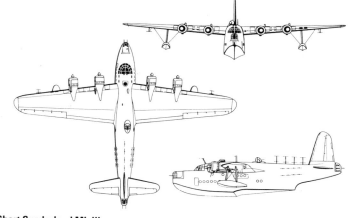

**Short Sunderland Mk III**

## Specification: Short Sunderland Mk V
**Origin:** UK
**Type:** 13-crew maritime reconnaissance flying-boat
**Powerplant:** four 1,200-hp (895-kW) Pratt & Whitney Twin Wasp R-1830 radial piston engines
**Performance:** maximum speed 213 mph (343 km/h) at 5,000 ft (1525 m); initial climb rate 840 ft (256 m) per minute; service ceiling 17,900 ft (5455 m); range 2,980 miles (4795 km)
**Weights:** empty 37,000 lb (16783 kg); maximum take-off 65,000 lb (29482 kg)
**Dimensions:** span 112 ft 9½ in (34.36 m); length 85 ft 4 in (26.01 m); height 32 ft 10½ in (10.01 m); wing area 1,487.0 sq ft (138.14 m²)
**Armament:** four fixed 0.303-in (7.7-mm) machine-guns in nose, four 0.303-in (7.7-mm)

machine-guns in tail turret, two 0.303-in (7.7-mm) machine-guns in bow turret and two 0.5-in (12.7-mm) flexible machine-guns in beam positions, plus a bombload of 2,000 lb (907 kg)

Obviously on account of its pre-war commercial ancestry, the Sunderland was a graceful sight, never more so than on take-off. This Mk III belonged to No. 201 Sqn based at Pembroke Dock in 1944 for patrols over the Western Approaches.

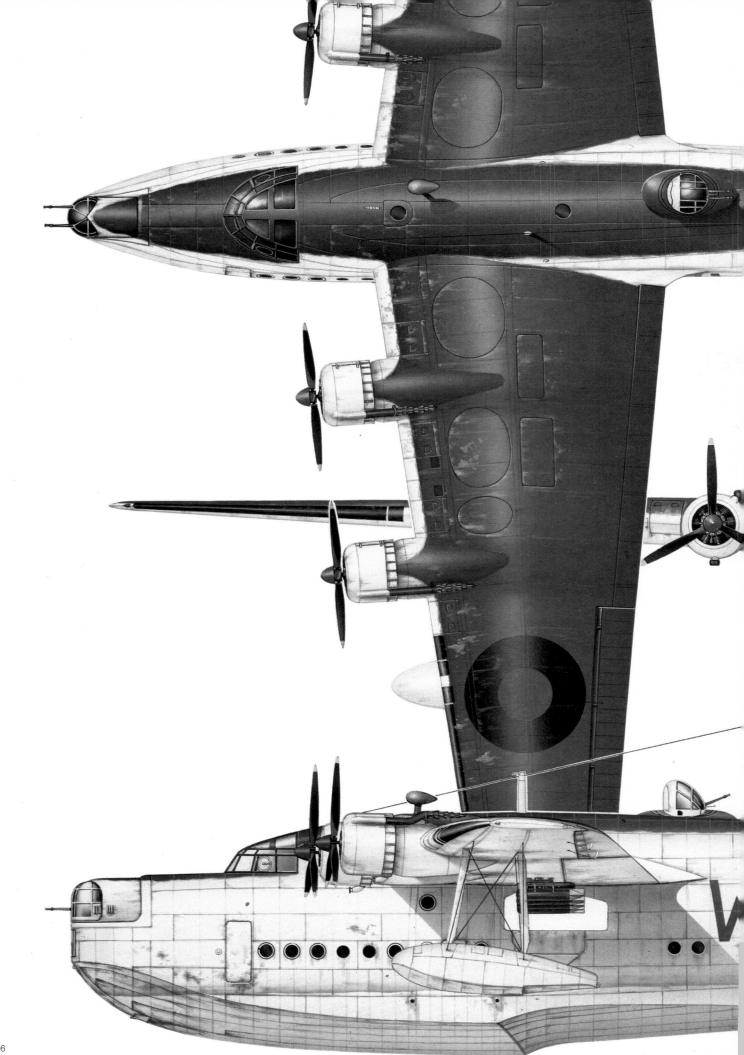

# Short Sunderland

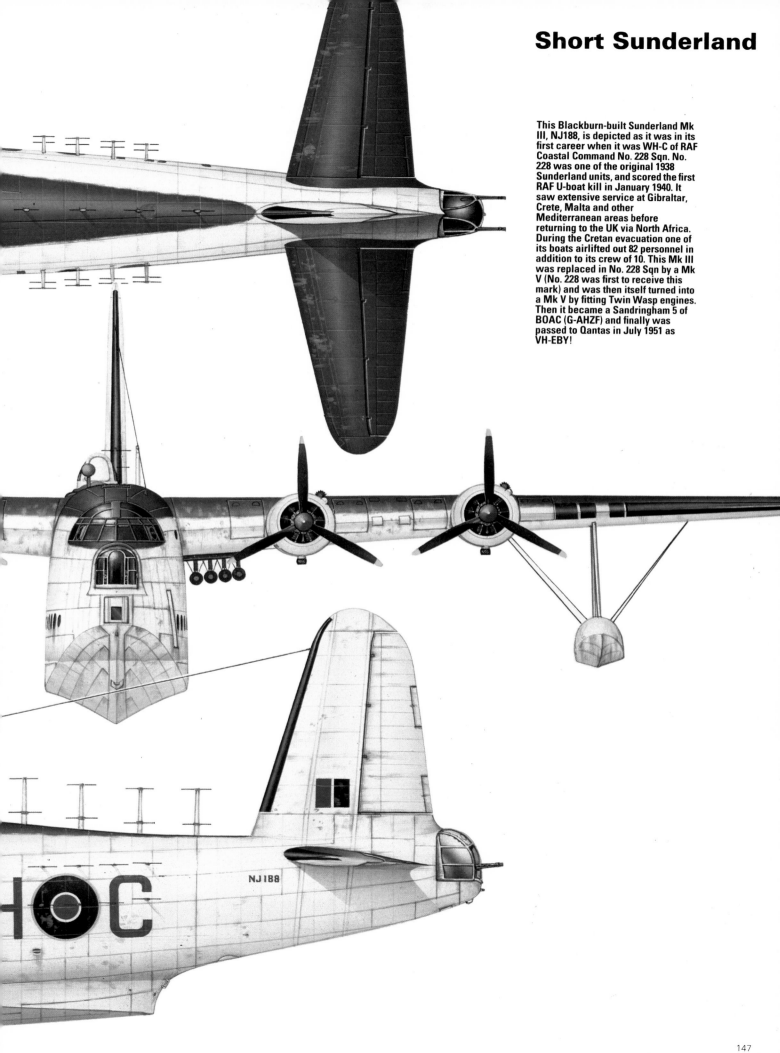

This Blackburn-built Sunderland Mk III, NJ188, is depicted as it was in its first career when it was WH-C of RAF Coastal Command No. 228 Sqn. No. 228 was one of the original 1938 Sunderland units, and scored the first RAF U-boat kill in January 1940. It saw extensive service at Gibraltar, Crete, Malta and other Mediterranean areas before returning to the UK via North Africa. During the Cretan evacuation one of its boats airlifted out 82 personnel in addition to its crew of 10. This Mk III was replaced in No. 228 Sqn by a Mk V (No. 228 was first to receive this mark) and was then itself turned into a Mk V by fitting Twin Wasp engines. Then it became a Sandringham 5 of BOAC (G-AHZF) and finally was passed to Qantas in July 1951 as VH-EBY!

NJ188

# Sukhoi Su-2

By 1942 the Su-2 was receiving such a battering from German fighters and flak (on account of poor performance and manoeuvrability) that it was quickly withdrawn as the Il-2 started to appear in numbers. The aircraft shown here belonged to a second-line unit in the Sverdlovsk area in 1942-3.

## History and Notes

Pavel Sukhoi's Su-2 proved something of a disappointment, as did so many of the world's single-engine attack aircraft of the late 1930s, being in the main undergunned, under-powered and overweight. In much the same class as the ill-fated Fairey Battle, the prototype ANT-51 (so-called after A.N. Tupolev, in whose bureau Sukhoi worked) had flown in August 1937 with an M-62 radial – a Russian copy of the Wright Cyclone – but later aircraft were powered by M-87s, developed from the French Gnome-Rhône 14K, before the aircraft entered production in 1940 as the BB-1 medium-range attack bomber. Maximum speed with bombload proved to be around 230 mph (370 km/h) (907 kg), and when the type was faced by German fighters in 1941 this proved disastrously inadequate, so a new version with 1,000-hp (746-hp) Shvetsov M-88B radial was quickly introduced as the Su-2 (reflecting the new Russian practice of recognizing the designer). However, without the heavy armour protection of the Il-2 and scarcely any worthwhile gun defence, the Su-2 continued to provide easy meat for Luftwaffe and flak alike, and although an Su-2 was flown with a 2,100-hp (1567-kW) M-90, which apparently increased the speed to around 340 mph (547 km/h) with bombload, the decision was taken to abandon the Su-2 in favour of the rugged Il-2, for which enormous manufacturing facilities had been prepared. The last Su-2s are thought to have been delivered in 1943.

**Specification:** Sukhoi Su-2
**Origin:** USSR
**Type:** two-seat attack bomber
**Powerplant:** one 1,000-hp (746-hp) Shvetsov M-88B radial piston engine
**Performance:** maximum speed 283 mph (455 km/h) at 8,200 ft (2500 m); service ceiling 28,870 ft (8800 m); range 739 miles (1190 km)
**Weights:** empty 6,614 lb (3000 kg); maximum take-off 9,645 lb (4375 kg)
**Dimensions:** span 46 ft 11 in (14.30 m); length 33 ft 7½ in (10.25 m); wing area 312.1 sq ft (29.00 m²)
**Armament:** four 7.62-mm (0.3-in) ShKAS machine-guns in wings and one or two 7.62-mm (0.3-in) ShKAS machine-guns in dorsal turret, plus an internal bombload of 882 lb (400 kg) and an external bombload of 1,323 lb (600 kg)

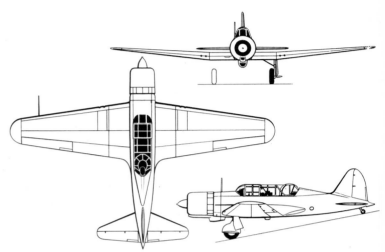

Sukhoi Su-2

An ASh 82-powered Su-2 equipped with ski landing gear; the 1,500-hp (1118-kW) engine was introduced in an attempt to give the aircraft a better chance of survival in the presence of German fighters, but to little avail.

# Supermarine Spitfire

Evidence of the high esteem in which the Americans held the Spitfire was the widespread use by the USAAF of this magnificent fighter. Most were Mk Vs and Mk IXs, but this aircraft, shown in desert finish, was a Mk VIII, flown by the CO of the 308th Fighter Squadron, 31st FG, in Italy, 1944.

## History and Notes

Classic creation of designer R.J. Mitchell, the Spitfire was the descendant of the race-winning Schneider Trophy seaplanes. First flown on 5 March 1936, the Spitfire Mk I with Merlin II engine and eight machine-guns entered RAF service in August 1938, this version being heavily committed to combat in the Battle of Britain. The Spitfire Mk II with Merlin XII followed in September 1940, the Spitfire Mk IIB being armed with two 20-mm guns and four machine-guns. The photo-reconnaissance Spitfire Mk IV was followed in March 1941 by the excellent Spitfire Mk V (of which 6,479 were produced) with 1,440-hp (1074-kW) Merlin 45; the Spitfire Mk VC fighter-bomber could carry one 500-hp (227-kg) or two 250-lb (113-kg) bombs. The Spitfire Mk VB remained the mainstay of Fighter Command between mid-1941 and mid-1942 when the Spitfire Mk IX, with 1,660-hp (1238-kW) Merlin 61 with two-stage, two-speed supercharger joined the RAF. The Spitfire Mk VI and Mk VII were high-altitude fighters with extended wingtips, but the definitive Spitfire Mk VIII fighter and fighter-bomber was used principally in the Mediterranean and Far East, being fully tropicalized.

The Spitfire Mk X and Mk XI were unarmed photo-reconnaissance versions and the Spitfire Mk XVI, with a top speed of 405 mph (652 km/h) was produced in fighter and fighter-bomber versions. All the foregoing (of which 18,298 were built) were powered by the Rolls-Royce Merlin, and the first with 1,735-hp (1294-kW) Griffon IV was the Spitfire Mk XII, introduced in 1943 to counter the Fw 190 fighter-bomber. It was followed by the 2,050-hp (1529-kW) Griffon 65-powered Spitfire Mk XIV fighter and fighter-bomber. The fighter-reconnaissance Spitfire Mk XVIII was just joining the RAF at the end of the war and had a top speed of 442 mph (712 km/h). In the Fleet Air Arm also served in large numbers both with Merlin and Griffon engines. Total production of the Spitfire was 20,351.

**Specification:** Supermarine Spitfire Mk VB
**Origin:** UK
**Type:** single-seat interceptor fighter
**Powerplant:** one 1,440-hp (1074-kW) Rolls-Royce Merlin 45/46/50 inline piston engine
**Performance:** maximum speed 374 mph (602 km/h) at 13,000 ft (3960 m); climb to 20,000 ft (6095 m) in 7.5 minutes; service ceiling 37,000 ft (11280 m); range on internal fuel 470 miles (756 km)
**Weights:** empty 5,100 lb (2313 kg); maximum take-off 6,785 lb (3078 kg)
**Dimensions:** span 36 ft 10 in (11.23 m); length 29 ft 11 in (9.11 m); height 11 ft 5 in (3.48 m); wing area 242.0 sq ft (22.48 m²)
**Armament:** two 20-mm cannon and four 0.303-in (7.7-mm) machine-guns in the wings

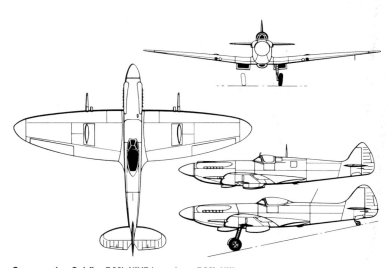

Supermarine Spitfire F.Mk XIVE (top view: F.Mk XII)

The immortal Spitfire seen here in its Mk VB form and in the markings of No. 303 (Polish) Sqn, probably late in 1942. The pilot is the squadron's CO at that time, Squadron Leader J. Zumbach, one of the highest-scoring Poles serving with the RAF.

Often quoted as the most perfect equation of grace with purpose in a military aeroplane, the Spitfire served in the RAF from 1938 until 1954. Seen here is the most-produced version, the Mk V, which led Fighter Command's cross-Channel offensive in 1941-2, and reigned supreme until the appearance of the Luftwaffe's Focke-Wulf Fw 190A.

# Tupolev SB-2

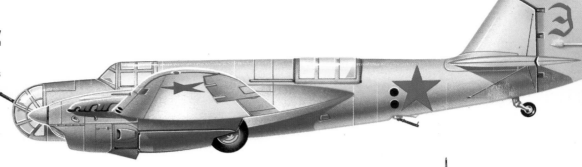

Late production SB-2bis, powered by the M-103 inline engine. This version had a top speed of 280 mph (451 km/h), but was painfully undergunned and suffered enormous losses in the opening months of Germany's Operation *Barbarossa*.

## History and Notes

In much the same category as the British Bristol Blenheim, the SB-2 was also a light twin-engine bomber with three-man crew. Designed by the bureau led by A.N. Tupolev, the prototype ANT-40 (later designated the SB-1) flew on 7 October 1934, and the type entered service early in 1936 as the SB-2 powered by two 750-hp (560-kW) VK-100 inline engines, which were in effect Russian copies of the Hispano-Suiza 12Y. Of all-metal stressed-skin construction, the SB-2 fought during the Spanish Civil War in 1936-9 when its 280-mph (450-km/h) top speed rendered it almost immune from interception by Nationalist fighters. It also served with the Chinese Central Government air force against Japan during 1938-9. In the Winter War of 1939-40 between the Soviet Union and Finland the SB-2 suffered heavily, in general on account of the harsh weather conditions' effects upon the liquid-cooled engines. Nevertheless a new version, the SB-2bis with 1,100-hp (821-kW) M-100A engines, started delivery in 1939 and, although production was phased out in 1942, this continued to serve until the end of the war, being employed as a night-fighter in the last two years. Production of all types was stated to be around 6,500, the bulk of these being produced during 1941-2.

## Specification: Tupolev SB-2bis
**Origin:** USSR
**Type:** three-crew light bomber
**Powerplant:** two 1,100-hp (821-kW) M-100A inline piston engines
**Performance:** maximum speed 280 mph (450 km/h) at 14,765 ft (4500 m); initial climb rate 1,310 ft (400 m) per minute; service ceiling 34,120 ft (10400 m); range 752 miles (1210 km)
**Weights:** empty 8,818 lb (4000 kg); maximum take-off 17,196 lb (7800 kg)
**Dimensions:** span 66 ft 8½ in (20.33 m); length 40 ft 3¼ in (12.27 m); height 10 ft 8 in (3.25 m); wing area 559.2 sq ft (51.95 m²)
**Armament:** two flexible 7.62-mm (0.3-in) ShKAS machine-guns in nose, one 7.62-mm (0.3-in) ShKAS machine-gun in dorsal turret and one 7.62-mm (0.3-in) ShKAS machine-gun in ventral position, plus a bombload of up to six 222-lb (100-kg) bombs

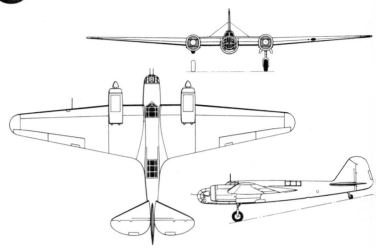

**Tupolev Tu-2S**

Often compared with the Bristol Blenheim, the SB-2 was in fact an older design, being the first Russian operational aircraft of metal stressed skin construction. Nevertheless it was ineptly flown during the Russo-Finnish Winter War of 1939-40 and suffered heavy losses at the hands of determined Finnish pilots.

# Tupolev Tu-2

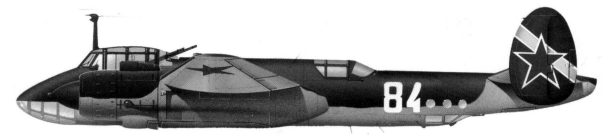

The Tu-2 underwent relatively little design modification during its long service life, reflecting a sound original concept, but was also evidence of the Soviet need to achieve uninterrupted production of large numbers of proven aircraft. The aircraft shown served in the last few months of the war.

## History and Notes

A.N. Tupolev's Tu-2 must be regarded as one of the best Russian aircraft to be produced during the war, in much the same class as the American B-25 and B-26 bombers, although reflecting a number of features regarded as outmoded in the West. First flown as the ANT-58 prototype in October 1940 and incorporating many of the fruits of early wartime experience, the Tu-2 was still undergoing flight development when Germany invaded the Soviet Union in the summer of 1941, and the first service deliveries were not made until a year later. Powered by the excellent 1,850-hp (1380-kW) Shvetsov ASh-82 FN radial and possessing a top speed of 342 mph (550 km/h) at medium level, and heavily armed and armoured the Tu-2 remained largely unchanged throughout its production life (which lasted until 1948), and started appearing in large numbers at around the time of the murderous Stalingrad campaign; during the great tank battles in the Kursk salient of July 1943 the 23-mm cannon was introduced for attacks on the less-heavily armoured German vehicles, although it proved inadequate to deal with enemy tanks. Renowned for its rugged structure, the Tu-2 was extremely popular in service, the engines in particular being regarded as among the most reliable of any produced during the war.

**Specification:** Tupolev Tu-2
**Origin:** USSR
**Type:** four-crew attack bomber
**Powerplant:** two 1,850-hp (1380-kW) Shvetsov ASh-82FN radial piston engines
**Performance:** maximum speed 342 mph (550 km/h) at 10,825 ft (3300 m); initial climb rate 2,295 ft (700 m) per minute; service ceiling 31,170 ft (9500 m); range 1,553 miles (2500 km)
**Weights:** empty 18,254 lb (8280 kg); maximum take-off 28,219 lb (12800 kg)
**Dimensions:** span 61 ft 10½ in (18.86 m); length 45 ft 3¾ in (13.80 m); height 13 ft 9½ in (4.20 m); wing area 525.3 sq ft (48.8 m²)
**Armament:** single 12.7-mm (0.5-in) UBT machine guns in forward dorsal position, rear dorsal position and ventral position, and two forward-firing 20-mm ShVAK cannon in wings, plus a bombload of 5,004 lb (2270 kg), later 6,614 lb (3000 kg)

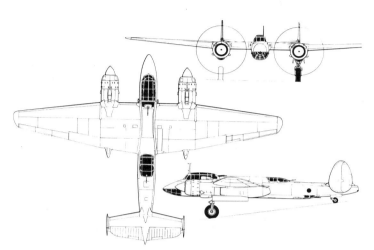

**Tupolev Tu-2S**

The Tu-2 was one of Russia's outstanding aircraft of the war, remaining in production from 1942 until 1948. Its nearest Western equivalent was probably the North American B-25 Mitchell.

153

# Vickers Wellington

Typical of the Wellington night bomber versions was this Mk IC of No. 150 Sqn, based at Newton in December 1940, a squadron which flew the bomber from October 1940 until October 1944, taking them to North Africa in December 1942.

## History and Notes

Employing the efficient geodetic lattice structure, the twin-engine Wellington continued in service with Bomber Command until 1943 – far longer than its contemporaries, the Hampden and Whitley. Designed to meet a 1932 requirement, the Wellington first flew on 15 June 1936 and in its Mk I form with Pegasus radials joined the RAF (No. 9 Squadron) in October 1938. The Wellington Mk IC with Nash and Thompson nose and tail gun turrets followed, together with the Merlin-powered Wellington Mk II and Hercules III- or XI-powered Wellington Mk III, and at the beginning of the war six squadrons were flying the Wellington. Early daylight raids resulted in heavy losses owing to the Wellington's large defenceless arcs and in 1940 the aircraft joined the night bombing force. On 1 April 1941 a Wellington dropped the RAF's first 4,000-lb (1814-kg) bomb. Subsequent bomber versions included the Twin Wasp-powered Wellington Mk IV, and Wellington Mk V and Mk VI high-altitude aircraft with pressure cabins; the latter versions did not see combat service. The Wellington Mk X with Hercules XVIIIs was the final bomber version, and the last raid by Bomber Command Wellingtons took place on 8-9 October 1943. In the meantime Wellingtons had been flying on maritime duties, the Wellington DW.Mk I with large mine-exploding hoops having operated in 1940 and Wellington Mk IC minelayers soon after this. Coastal Command versions included the Wellington GR.Mk VIII with Pegasus engines and ASV radar, the Wellington GR.Mks XI and XII with Hercules, Leigh Light and provision for two torpedoes; the Wellington T.Mks XVII and XVIII were trainers, and many Mk Xs were converted to 'flying classrooms'. Wellingtons were also used as test-beds for early jet engines. The Wellington C.Mks XV and XVI were transport conversions of the Mk IC. A total of 11,461 aircraft was produced.

**Specification:** Vickers Wellington Mk III
**Origin:** UK
**Type:** six-crew night medium bomber
**Powerplant:** two 1,500-hp (1119-kW) Bristol Hercules XI radial piston engines
**Performance:** maximum speed 255 mph (411 km/h) at 12,500 ft (3810 m); initial climb rate 930 ft (283 m) per minute; service ceiling 19,000 ft (5790 m); range with 4,500-lb (2041-kg) bombload 1,540 miles (2478 km)
**Weights:** empty 18,970 lb (8605 kg); maximum take-off 34,000 lb (15422 kg)
**Dimensions:** span 86 ft 2 in (26.26 m); length 64 ft 7 in (19.68 m); height 17 ft 5 in (5.00 m); wing area 840.0 sq ft (78.04 m²)
**Armament:** two 0.303-in (7.7-mm) machine-guns in nose turret, four 0.303-in (7.7-mm)

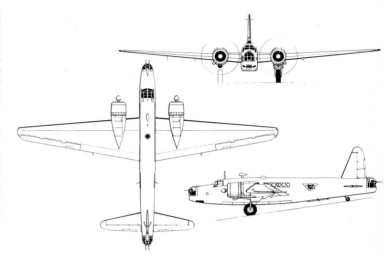

**Vickers Wellington Mk IC**

guns in tail turret, and two flexible 0.303-in (7.7-mm) machine-guns in beam positions, plus a maximum bombload of 4,500 lb (2041 kg)

**Product of Dr Barnes Wallis' prolific drawing board was the famous Wellington bomber, which served throughout the war in a variety of roles. It was the best of the RAF's night bombers in the early months of the war and served on a total of 57 squadrons in various versions.**

# Vought F4U Corsair

This F4U-1A (with carrier equipment removed) served with No. 18 Sqn of the Royal New Zealand Air Force, flying from Bougainville in the Solomons in 1945; the Corsair was this air force's principal fighter in the last year of the war.

## History and Notes

Distinctive yet not unattractive with its inverted gull wing, the F4U Corsair was unquestionably the best shipborne fighter of the war, and gained an 11:1 kill:loss ratio in the Pacific. Designed by Tex B. Beisel, the XF4U-1 was flown on 29 May 1940, the first production F4U-1s being delivered to VF-12 in October 1942, although most of the early aircraft went to the US Marine Corps. It was a land-based US Marine squadron, VMF-124, that first flew the Corsair into action, on 13 February 1943 over Bougainville. Additional production lines were set up by Brewster and Goodyear, these companies producing the F3A-1 and FG-1 respectively. To improve the pilot's field of vision, later aircraft introduced a raised cockpit, and the F4U-1C had a four 20-mm cannon armament. The F4U-1D, FG-1D and F3A-1D were powered by water-injection boosted R-2800-8W engines, and could carry two 1,000-lb (454-kg) bombs or eight 5-in (127-mm) rockets under the wings. Late in the war a night-fighter version, the XF4U-2, saw limited service with VFN-75 and VFN-101. Wartime production of the Corsair (which continued until 1952 with later versions) reached 4,120 F4U-1s, 735 F3A-1s and 3,808 FG-1s; of these 2,012 were supplied to the UK's Fleet Air Arm and 370 to New Zealand. Indeed it was the Royal Navy's Corsair Mk IIs of No. 1834 Squadron that were the first Corsairs to operate from a carrier when, on 3 April 1944, they took part in operations against the *Tirpitz*.

**Specification:** Vought F4U-1 Corsair
**Origin:** USA
**Type:** single-seat shipboard fighter
**Powerplant:** one 2,000-hp (1492-kW) Pratt & Whitney R-2800-8 radial piston engine
**Performance:** maximum speed 417 mph (671 km/h) at 19,900 ft (6066 m); initial climb rate 2,890 ft (881 in) per minute; service ceiling 36,900 ft (11245 m); range 1,015 miles (1633 km)
**Weights:** empty 8,982 lb (4074 kg); maximum take-off 14,000 lb (6350 kg)
**Dimensions:** span 41 ft 0 in (12.50 m); length 33 ft 4½ in (10.17 m); height 16 ft 1 in (4.90 m); wing area 314.0 sq ft (29.17 m²)
**Armament:** six forward-firing 0.5-in (12.7-mm) machine-guns in the wings

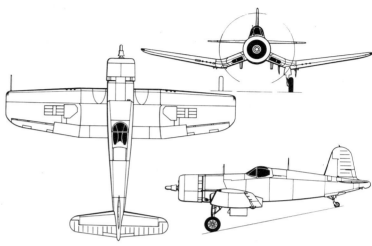

Vought F4U Corsair

Generally regarded as the best shipboard fighter of the war, the Corsair in its F4U-4 version had a top speed of 446 mph (718 km/h); the aircraft is seen here carrying a 1,000-lb (454-kg) bomb under the fuselage.

# Westland Lysander

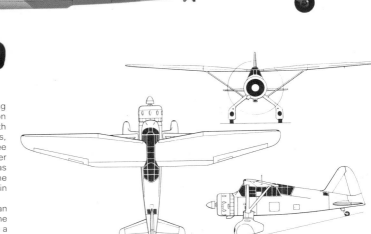

Among the RAF army co-operation squadrons sent to support the British Expeditionary Force in France at the outbreak of war was No. 13 Sqn, one of whose Lysander Mk IIs is depicted here. The squadron suffered heavily during the German attack in the West of May 1940, but continued to fly the Lysander until September 1941.

## History and Notes

First flown in prototype form during June 1936, the Lysander was a two-seat high-wing monoplane army co-operation aircraft with excellent STOL capabilities. The first production series was the Lysander Mk I, and aircraft of this version entered service in late 1938 with No. 16 Squadron, based at Old Sarum. Lysanders went on to equip some 30 RAF squadrons, and these served in Europe, the Middle East and the Far East. The type was built in three marks, these being distinguished mainly by the different powerplants used. The Lysander Mk I featured the 890-hp (664-kW) Bristol Mercury XII radial; the Lysander Mk II, which was built in the UK by Westland and in Canada by the National Steel Car Corporation, had the 950-hp (709-kWP) Bristol Perseus XII radial; and the Lysander Mk III, which was also built in the UK and Canada, used the 870-hp (649-kW) Mercury XX or Mercury XXX radial.

The Lysander operated in its intended role for only a short time in the war, European operations confirming that such large and relatively slow aircraft were deathtraps in the presence of determined opposition, both ground and air. However, the type went on to a notably successful second career in air-sea rescue, radar calibration and, perhaps most significantly, agent dropping and recovery in occupied Europe. Total production was 1,368 aircraft.

## Specification: Westland Lysander Mk I

**Origin:** UK
**Type:** two-seat army co-operation aircraft and short-range tactical reconnaissance aircraft
**Powerplant:** one 890-hp (664-kW) Bristol Mercury XII radial piston engine
**Performance:** maximum speed 229 mph (369 km/h) at 10,000 f (3050 m); climb to 10,000 ft (3050 m) in 5.5 minutes; service ceiling 26,000 ft (7925 m); range 600 miles (966 km)
**Weights:** empty 4,065 lb (1844 kg); normal loaded 5,920 lb (2685 kg)
**Dimensions:** span 50 ft 0 in (15.24 m); length 30 ft 6 in (9.30 m); height 11 ft 6 in (3.51 m);

### Westland Lysander

wing area 260.0 sq ft (24.15 m²)
**Armament:** two forward-firing 0.303-in (7.7-mm) machine-guns in wheel fairings and two 0.303-in (7.7-mm) machine-guns in the rear cockpit, plus provision for eight 20-lb (9.07-kg) bombs on stub winglets

**Possessing an excellent short-field performance, the Lysander proved a useful army co-operation and short-range reconnaissance aircraft and served on many wartime fronts. These aircraft, probably of No. 208 Sqn, are seen over the Suez Canal.**

# Yakovlev Yak-1/-3/-7/-9

Although being replaced by later Yak fighter developments in 1944 the Yak-3 continued to serve, particularly as personal mounts of senior officers. This aircraft was flown by Major-General G. N. Zakharov, commanding the 303rd Fighter Aviation Division.

## History and Notes

It is said that 37,000 Yakovlev fighters were produced during the war, of which the vast majority were Yak-9s, superb fighters that could outfight the German Bf 109G as early as the time of the Stalingrad campaign. Developed progressively from the Yak-1 (which first flew in March 1939), through the Yak-7B which served from early 1942, the Yak-9 was first flown in its production form in the summer of that year, returning a speed of 373 mph (600 km/h). Numerous versions of this versatile fighter were developed, including the Yak-9T anti-tank fighter with 1,260-hp (940-kW) Klimov VK-105PF inline engine and 37-mm hub-firing cannon, the Yak-9B fighter-bomber with provision for 882 lb (400 kg) of bombs, the Yak-9D long-range fighter and the Yak-9DD very long-range escort fighter, the latter being flown as escort for USAAF bombers on shuttle raids between the UK and the Soviet Union late in the war. The Yak-9U fighter, with 1,650-hp (1231-kW) VK-107A engine and a top speed of 435 mph (700 km/h), was the final version to see combat during the war and represented the point at which Soviet technology may be said to have finally caught up with that of the West, and came to be much respected by the best Luftwaffe pilots in their final generation of Bf 109K and Fw 190D fighters.

**Specification:** Yakovlev Yak-9U
**Origin:** USSR
**Type:** single-seat fighter
**Powerplant:** one 1,650-hp (1231-kW) VK-107A inline piston engine
**Performance:** maximum speed 435 mph (700 km/h) at 22,640 ft (6900 m); initial climb rate 4,920 ft (1500 m) per minutes; service ceiling 35,925 ft (10950 m); range 609 miles (980 m)
**Weights:** empty 5,093 lb (2310 kg); normal loaded 6,989 lb (3170 kg)
**Dimensions:** span 32 ft 9¾ in (10.00 m); length 28 ft 6½ in (8.70 m); height 8 ft 0 in (2.44 m)
**Armament:** one 23-mm hub-firing VYa-23V cannon and two 12.7-mm (0.3-in) UBS machine-guns, plus provision for two 220-lb (100-kg) bombs

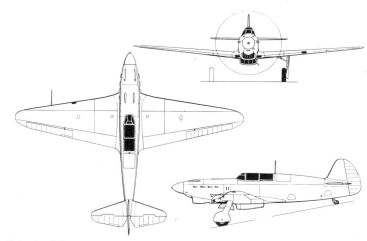

Yakovlev Yak-1

Formation of Yak-9Ds of a Guards Regiment in the Crimea, the nearest aircraft being flown by Colonel M.V. Avdyeyev, holder of the Gold Star of a Hero of the Soviet Union. The two insignia on the Yak's nose are the Guards unit insignia and the Order of the Red Banner.

# Yokosuka D4Y 'Judy'

A Yokosuka D4Y3 Suisei Model 33 of the 601st Kokutai; later versions of the D4Y3 were frequently equipped with three solid-fuel RATOG units under the rear fuselage when operating from the smaller Japanese carriers.

## History and Notes

Well-proportioned and purposeful in appearance, the Yokosuka D4Y possessed an excellent performance and owed much of its concept to the German He 118, for whose manufacturing rights Japan negotiated in 1938. Designed as a fast carrier-based attack bomber and powered by an imported Daimler-Benz DB 600G engine, the D4Y1 was first flown in December 1941; D4Y1-C reconnaissance aircraft were ordered into production at Aichi's Nagoya plant, the first of 660 aircraft being completed in the late spring of 1942. The first service aircraft were lost when the *Soryu* was sunk at Midway. Named Suisei (Comet) in service and codenamed 'Judy' by the Allies, many D4Y1s were completed as dive-bombers, and 174 Suiseis of the 1st, 2nd and 3rd Koku Sentais were embarked in nine carriers before the Battle of the Philippine Sea; however, they were intercepted by American fighters long before reaching the American carriers, and suffered heavy casualties without achieving any success. A new version with 1,400-hp (1044-kW) Aichi Atsuta 32 engine apeared in 1944 as the D4Y2 but, in the interests of preserving high performance, nothing was done to introduce armour protection or crew for fuel tanks, and the sole improvement in gun armament was the inclusion of a 13.2-mm (0.52-in) flexible gun (replacing the previous 7.92-mm/0.31-in gun) in the rear cockpit. This version suffered heavily in the battle for the Philippines. Problems of reliability with the Atsuta inline engine led to adoption of a Kinsei 62 radial in the D4Y3, and this engine was retained in the D4Y4 which was developed in 1945 as a single-seat suicide dive-bomber. A total of 2,033 production D4Ys was completed.

## Specification: Yokosuka D4Y3 'Judy'
**Origin:** Japan
**Type:** two-seat carrier-borne dive-bomber
**Powerplant:** one 1,560-hp (1164-kW) Mitsubishi MK8P Kinsei 62 radial piston engine
**Performance:** maximum speed 357 mph (575 km/h) at 19,850 ft (60.50 m); climb to 9,845 ft (3000 m) 4.55 minutes; service ceiling 34,450 ft (10500 m); range 945 miles (1520 km)
**Weights:** empty 5,514 lb (2501 kg); maximum take-off 10,267 lb (4657 kg)
**Dimensions:** span 37 ft 8¾ in (11.50 m); length 33 ft 6⅜ in (10.22 m); height 12 ft 3¼ in (3.74 m); wing area 254.03 sq ft (23.60 m²)
**Armament:** two fixed forward-firing 7.7-mm (0.303-in) Type 97 machine-guns in nose and one 13.2-mm (0.52-in) Type 2 flexible gun in rear cockpit, plus a maximum bombload of 1,234 lb (560 kg)

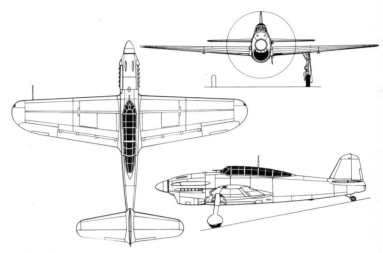

**Yokosuka D4Y 'Judy'**

The D4Y2 variant of the Suisei (Comet) was fitted with the Aichi Atsuta 32 inline engine, an engine whose constant unserviceability plagued the early operational life of the aircraft until replaced by the Kinsei radial of the D4Y3.